MULTINATIONALS ON TRIAL

Multinationals on Trial
Foreign Investment Matters

JAMES PETRAS
SUNY at Binghamton, USA

HENRY VELTMEYER
Saint Mary's University, Canada and
Universidad Autonoma de Zacatecas, Mexico

ASHGATE

Published by
Ashgate Publishing Limited
Gower House
Croft Road
Aldershot
Hampshire GU11 3HR
England

Ashgate Publishing Company
Suite 420
101 Cherry Street
Burlington, VT 05401-4405
USA

Ashgate website: http://www.ashgate.com

British Library Cataloguing in Publication Data
Petras, James F., 1937-
Multinationals on trial : foreign investment matters
1. Investments, Foreign - Political aspects
2. International business enterprises - United States
3. Imperialism - Economic aspects 4. United States -
Foreign relations - 21st century
I. Title II. Veltmeyer, Henry
327.1'11'0973

Library of Congress Cataloging-in-Publication Data
Petras, James F., 1937-
Multinationals on trial : foreign investment matters / by James Petras and Henry Veltmeyer.
p. cm.
Includes bibliographical references and index.
ISBN-13: 978-0-7546-4949-6 1. Investments, Foreign. 2. International business enterprises. I. Veltmeyer, Henry. II. Title.

HG4538.P457 2006
332.67'3--dc22

2006025021

Printed and bound in Great Britain by MPG Books Ltd, Bodmin, Cornwall.

Contents

List of Tables and Figures

Author Notes

James Petras is Professor Emeritus in Sociology at Binghamton University in New York and Adjunct Professor in International Development Studies at Saint Mary's University (Halifax, N.S., Canada). He is the author of over 60 books and numerous other writings on the dynamics of world and Latin American developments, including *Unmasking Globalization: Imperialism of the 21st Century* (2001); System in Crisis (2003); *The New Development Politics* (2003); *Social Movements and the State: Argentina, Bolivia, Brazil, Ecuador* (2005) and *Empire with Imperialism* (2005). A list and an actual file of his periodical writings and journal articles are maintained and can be accessed via www.rebelion.com.

Henry Veltmeyer is Professor of Development Studies at the Universidad Autónoma de Zacatecas (UAZ) in Mexico and Professor of Sociology and International Development Studies at St. Mary's University (Halifax, N.S. Canada). He is author of, among other works, *The Labyrinth of Latin American Development* (1999); *Transcending Neoliberalism: Community Based Development in Latin America* (2001); and, with James Petras, of *Unmasking Globalization: Imperialism of the 21st Century* (2001); *System in Crisis* (2003); *Social Movements and the State: Argentina, Bolivia, Brazil, Ecuador* (2005) and *Empire with Imperialism* (2005).

Introduction

The economic power of the corporations that dominate the world economy and their role in the development process generate controversy. The dynamics of corporate power and the role of foreign direct investment (FDI) have been the object of innumerable studies over the years. The most heated debate surrounding the role of multinational corporations has to do with the type of capital that they deploy in their operations and the conditions associated with it. On this issue it is an article of faith for policy analysts and many governments that whatever its social, economic and political costs, and its negative impacts, FDI is an indispensable means of accessing much-needed financial resources – the backbone of global development finance. It is also assumed, and often argued, that FDI brings with it all sorts of collateral benefits, particularly in the form of technology transfers and employment generation; and that as a result, as the bearer of needed investment and technology, it is a catalyst of development. For these and other reasons, governments of all ideological types and the most diverse political persuasion have tended to pursue policies designed to attract foreign investment. And of course, such policies have been and still are widely viewed as the only way forward – an indispensable and the best means of facilitating a process of globalization, integrating countries across the world into the 'new world economic order'.

This book takes an entirely different view of the role of the multinationals and of the development impact of FDI. First, it is argued (Chapters 1-2) that imperialism is much more useful as a concept for describing and explaining the dynamics of world development than globalization. In Chapter 2, it is argued that imperialism is the driving force of empire building; that the multinationals not only function as agents of this imperialism but they work very closely with their imperial states. The all too dominant focus today on the dynamics of globalization, rather than imperialism, fosters the illusion of a world under the command of stateless corporations that have no national interest to protect and advance, and that have marginalized and encroached on the power of the nation-state. But this book sees the issue differently. We view FDI is a mechanism for empire-centred capital accumulation, a powerful lever for political control and for reordering the world economy.

Chapter 3 explores the economic dynamics associated with FDI and other forms of 'international financial resource' flows. It is shown, for example, that in the 1980s and 1990s, in the context of the Washington consensus on correct policy, the operations of global capital facilitated a South-North net transfer of US$1.5 trillion, draining from countries in the South potential capital for developing their economies. And FDI plays a major role in this process, its economic, social and political costs far outweighing its presumed benefits.

Chapter 4 turns towards the social dynamics involved in the flow of 'international financial resources'. At issue in these dynamics is a process of growing disparities in the international distribution of productive resources and incomes – increased social inequalities among and within regions and countries. The evidence is clear enough: neoliberal policies of structural adjustment to the requirements of the new world order have brought about an increase in these and other forms of social inequality, and with this 'development' ('underdevelopment'?) new forms of world poverty, deprivation and social exclusion. The chapter examines the substantial statistical evidence on these issues and reviews associated studies that are advanced from different theoretical and political perspectives. The chapter also critically examines and dissects the 'war on poverty' waged by the 'international development community' and the associated strategies orchestrated by the World Bank.

Chapter 5 turns towards the policy dimensions of FDI in the context of two theoretical models that have been constructed to promote a process of economic and social development: a state-led model in force from the 1950s to the 1970s and used to direct the development process in Asia; and an alternative neoliberal model of capitalist development predicated on the working of the forces of 'economic freedom' in a new world economic order. These two models, and associated polices regarding FDI, are exemplified by South Korea and Mexico.

With Chapter 6 the book turns to the dynamics of state policy, particularly in regard to policies used by virtually all governments to attract FDI in the mistaken belief that there is no alternative form of development finance. Foreign investment by the multinationals is shown to be highly prejudicial to most countries in the Developing World because of the non-market incentives that it demands. Much of what passes as favourable 'market conditions' are in large part political decisions that maximize benefits to the multinationals at the cost of the local economy, its tax payers, consumers and workers. The meaning is clear: investments are not merely market transactions in which the multinationals justify their profits on the basis of the risks they run, the innovations they introduce, the capital they invest. But abundant evidence is available to demonstrate that most foreign investment is subsidized and risk-free, and relies on securing monopoly profits based on the appropriation of existing national (state) enterprises and control of strategic markets. The dynamics of these policies are examined vis-à-vis their negative outcomes for developing countries.

Chapters 7 and 8 turn towards possible and available alternatives to FDI and associated policy regimes. Chapter 7 argues that foreign investment is a risky, costly and limiting development strategy. For one thing, the benefits and costs of foreign investment are unevenly distributed between the 'sender' and 'recipient', with most of the benefits accruing to the former and the costs largely assumed by the latter. In this context it is not surprising that not one of the early, late or latest developing countries put foreign investment at the centre of their development process. Neither the US, Germany and Japan in the nineteenth and twentieth centuries; nor Russia, China, Korea and Taiwan in the twentieth century relied on foreign investment to advance their industrial and financial institutions. Given the pitfalls and disadvantages of foreign investment cited in the text, it is clear that the way ahead for developing countries is through minimizing FDI and maximizing national ownership and investment of local financial resources, skills and enlarging and deepening local and overseas markets through a diversified economy.

Chapter 7 also provides a systematic analysis of the arguments pro and con FDI, dissecting the associated myths that prevent governments in the developing countries from seeking viable socialist alternatives to FDI, leading them to institute a capitalist and imperialist (that is, FDI) regime. The book concludes with a discussion of the construction of an alternative anti-imperialist, non-FDI, regime. Discussing various alternatives, and advancing a Worker-Engineer Public Control (WEPC) model, the chapter and book concludes with an analysis of policies useful for sustaining an anti-imperialist regime that pursues national development without recourse to foreign investment.

Chapter 1

Empire and Imperialism

The 1980s ushered in a series of sweeping, even revolutionary, changes in the forms of economic and social organization that have been conceptualized as a 'new era', that of 'globalization', in which economies across the world are integrated by one means or the other (mostly by way of 'structural reforms' in macroeconomic policy) into a 'new world economic order'. A more accurate description of these changes and their dynamics would be the travails of 'the American Empire'. The various efforts of the regime that has captured the apparatus of the US state to launch the 'US Century' of world domination and to build an empire provides a historic context for understanding the role and contemporary dynamics of foreign investment – the central object of analysis in this book. In this chapter we briefly review the state of conditions associated with these dynamics.

Building an Empire

The end of the Second World War brought about a radical realignment in global power relations. The sun had definitely set on the British empire and the system of European colonialism was in disarray, rift by the economic devastation of war-torn Europe and growing movements for national liberation across the system. The predominant position of the US is reflected in its domination of the Bretton Woods negotiations leading to the construction of a capitalist world order, the emergence of the US dollar as the reserve currency for the world economy and its economic pre-eminence, accounting as it did for about 50 per cent of the world's productive and financial resources, its wealth (Kennan, 1968). In this context, notwithstanding the institution of a system of multilateral international relations (the United Nations) designed to prevent any one country acting on a possible dream of world domination, the US foreign policy establishment initiated a longstanding and still ongoing debate about how the US might maintain its economic pre-eminence and establish its hegemony. The dynamics of this policy debate can be traced out from some influential musings, in 1948, by George Kennan, a US state policy analyst, about the burden of a US-led empire to a series of policy briefs prepared in the 1990s by a host of neoconservative think-tanks and reactionary foundations such as the Heritage Foundation.[1] These policy debates about the need for the US, with

1 'We have about 50% of the world's wealth, but only 6.3% of its population.... In this situation ... [o]ur ... task in the coming period is to devise a pattern of relationships which will permit us to maintain this position of disparity.... To do so, we will have to dispense with all sentimentality and day-dreaming; and our attention will have to be concentrated everywhere on our immediate national objectives.... We should cease to talk about vague and ... unreal

the threat of the spread of international communism and the institution of the Soviet empire, for the US to assume the burden and mantle of empire are also reflected in a process of empire building. Like the policy debates, this process can also be traced back to the end of the Second World War if not earlier.

The resulting empire was centred on the US, constructed with a series of formal alliances with a grouping of west European partner states – the Organization for Economic cooperation and Development (OECD) and NATO – as well as a more global network of working agreements with allied satellite states and their elites, was built on the foundation of the transnational corporation, the economic 'shock-troops' of the system and its major operating units of the system. By 1970, after two decades of unprecedented rapid growth (the 'Golden Age of capitalism') the Euromerican empire was well established, although not without internal tensions. In fact, the system as a whole was in crisis, subject to conditions of economic stagnation, sluggish productivity growth, a profit crunch on capital, and a destabilizing level of inter-imperialist rivalry and competition for the world market (Brenner, 2000). One manifestation of this crisis was a large and growing, and quite unsustainable, deficit in the US trade account vis-à-vis, in particular and ironically, Germany and the Japan, two erstwhile enemies of the US state that in its own economic and political interest it as nevertheless compelled to help reconstruct and develop. Concerted action and a trilateralist strategy designed to stabilize the system as a whole ensured that this rivalry and competition was kept within system-preserving limits. The next chapter elaborates on the dynamics involved in this process.

State of the Empire

Imperial policymakers do not pursue a single strategy in pursuit of empire building. Even a cursory view of recent and contemporary policy-making reveals a multiplicity of strategies based on various contingencies in different times and locations (Ikenberry, Lake and Mastanduno, 1988; Kagan, 2003). To the extent that the current regime in Washington has attempted to foist a single strategy – an aggressive unilateralist and militarist approach – regardless of specific contingencies, it has led to severe setbacks and what many analysts view as an 'erosion' of empire (Johnson, 2000, 2004; Eland, 2002; Mann, 2003; Pollin, 2003; Todd, 2003). However, while tactics are flexible and vary enormously, the strategic goals of US foreign policy remains constant: to enhance US hegemony and its domination of the new world order.

The pursuit of strategic imperial goals is not a linear process of advance or decline. It evolves in response to diverse contingencies, some within the reach of

objectives such as human rights, the raising of the living standards, and democratization. The day is not far off when we are going to have to deal in straight power concepts. The less we are then hampered by idealistic slogans, the better.... We should recognize that our influence ... in the coming period is going to be primarily military and economic. We should make a careful study to see what parts of the ... world are absolutely vital to our security, and we should concentrate our policy on seeing to it that those areas remain in hands which we can control or rely on' (Kennan, 1948).

imperial policymakers and others beyond the immediate control of the architects and administrators of US foreign policy.

Any study of imperialism, or more specifically of empire building, should recognize that imperial policies are not simple products of vague abstractions such as the 'logic of capital accumulation' or projections of political ideologues or the 'political will' of key policy elites. While some contemporary leading policymakers may believe that 'willing' a policy will result in its realization, actual practice and results point to gross underestimates of the obstacles and forces of resistance, leading to a weakening of imperial power and disastrous outcomes such as a war that is going nowhere and the occupation of a country (Iraq) that is spinning out of control.

Imperial Power: Contingencies that Count

While the structures of the imperial state and the scope and depth of its private economic institutions are expressions of the global power of the empire, the exercise of power in concrete instances is dependent on specific contingencies.

One of these 'contingencies' is past or present military defeats or victories in prolonged warfare. The outcomes of imperial warfare have a strong impact on inhibiting or multiplying the exercise of military power. For example, the US defeat in Vietnam weakened the military's willingness to engage in subsequent invasions in Iran, Nicaragua and Angola, despite their strategic importance. Similarly, the enormous costs of prosecuting the Iraq War have made it difficult, if not impossible, for the US to attend to other issues of imperial rule, be they related to Iran, Latin America or other redoubts of the empire. On the other hand, successful US military intervention in the first Gulf War, the invasion of Yugoslavia and Afghanistan convinced Washington of its 'unlimited power to engage in several wars throughout the world.' But the prolonged, ongoing and growing resistance in the aftermath of the Iraq invasion and occupation certainly has at least temporarily set back the US war plans for further conquests of neighbouring Iran and Syria.

Related to the outcomes of imperial war, the level of domestic political support (passive or active) is another contingency effecting imperial strategy. Prolonged wars with high military casualties and economic costs inevitably result in loss of citizen support, which, as with Iraq today, may eventually result in institutional and political opposition. However, more crucial than the isolated congressional critic, even perhaps than the loss of control over legislative power and political support, growing citizen discontent can manifest itself in large-scale desertions, sharp falls in military recruitment and re-enlistment and decline in morale, especially of 'reserve forces.'

The third contingency, which affects imperial military strategy, is the composition, strength or weakness of collaborators and adversaries in the locus of warfare. Weak, discredited collaborator regimes with little or no domestic support, a weak intelligence system and a vulnerability to constant, bloody direct attacks require a prolonged, deep involvement of imperial forces. Strong, organized, deeply entrenched and highly motivated anticolonial resistance movements, with extended intelligence networks, can effectively limit the apparent 'structural advantages' (armaments, numbers, technology, military budgets and so on) of the imperial occupation forces.

Successful or failed imperial strategies are contingent on securing large-scale, long-term commitments and support from allies – other imperial powers – supplying soldiers and financial, diplomatic, political and propaganda support. The US's 'successful' wars – Yugoslavia (Bosnia, Kosovo), Afghanistan and Haiti were based on Euro-Latin American alliance with the US imperial regime. The relative lack of imperial alliances in the Iraq invasion, and the withdrawal of limited allied support have weakened the capacity of the US to consolidate its colonial occupation in Iraq.

While the imperial state has a vast global network of military bases (at least 120 identified), a $500 billion plus budget, and a dozen espionage and paramilitary organizations operating worldwide, these and other structural underpinnings of empire depend on the internal cohesion of the policy elites. While there are always bureaucratic frictions, jurisdictional conflicts, and competition over budgeting allocations among imperial agencies, they usually converge on the goal of enhancing US imperial power. US imperial interests are normally the central and dominant concern of the policy elite, whatever its internal factional or ideological disputes.

However, political contingencies that challenge the norm of US 'empire first' can emerge and in fact have done so in the context of the Iraq war: US policy in the Middle East was definitively shaped and defined by a section of the policy elite whose primary concern was to promote Israeli power in the Middle East and to use US war powers to destroy Israel's real and potential Middle East adversaries. On the complex political dynamics of this issue (the power and virtual stranglehold of the Israeli lobby over US foreign policy in recent years) see Petras (2006).

This unanticipated contingency seriously divided the imperial state, setting off a conflict between the Israel 'Firsters' in The Pentagon, the Executive and Congress and the US military, intelligence agencies, diplomatic corps and sectors of public opinion.[2] These profound divisions led to the 'Israel Firsters' setting up parallel intelligence and propaganda agencies, the preparation and dissemination of a mass deceitful pro-war propaganda campaign, the distortion and fabrication of intelligence reports, blatant espionage for the Israeli state, including the turning over of highly classified war documents. The result was a war, which was a disaster from

---

2 The struggle within the US power structure between the economic empire builders (EEB) and the civilian militarists/Zioncons over US Middle East and global policy is now out in the open and intensifying. The EEB now have a politically powerful organizational expression, the Baker Commission (known officially as the Iraq Study Group) led by the formidable former Secretary of State, James Baker. The EEB is backed by a group of bipartisan congressional leaders, sectors of the traditional military elite, a powerful coalition of Texas-based oil and gas groups and sectors of Wall Street financial houses and potentially a large majority of public opinion. Against this unofficial more pragmatic (less ideological vis-à-vis Israel) coalition of forces are the civilian militarists in The Pentagon, State Department and White House (Rumsfelt, Cheney, Rice, Bolton and Bush), a declining majority of Congressional Democrats and Republicans, the Presidents of the Major Jewish Organizations headed by the America-Israel Political Affairs Committee (AIPAC) and their influential apparatchiks in the mass media and their numerous 'grassroots' political fronts (political action committees).

the perspective of the US empire builders, and a major success for the Israel boosters – in Iraq, quite apart from the unsettled debate as to the geopolitics of oil involved, they destroyed the one Arab country in the Middle East with a solid secular state, a scientific elite and modern economy and military structures.

The Zioncon-civilian-militarist (ZCCM) policy of colonial invasions and military occupation in pursuit of destroying Israel's adversaries and enhancing its dominance of the Middle East has weakened US efforts to sustain its global dominance. The vast absorption of military resources, troops, reserves and logistical support systems in pursuit of a prolonged guerrilla war without end, has severely weakened Washington's capacity to apply military force to intimidate and enforce or intervene in other strategic regions or countries of conflict. Military losses in Iraq have undermined domestic public support for present and future overseas military interventions in support of empire building. The sustained military and political resistance to the vast US military occupation army has lowered the intimidation factor so necessary in sustaining imperial diplomacy. In a word, the Iraq war has become a major impediment to empire building, its defence and its domestic economic and political support, a principal motivating factor in the set up of the Baker Commission.

The 'resources' of the US imperial state are formidable, both in quantity and quality: a military budget bigger than the next 20 other countries, a highly trained officer corps, with a high-tech infrastructure and weapon systems. However, this 'structure' and its resources operate in and confront a series of contingencies, which can reduce or neutralize the effective exercise of these 'resources'. Clearly, imperial structures depend on contingencies which can escape the control of imperial policy elites, creating a degree of uncertainty in the outcome of imperial induced conflicts, especially in the context of policymakers with dual loyalties and infected by a high degree of ideological voluntarism.

Imperialism: Omnipotence, Impotence and Class

Some writers and many pundits confuse the omnipresence of the imperial state and the multinational corporations with omnipotence (Brightman, 2004). This is the case, for example, with Hardt and Negri's *Empire*, a book purportedly on the Left that captured the political imaginary of the liberal and conservative intellectual establishment and the International Business press.[3] A similar conflation of omnipresence and omnipotence is characteristic of the stream of studies and briefs written by the foreign policy analysts connected to the White House. Even in discussing the omnipresence of imperialism, the term has to be stretched to include an indirect presence via collaborator regimes and client political, cultural and social organizations. Describing the presence of imperialism does not tell us about its power to successfully realize policy outcomes in specific circumstances and time frames. There are numerous cases where there is a substantial military and economic presence of imperial force but where imperial policies are setback and US interests

3 For a critical analysis of *Empire* see Petras and Veltmeyer (2005b).

are adversely affected (Todd, 2003; Wallerstein, 2003). Iraq is a notable case, but on a different level Venezuela is another example.

The source of the confusion between the presence of imperialism and its power is a result of thinking of power merely in terms of 'global structural attributes' (the overall size and scope of US military – economic institutions) and of believing that 'power' is a structural fact, an attribute embedded in hierarchical structures in which power is concentrated at the top. 'Power', according to this view, is always and everywhere associated with the dominant classes, and the wealthiest and most militarist state.

This approach fails to see that power is a relationship between classes and states, contingent on the direction and outcome of class and national struggles. The location or position in the international system; and ownership of the means of production, media, consumption, military force and cultural outlets are extremely powerful levers in any equation of political power. But they are not the only source or 'resources' of power. Mass organizations of class conscious workers and direct producers, their degree of combat readiness, the capacity of their leaders and quality of their programs, the strength of their tactics and strategy are also power sources: in fact, policy outcomes often are the result of a confrontation between the structural power of imperialism and the alternative power of the exploited and the oppressed. On this point we need but point towards the effectiveness in certain conjunctures of the 'antiglobalization' movement and the forces of anti-imperialism, which in Latin America have joined with the antisystemic social movements of the rural landless workers, indigenous communities and peasant farmers to halt in its tracks the 'structural reform' agenda of globalizing capital, in some contexts bring about a reversal of major neoliberal polices and in others a serious challenge to imperial rule (Petras and Veltmeyer, 2005b).[4] The key factors in the equation of economic and military power are not only the quantitative sum of structural resources of the empire, or the number of organized poor and exploited, but how effectively potential power is applied in specific conflictual situations. The conversion by imperialism of its quantitative resources (for example big economic firms, military backing) into

4 The antiglobalization and the antiwar movements contain both anti-imperialists and reformers – groups which generally support US imperial power but oppose the particular way power is exercised. Others oppose the behaviour of the multinational corporations but not the imperial state and system in which they are embedded. These movements are anti-imperialist to the degree that they mobilize popular forces to oppose an important manifestation of imperial expansion, raise popular consciousness about the motives of the US and EU regimes and open the possibility of deepening and extending resistance to imperialism as a system. By the end of the twentieth century there emerged three variants of anti-imperialism: i) *Rightwing anti-imperialism*, articulated by US client dissidents in Eastern Europe, the Balkans, and Caucasus as an instrument to shift allegiances from Soviet domination to the US Empire; ii) *Clerical anti-imperialism*, based on religious (Muslim) opposition to US military aggression, political conquest, cultural influence, economic depredations and racial hostility; iii) Modern anti-imperialism, which opposes imperial wars and the operations of the Multinational Corporation, the WTO, *ALCA*, and support national liberation in the Developing World that normally also have a social change agenda.

favourable policy outcomes is not automatic; far from it. It depends on the resources available to, and relative effectiveness of, its adversaries.

On this point, Lenin's thesis that imperialism, as he defined it,[5] is the most advanced stage of capitalism, and Marx's dictum that capitalism cannot help but create its own gravediggers, seem to hold up. Wherever found today imperialism in its diverse forms appears to be the bearer of capitalism (economic liberalism) and the gospel of its virtuous marriage with democracy (political liberalism); and everywhere where imperial power is projected in one form or the other the end result is an accumulation of diverse forces of resistance and opposition. Although these forces are fragmented and divided, and thus difficult to mobilize, they are found in virtually every 'popular' sector of 'civil society', particularly in the organizations of the urban and rural poor, the rural landless workers and 'peasants', many of which are both proletarianized and impoverished.[6] In diverse contexts and conjunctures, these forces have been successfully mobilized against imperial policies and imperialist rule. In fact, the 1980s and 1990s saw a series of setbacks in the capacity of the US state to project both its economic and military power.

The reason why 'globalists' on the left and right overstate the power (or omnipotence) of imperial institutions (or the irresistible force of 'globalization') is that they look only at 'structural' or institutional attributes of power and ignore its political and social subjective conditions.

Moreover, the omnipresence of imperialist institutions requires the spreading out of forces, the multiplication of points of conflict and the increasing vulnerability to global disruption at particular strategic points in the production and consumption chain. This suggests that omnipresence can lead to relative imperial impotence. In other words omnipresence can be a weakness rather than a strength.

As noted earlier, imperial pundits, publicists and propagandists often pretend that being everywhere signals omniscience. Unfortunately, many leftist writers take the imperial propaganda images of 'omnipresence equals omnipotence' at face value, as a point of departure for their 'harsher' critique of empire building. This is a great disservice since it obscures the limits of imperial power, its vulnerability and, worst of all it discourages mass opposition by putting premature closure on direct action.

5 Lenin essentially defined imperialism in economic terms – as a phase of capitalist development characterized by the fusion of industrial and financial capital; a tendency towards monopoly; the export of capital; and the territorial division of the world by European powers as a result of these economic forces. The undoubted imperialistic ambitions of leaders in power in the Soviet Union and China in the Twentieth Century would have to be explained in a very different way – more likely in terms of 'power begetting power'.

6 The literature documenting and analyzing from diverse theoretical perspectives these growing forces of resistance to neoliberal globalization, global capitalism and imperialism is immense, but see for example (Petras and Veltmeyer, 2003; Wallerstein, 2003; Johnson, 2004).

Imperial Projections of Power: Rationality, Coherence and Realization

Some writers, journalists and academics from both the right and the left assume that the projections of power, or claims, plans and ideological pronouncements are the same as the realization of the same. In fact, many of the empire's projections and proposals are not successful and failures are not uncommon. At the same time, some writers go to the opposite extreme, automatically assuming that failures spell the 'erosion' if not demise, of the empire (Todd, 2003; Wallerstein, 2003).

Under the Bush regime, the ideologues of imperial power laid out a schema for world conquest based on a sequence of wars, through unilateral projections of power.[7] The claims to being the only superpower, the driving force of globalization, the most powerful military power with capacity for multiple simultaneous wars based on preventive war doctrines and establishing an uncontested world empire was in large part wishful thinking or imperial hubris. The ideologues of empire fell victim to their own lies and deceptions because many of them – especially the key Zionist policymakers – cynically manipulated Washington's doctrine of invincibility to commit the empire to an unwinnable war in Iraq, to the advantage of Israel's regional ambitions.

From the first Gulf War, through the Clinton decade of the 1990s, to the Bush regime in the 21st century, US imperial ideology made grandiose claims on global power, some of which was realized, but most of which was proven to fall far short of realization. The first US war against Iraq did not lead to US domination in the Middle East; nor did it marginalize Europe, China or Russia from world politics, as Wolfowitz's 1992 working paper had projected. The US invasion of Yugoslavia increased the number of US client states in the Balkans, but it was shared influence with Western Europe – the US gained regional political influence, the EU gained economic advantage.

The US Zionist militarist plans for world domination found in the proposal for a new US imperial century, signed off by Perle, Wolfowitz, Feith, Abrams, Kagan, Kristol, Cohen, and Wurmster among others, were put in practice when they entered the Bush regime. Two prolonged colonial wars later, the projection of power and the doctrine of sequential offensive wars are in tatters. The US state is tied down, desperate in its efforts to train a surrogate colonial force so as to allow it to extricate itself from a war that most Americans, even erstwhile supporters and boosters, oppose.

---

7 The neoconservative project of global American empire – its plan for global dominance, for a new imperialism that would not 'hesitate to use [coercive] force if, when and where necessary', and do so unilaterally – was at least a decade in the making and hatched within George Bush Senior's presidency, if not earlier. In 1992, *The Washington Post* made public a secret Pentagon document – the infamous 'Wolfowitz Report'. The existence and paternity of the Report was denied but it did nevertheless arouse controversy, especially among US 'allies'. The Report anticipated what would later be asserted by Kohl and Feldstein: 'We must discourage the other industrialized nations from challenging American leadership and from bringing into question the economic and political established order. We must keep such a military supremacy that potential rivals will be dissuaded from aspiring to a larger regional or global role'.

The boasts and arrogance of the biggest Jewish American organizations backing Israel via the war (The Presidents of the Major Jewish Organizations, AIPEC and a host of other fronts) are deflated by a major espionage case involving key officials in AIPEC and the hurried departures from high Pentagon positions of two major neoconservative architects (Wolfowitz and Feith) of US military attacks on Israel's adversaries.

Many writers attribute a rationality and coherence to imperial policy that is simply not there. This attribution flies in the face of irrational projections of power based on myths about conquered peoples' receptiveness to US aggression and the assumption of the unlimited capacity of Americans to sustain multiple prolonged wars. But there is no necessary congruence between the pursuit of imperial interests and the policy instruments fashioned to pursue them. The facile assimilation of US and Israeli interests in the Middle East by an army of Congressional and Pentagon insiders all too ready to support the powerful Israel lobby of Zionist organizations is but one example of the failure of imperial policy at odds with itself and of the now widely recognized 'failed policies' in Iraq, Iran and Syria. Success has many claimants to paternity; but the Bush administration's Middle East policy is fast losing support, the wagons of support being closely drawn around Bush himself and perhaps Condoleezza Rice. Everyone else, including many erstwhile supporters within the administration and both houses of Congress, are jumping ship as the administration's imperial policy towards Iraq and the middle east sinks under the weight of its internal contradictions.

The irrational dynamics of imperial policy are not restricted to the Middle East. Similar blindspots and irrationalities of neoconservative Cuban-American policy elites in shaping a destabilization policy toward Venezuela has led to endangering the supply of strategic energy resources and the large-scale presence of US petroleum corporations. The failed US policies toward Venezuela (coup, referenda, elections and funding client NGOs) have clearly radicalized Venezuelan public opinion, strengthened Chavez and weakened US client groups. A 'rational analysis' of the positive mass impact of Chavez social welfare programs, his continuing openness to US oil multinationals, and the rising state income from petroleum sources should have told the empire builders that 'accommodation' and long-term deep penetration would have been a more effective policy.

However, pointing out the irrationalities, incoherence, failed policies and contradictory nature of imperial policy makers – in terms of their own empire building goals – should not lead to an underestimation of the acute dangers from imperial policy. Failed policies (even repeated defeats) do not spell the demise of empire or even its retrenchment. With its vast resources, the US Empire has a wide margin to commit numerous errors, to employ mediocre policymakers, engage in severe internal disputes and still launch a new wave of aggressive policies. For imperialism there are numerous chances for success; for Third World progressive regimes, one fateful error can end its tenure in office. Despite several major defeats in Venezuela, the US continues a new onslaught – attempting to provoke border warfare with Colombia, co-opt right wing elements in the Chavez regime and so on. President Chavez needs to stay in power at least in the short-term, for a single election defeat would lead to massive historical reversal of nearly a decade of progress, as the electoral defeat of the Nicaraguan Sandinistas demonstrated.

Characteristics of Empire Building

Empire building does not follow a linear upward trajectory. On the contrary, there are upward and downward movements, including near breakdowns, and almost permanent instability and continuous wars with a variety of anti-imperial forces in diverse geographic regions. There is no one 'weak link' – the points at which the empire is most vulnerable to change over time and location. At one point (1960–75) it was in South-East Asia and at another in Latin America (1970–76); at other times it was Central America (the 1980s); and in the new millennium it is the Middle East and South Asia and the northern rim of South America (Venezuela and Colombia). And despite all the resources and political will at its disposal the US state has been unable to come to terms with the Government of Cuba, which has managed to resist the most overt forms of US imperial power short of invasion, a strategy that the government is loath to pursue because of its likely exceedingly high costs deriving from the fact (of which the government is well aware, notwithstanding its pronouncements to the contrary) that the Cuban Revolution has the readily mobilized support of a majority of Cubans. The social composition of the resistance to imperialism varies: in the late 20th century it was secular urban nationalists and revolutionary socialists; in the early 21st century it includes radical Muslims in Asia and indigenous peasants in Latin America.

Imperialism by its intrusive, disruptive, destructive and exploitative character inevitable generates permanent political, social and cultural forms of opposition. As a result, brief periods of consolidation are typically followed by prolonged periods of instability. The cycles of 'consolidation' and 'instability' reflect the sequence of imperial conquest: initial occupation and severe repression, followed by the fostering of imperial sponsored selection-elections, and the emergence of an apparently 'hegemonic' elite – followed by new waves of popular resistance in response to corruption, pillage and incompetence, leading to new revolts and perpetual warfare until the imperial regime withdraws or engages in genocide.

History teaches us that the extended consolidation of empire requires the forcible mass eviction-destruction of a people; otherwise it takes the form of perpetual tension and conflict between the conquered people and the 'colonized elites' assigned the responsibility of maintaining order.

The Geography of Empire

Empire builders operate through a variety of unequal 'treaties' and agreements. These include: 1. Bilateral relations between the empire and client state; 2. *Multilateral agreements* – relations between the empire and regions (Central American Free Trade Area, LAFTA – Latin American Free Trade Area) 3. *Sub-regional pacts* – relations between the empire and specific clients.

These agreements are based on the scope and degree of subordination of the particular ruling elite(s) in each geographical unit. The 'easiest' and least complicated mode of empire building is to move step-by-step – the salami tactics – of incorporating countries with compliant rulers via bilateral agreements. This does not preclude imperial policymakers from looking toward incorporating broader geopolitical units into the empire. The playing off of one region over another in terms of marginal trade and loan concessions and regimes changes in neighbouring countries can set the stage for the incorporation of sub-regions into the empire. Eventually, the empire builders may 'go for' entire regions, via continent-wide agreements.

Two fundamental limitations to the strategy of empire building via geographical incorporation have emerged: 1) The internal opposition of the majority of the population adversely affected by imperial domination and 2) the non-reciprocal nature of the treaties adversely affecting the elites within the country to be incorporated in the empire. The latter contradiction is more acute in the everyday debates, negotiations and conferences between the empire and its clients. The US and European imperial states depend on the political support of non-competitive groups, especially in the powerful agricultural sector to sustain imperial expansion. There is also an important dialectic of conflict and complementarity between the 'advanced' sector of the capitalist system represented by the global multinational corporations, and the relatively backward, highly subsidized and government protected local capitalists.

In order to secure the support of client states and the ruling elites in the Developing World for the incorporation of their countries into the empire (i.e. globalization), imperial policy makers in the US and Europe, and Japan, are forced to lower trade barriers and end protectionism and subsidies to the backward sectors and industries that are unable to compete against Third world producers. However, while Third World export elites are quite willing to shortchange workers, manufacturers, and public employees, they are not willing to commit economic suicide. The dilemma for the empire builders is that they need the political support of both their own country's backward (in terms of the globalization imperative) economic sectors and the export-oriented elites in the Third World, in countries such as Brazil and India, whose economic interests are directly opposed to them. This conflict has resulted in the collapse of the Doha round of WTO free trade negotiations and it has killed the Bush regime's proposal of a continental free trade zone in the Americas.

Concessions to the export elites included limited market access, delayed entry, quotas and free access for selective producers. Nevertheless, in many cases comprehensive agreements have been stalled by the desire of empire builders to have it both ways: free trade and open market access for their corporations and protection for their noncompetitive but politically powerful economic interests.

Tactics of Empire Building

Given the finite resources of the empire, empire builders must rely heavily on tactical maneuvers to maximize 'outside' resources. This means involving outside collaborators, subsidized clients, bridge building to protected 'Trojan Horses' in adversarial states. Many of the tactics employed by US empire builders have a long ignoble history, but in many cases, past and present, they have worked, where large-scale warfare has failed.

The most frequent tactic is 'divide and conquer', in its many and diverse forms.

The most prominent of these has been the fomenting of ethnic, religious and tribal separatism to break up adversarial nation-states and create mini-client states. The imperial powers, namely the US and the EU, have been in the forefront of selectively politicizing social, cultural, religious and ethnic differences, funding, training and supplying minorities with arms and media outlets, providing favourable propaganda in favour of their claims and actions (including 'justifying' wars and ethnic terrorism) in order to secure regimes whose dubious subsequent claims to 'independence' is belied by the military bases established by the US, the US-European takeover of strategic financial and productive activities, services and media and their subordination to the IFIs controlled by the imperial powers.

The imperial 'divide and conquer' tactic, via ethnic separatism was successful in Yugoslavia, Afghanistan and Iraq – where the US and EU created mini-client regimes in Montenegro, Kosovo, Macedonia, the 'de facto' mini Kurdish state in Northern Iraq as well as the division of Afghanistan among tribal warlords.

In Bolivia, the US strongly backs a 'separatist' regional movement based in the south and centred in the oligarch-dominated city of Santa Cruz. The purpose is to separate the oil and gas rich south from the rest of the highlands where Indian-peasant and worker power is a dominant force. In Russia, the US and the EU have been training and propagandizing in favour of all sorts of ethnic-based separatist groups, headed up by the Chechen terrorists in an effort to further debilitate the Russian state and further extend US and EU empire building.

On the other hand, the EU and the US oppose national anti-imperialist movements like the Iraqi, Haitian, Afghan, Basque and Irish, which challenge the US or its EU allies.

Imperial policy is coherent with a class-imperial perspective: Separatism which contributes to empire building is good and to be supported; self-determination against the empire or its allies is bad. There is no hypocrisy, as some critics charge, in not holding 'universal standards', because politics is based on universal class criteria.

Separatism, as a weapon in empire building, is a formidable weapon that has been successfully wielded as a propaganda tool to discredit adversaries. Once ethnic animosities have become confrontational, the US and EU propaganda machines move into high gear, publicizing the 'atrocities', 'injustices' and 'human rights' violations committed against their client 'rebels'. To the extent that most NGO 'progressives', liberals and 'socialists' lack any sense of the underlying class-imperial issues at stake they are drawn into a tacit alliance condemning US adversaries. What is curious about this 'unholy alliance' between empire-builders and the 'Western progressives' is that while the imperialist countries seize all the advantages of any successful separation (bases, resources, media, factories and cheap labour) to 'clientelize' the state, the progressives never look back self-critically on their policies. In the name of the lofty abstract principles of 'self-determination' they have contributed to empire building by legitimating future clients-in-the-making.

Military warfare is a key tool of empire building, in many cases with the support of client separatists who act as military and police mercenaries in occupied countries. Where surrogates fail, where powerful civilian militarist political forces are in charge of US policy, the empire resorts to ferocious military violence.

In all circumstances, the empire pursues an international inspection program of the targeted adversary prior to attack – to disarm the gullible, to force political concessions, to secure intelligence of all essential military and civilian installations and to recruit any civilian or military turncoats. The purpose of the military attack is to destroy the anti-imperialist regime, or simply a dissident national leadership, or an adversary of a close ally and to put in place a new state apparatus and party regime willing and able to serve imperial economic and military interests.

Historical experience has demonstrated that colonial wars are very costly and rarely lead to imperial consolidation as they destroy and displace millions and violate every social-cultural institution of the conquered society. Political destabilization of adversarial regimes is much more common and effective in the current phase of empire building. A wide spectrum of imperial agencies operate an ever broader network of 'civil society' client groups in fomenting unrest, while higher echelons of the intelligence services recruit high level military and intelligence counterparts to 'tolerate' the use of violent extra-parliamentary seizures of power. Specific tactics accompanying 'directed' mob action, include selective assassinations of expendable allies (creating martyrs) or popular regime figures, exaggerated or invented corruption or atrocity propaganda campaigns and demands for elections where the incumbents have become discredited and the client insurgents are made 'heroes'. If surrogates and separatists are defeated and destabilization does not work, the empire builders frequently resort to direct or 'third party' military attacks.

'Third party' conflicts are usually provoked by the empire builders to force the entry of UN peacekeepers under imperial tutelage to intervene and leads to 'regime change'. This in turn leads to client building, military bases and pillage of lucrative resources and wholesale privatization-denationalization of the economy. In some cases the imperial power will directly intervene in third party conflicts under the pretence that the aggressor is a 'victim' of the anti-imperialist adversary. In some cases 'third countries' become 'launching pads' for imperial attacks, either directly or through mercenary clients.

Most empire loyalist regimes are very vulnerable because of the harsh conditions they impose on the population to pay tribute to the empire – in the form of debt payments, profit remittances and wealth transfers. Therefore empire-building policymakers are always faced with unstable clients. The most prominent tactic is to 'rotate' personalities, parties and elites in and out of regimes to avoid popular upheavals, which challenge the state (military, civil bureaucracy, police and so on), which is the foundation of imperial power in each nation. In other worlds imperial policymakers sacrifice specific regimes to save the state – from revolution. The discourse of US imperial elites about favouring 'constitutional' or 'democratic' change – when it involves a client regime – is precisely about ensuring that the change occurs within and among the range of client politicians compatible with imperial interests. The existence of 'alternative' clients is crucial to demobilizing popular insurgents and turning them to elite-dominated institutions.

Conclusion

Empire building is the result of deliberate, calculated acts and improvised interventions in circumstances and contingencies, which are out of the control of imperialist elites. Imperial policymakers utilize a vast array of policy tools in destroying adversaries and supporting clients, but they neither control all political resources nor dominate the conditions or social forces, which act against them.

Imperialism is not a form of political architecture, immobile, daunting and immovable. Imperialism is a set of class-national relations, which operate in conflictual fashion in every aspect of social, cultural and political life on every level of the class structure. It makes no sense to enumerate the 'power' of imperialism by listing its MNCs, IFIs, military budget and aggressive bellicose rhetoric, and forget that the empire builders lose, are defeated in war, social struggles and political conflicts. Power is not only embedded in 'structures' but is equally measured in class relations, organization, leadership, morale, combativeness and strategic and tactical moves.

Profound reversals of imperial structures occur when far-reaching class-national struggles set in motion new quasi-state, dual power structures – guerrilla armies, local governments, autonomous regions, entrenched militant neighbourhoods and popular militias. The formidable face of the empire, the big military budget and the giant multi-nationals begins to crack as contingencies resulting from the class struggle impinge on their activity: capital flees, military morale declines, domestic support wavers and allies abandon ship. Imperial structures are only as strong as the underlying class forces, which support them, and they depend on the degree and depth of the class and national struggle, which as Marx once pointed out is the 'motor force of history'.

Chapter 2

Imperialisms, Old and New

Foreign investment, fundamentally, is a matter of capital accumulation and the international flow of privately owned 'capital'. For over a hundred years capital accumulation has been the fundamental driving force of economic growth, capitalist expansion and societal transformation. The process can be traced out in the dynamics of 'economic growth' and associated social changes. There are six phases of this development:

1. from the beginning of the nineteenth century to around 1870, a period of capitalist industrialization based on the factory system, the market and an extension of the social relation of wage labour;
2. a period, from around 1870 to 1914, characterized by the fusion of industrial and financial forms of capital, a trend towards the concentration of capital and the emergence of monopolies, the export of capital, the globalization of trade migrant u, and the territorial division of much of the world among capitalist powers and European colonialism;
3. a period of imperial war, economic depression, mass-production based on the 'scientific management' of labour (Fordism), the 'taming of capitalism' based on government-led social reforms, and the rise and defeat of fascism (1914–1945);
4. a period of exceptionally high growth ('the golden age of capitalism') accompanied by a process of decolonization, nation-building and state-led 'international development' (1945–1973);
5. a transitional period of crisis and restructuring (the 1970s);
6. a period of neoliberal globalization and free market 'reforms' – and 'neoimperialism' (1980–2007).

The term 'imperialism', in this historic context, defines the dynamics of a long-term process of social change and transformation, together with associated class struggles. Imperialism in this historic context has taken diverse forms, old and new. These transformations provide changing contexts for understanding the dynamics of capital accumulation, foreign investment and anti-imperialist movements. It also provides the framework for our analysis of these dynamics.

Old and New Imperialisms

The 'old imperialism' emerged in the late nineteenth century as direct consequence of industrial capitalism and engaged Europe, the US and Japan and in a competitive struggle for markets and territorial control, carving up much of Africa and Asia among them. Imperialism was based on an 'international division of labour' in which the imperial states produced and exported manufactured goods in exchange for raw materials, minerals and other industrial inputs or consumer commodities from their colonies or semi-colonies. The imperial system was set up in the nineteenth century but continued well into the twentieth century even in the context of two devastating world wars that brought on a decolonization and national liberation movement. It found support in the ideas advanced by proponents of a neoclassical theory of economic growth – a theory that saw the world market as the fundamental agent of economic growth and the existing international division of u as a system that would provide 'mutual benefits' to countries both North and South.

The actual workings of this system, adumbrated by orthodox economists in terms of the law of comparative advantages, also gave rise to a very different school of thought, one much less sanguine about the anticipated outcomes of this economic system. In fact, most theorists at the time were generally critical, arguing that rather than providing mutual benefits to countries that were well along the path towards development and those seeking to enter this path, the economic structure of the system (world capitalism) did not provide 'mutual benefits' but worked to the advantage of the countries at the centre.

This system has been analyzed from different theoretical perspectives, giving rise to various debates about the development process. One of these theories was that the centre-periphery structure of the world capitalist system was particularly advantageous to the transnational corporations, allowing them to accumulate capital via relations and conditions of 'unequal exchange' and 'unequal development' (Amin, 1976) and 'deteriorating terms of trade' (Prebisch, 1949). In effect, it was argued that the economic structure and imperialist domination of the world capitalist system works to siphon off an economic surplus produced by workers and producers on the 'periphery' of the system.

This theory of 'dependent capitalist development' or 'dependency' was advanced with diverse permutations in the 1960s and 1970s (Kay, 1989). It was countered by several other theories, including a theory of imperialism that drew attention to the absence of class analysis, a presumed failing of 'dependency theory' in its diverse formulations. At the very least a theoretical focus on dependency shifts the attention of analysts away from relations of production, i.e. class relations of property in the means of production, to relations of economic exchange among countries. Nevertheless, 'dependency theory' caught the imagination of many on the political left, with a consequent inattention to class analysis and the dynamics of imperialist domination.

The basic argument advanced by 'dependency' or 'world system' theorists was that the centre-periphery structure of the world system inhibited the capitalist development of economies on the periphery, resulting in an 'underdevelopment' of these economies, including a disarticulated structure of capitalist production, a deepening of social inequalities worldwide and a growing social divide between the wealthy few (within the transnational capitalist class) and the many poor (the direct producers and the working class). The basic theory was that the system of global capitalist production worked to the advantage of countries at the centre and to the disadvantage of those on the periphery; that, in effect, the critical structural factor explaining the development of some economies and the underdevelopment of others was location in the world capitalist system.[1]

The growing and deepening global inequalities that have emerged over several decades of globalizing capitalist development suggests that the theory, which had been largely abandoned, a victim of trenchant criticism from both the left and the right, retains some explanatory power. Table 2.1 (see Chapter 4 for more details) provides a snap shot of some regional dynamics of this unequal development and associated social inequalities over the past 25 years of capitalist development.

Table 2.1 Per capita income as a percentage of OECD, by developing region

	(per capita, in constant US$)					
	1980	1981–85	1986–90	1991–95	1996–00	2001
Sub-Saharan Africa	3.3	3.1	2.5	2.1	2.0	1.9
Latin America/ Caribbean	18.0	16.0	14.2	13.5	13.3	12.8
South Asia	1.2	1.3	1.3	1.4	1.5	1.6
East Asia	1.5	1.7	1.9	2.5	3.1	3.3

Source: UN, The Inequality Predicament, 2005, p. 46.

The income statistics presented in Table 2.1 expose little of the basic structure and changing regional patterns of global income disparity (on this see Chapter 4). Economists have theorized a tendency for income levels across the world to converge after an initial period of increasing disparities.[2] And indeed it is possible to detect a slight tendency towards convergence between 1950 and 1973.[3] But developments in the subsequent period of capitalist development, marking 25 years of free-market

1 There are diverse formulations of this theory but see in particular Wallerstein (2003). Regarding the Latin American contributions to this theory see Kay (1989); as for its permutations in the Caribbean see in particular Girvan (2006).

2 On this theory – that economies across the world, regardless of their location, would tend toward similar income levels and then to analogous growth rates whose long-term trend would be towards convergence toward common productivity levels of the factors themselves and of the living standards – see, inter alia, Romer (1990); Barro (1996) and Sachs and Warner (1995).

3 In the 'golden age of capitalism' (1950–1973), Europe's per capita income grew more than 4 per cent per annum and Japan's 8 per cent (Maddison, 2003). Even the Socialist countries raised income to annual rates of over 3 per cent. In addition, if we compare per capita GDP rates of the US and those of a considerable number of developing countries, those years seem to be a period of income-level convergence on a global scale. Nonetheless, even within the generalized prosperity, some regions already began to fall behind. Thus, whereas world per capita GDP was growing at a rate of 2.9 per cent per annum, Africa (2.2 per cent) and Latin America as a whole (2.5 per cent) were losing ground (Maddison, 2003).

'structural reforms' under the Washington Consensus, show no such convergence, even when the atypical trend towards rapid economic growth in East Asia and China, and more recently in India, are taken into account. Breaking down world income statistics by 'region' and isolating the poorest and richest countries, as well as the countries that once constituted the socialist bloc (now 'in transition' towards capitalism), shows that the North-South disparity in national incomes, the product of decades of uneven development, has worsened in recent decades.

Economic Mechanisms of Imperialism

The major mechanisms of exploitation and surplus transfer identified by *dependistas* are aid (Hayter, 1971), monopoly over technology (Dos Santos, 1970), unequal exchange (Amin, 1986),[4] the structure and terms of trade (Prebisch, 1949), foreign debt payments (George, 1986) and, more generally as in this volume, foreign direct investment. Through a combination of these and other mechanisms a substantial part of the social product is sucked out of the periphery and transferred to the centre, there converted into capital, leaving workers and producers on the periphery to bear the heavy social costs of this 'development' and survive in the wreckage left in its wake.[5] In this context the concept and theory of dependency can be viewed as particularly

4 'In theory, the new [worldwide] unequal division of labour would suit the bourgeoisie of the peripheries and the monopolies of the centres. For the transfer of industries would make it possible to recreate in the centre a reserve army of unemployed which a quarter of a century of growth had reduced to such an extent that the system has lost its 'normal' flexibility. And this unemployment would raise the rate of surplus value in the centre itself' (Amin, 1976).

5 As for the external debt, it is clearly more than a mechanism of surplus transfer (debt repayment); it s used as a lever on economic policies designed in the interest of the creditors and with significant negative social, economic and political costs to the debtor countries. This issue has been extensively analyzed over the years but a discussion of the US Senate Foreign Relations Committee, in August 1977, of the situation of countries with imminent debt problems (mainly Brazil, Mexico, Chile, Argentina, in Latin America) in relation to the IMF's measures is very revealing. Part of the records of this discussion read as follows: 'The measures that the IMF and the private banks stimulate the deficit countries to adopt usually include limitations to the growth of the money supply, reductions in public spending and devaluation. These measures are destined to maintain the level of domestic consumption low and to reduce the demand for imports. The growth of export industries are regarded as very important to help equilibrate the balance of trade and to assure that the country receives enough foreign exchange to service its foreign debt. Countries may also be stimulated to create a favourable climate for foreign investment and for private sector in general.... The problem with these measures is that, although they may be the most effective way quickly to compensate the balance of payments deficit of a country, they can also lead to greater unemployment, to the reduction in social welfare and to a lower standard of living for the people.... In the poorest countries, in which the majority of the population barely reaches a minimum level of subsistence, the government decision to impose a program of strict economic austerity can create social and political disturbance.... Finally, and as we have shown, in many countries there seems to be a direct correlation between economic difficulties and political repression. The ... government, therefore, may see itself obliged to choose between continuing its efforts in favour of human rights or to support the creditor demands to implant drastic economic

relevant. However, this book and recent studies point towards imperialism rather than dependency as the more relevant concept. Linkages among bankers, investors, agro-mineral elites and their Euroamerican counterparts and allies, as well as subsequent polarized socioeconomic and political developments, suggest that a dependency analysis has to be supplemented with class analysis and an analysis of international power relations derived from a theory of imperialism rather than dependency.

Multinational Corporations in the World Economic Order

In the 1970s, the UN Centre for Transnational Corporations (UNCTC)[6] documented the existence and workings of a 'billion dollar club', with reference to a small cluster of TNCs whose assets exceed the GDP of most countries and that dominate the world economy. The size and economic power of these MNCs, if not their position in the world economy and their functioning as imperial agents, are reflected in the assets and sales of the top corporations. Total annual sales of each of these corporations exceed the revenues of all governments except for the US and the GDP of all but the largest economies in the Developing World; of the 100 biggest economies in the world almost one-half are transnational corporations. Globally, in 2002, UNCTAD (2004: xvii) estimate that the world's 100 largest MNCs, representing less than 0.2 per cent of the global universe of MNCs, accounted for 14 per cent of sales by foreign affiliates worldwide, 12 per cent of their assets and 13 per cent of their employment. The top 500 MNCs, however, command the global economy with a share exceeding 25 per cent of global production and a monopoly position in the most strategic areas of production. The MNCs as a global entity accounted for well over 90 per cent of world trade in commodities and services and from 30 to 40 per cent of this trade was intra-firm, thus protecting and insulating the MNCs from the competitive forces of the market (Chakravarthi Raghavan / IFDA, June 10 1986). In the light of both the power and the effective role played by the MNCs in the global economy it is not at all unreasonable – in fact it is more than possible – to conceive of them as functional units and an agency of economic imperialism. At least, this is what we will argue.

Dynamics of Intra-Imperialist Competition

In the immediate post WWII context, high-level representatives and officials from the US, the UK and other 'capitalist democracies' of Western Europe met at

austerity programs that could only be imposed at the expense of civil liberties in the countries that adopt them' (Senate Foreign Relations Committee, 1977, pp. 179–180).

6 The UNCTC was more or less dismantled in the 1980s, in the wake of a major campaign and an assault on it by the Heritage Foundation and other Washington-based conservative and neoliberal institutions, concerned to establish a 'new world order' in which capital in its movements and TNCs in their operations are liberated from the shackles of government regulation. The UNCTC now survives in emasculated form but still manages to produce every three years a *World Investment Report* with very useful data on TNCs.

Bretton Woods to establish the institutional framework of a world order designed to reactivate the capital accumulation process, and to do so on the basis of the market and a project designed to ensure that those economically backward countries liberated from the yoke of European colonialism would pursue a capitalist path of economic development. Behind this project was the geopolitical interest of the US imperial state in establishing its hegemony, which was to some extent precluded by the construction of the multilateral system of the United Nations.

A systemwide crisis in the early 1970s brought the 'golden age of capitalism' (two decades of unprecedented rapid growth) to an end. It also saw important changes in the dominant forms of capital export – or what in the relevant academic and official discourse is termed 'international resource transfers'. In the 1950s and the 1960s there were two major forms of capital export: foreign direct investments (private capital transfers); and foreign aid, the 'official' transfer of financial resources and technical assistance made by governments and international organizations in the industrialized and developed North to governments in the South.

The entire manufacturing sector, which led the process of capitalist industrialization and rapid economic growth, was in crisis. On the one hand, the major markets for northern manufactures were saturated under conditions of intense competition among US, Japanese and German MNCs.

By 1970, in the throes of a system-wide production crisis, German and Japanese MNCs were winning the battle for the world market, having substantially increased their market share relative to their American competitors. Towards the end of the the Second World War, the US dominated the world's industrial and financial resources at its disposal. With just 6 per cent of the world's population, it had over 59 per cent of the world's developed oil reserves; generated 46 per cent of electricity worldwide; accounted for 38 per cent of world industrial production; and possessed 50 per cent of the world's monetary gold and currency reserves (Semmens, 2002). If it were not for the threat to US power represented by the enormous potential for industrial production in the USSR and the imminent formation of a socialist bloc, the US quite possibly would have acted unilaterally in support of its economic power with a corresponding political power, to consolidate its dominance. But under the circumstances the US was constrained to act within the UN system devised to prevent any one superpower from acting on a possible dream of world domination. The US state was also pushed into the creation of a program of international cooperation for international development, to ensure thereby that the countries in the process of liberating themselves from the yoke of colonial rule would not fall prey to the lure of communism and would pursue their process of nation-building (and economic development) along a capitalist path, within the institutionality of the world order set up in 1994 at Bretton Woods. But by 1970, after several decades of system-wide rapid economic development, the US had lost its command of the world economy, the victim of its own success in helping to reconstruct, in its own national interest, a Europe and Japan devastated by war. In 1950 the US accounted for 20 per cent of world export trade, while Germany and Japan between them accounted for only 6.3 per cent. By 1970 the US share had been cut 25 per cent while Germany and Japan's share of world exports tripled to 18.8 per cent.

This situation, reflected in these statistics on world trade shares as well as the statistics on a growing deficit in the US's merchandise trade account (see Table 3.6), led to US Government counter-measures designed to bolster the performance of the US corporations (Arrighi, 1982). This 'performance' was vital to the 'interests' of the US and a healthy balance of its international payments. The first consequential measure was taken by the US Government under Richard Nixon's presidency in its unilateral decision to let the US dollar float on the world market, abandoning a fundamental institution of the Bretton Woods system. Other measures include a series of efforts, adopted over the decade and in to the next, to manipulate the exchange and interest rates, attempting thereby to improve conditions for US exports as well as attract investments from abroad to help balance the national account. Arrighi (1982) details and analyses these measures, and the strategy underlying it, in a study that sheds light on the intra-capitalist competition that was threatening to tear the world system apart and on the trilaterally state efforts to contain this competitive struggle and to protect the world system in the common interest.

US efforts to rearrange the deck of the world market was a strategic response to the global production crisis, the conditions of which were reflected in a recessionary trend in world production – down 50 per cent from an annualized average rate of 4.5 per cent in the 1950s and 1960s. Other strategic responses included a direct assault of capital against labour, abrogating a long-standing social accord on sharing the fruits of any productivity gains, and a corporate strategy to separate its labour-intensivelabor-intensive production operations and relocate them overseas closer to sources of cheaper labour (Fröbel et al., 1980). The unintended consequence of this strategy, which can be traced out through various shifts in the pattern of distribution in FDI flows, included the creation of a new international division of labour; the appearance of several 'newly industrializing countries' and 'emerging markets' in Asia (South Korea, Taiwan, Singapore and Hong Kong) and Latin America (Brazil, Mexico); and the construction of a global production system, that in the 1980s became a cornerstone of a new global economy.

The spatial relocation of production and labour processes entailed a tactical rather than a strategic response of the multinationals seeking to improve their bottom line. However, the strategic ramifications of these corporate decisions were well understood at the time. One of a number of diverse strategic assessments was provided in 1969 by the then Vice-President of the US, Nelson Rockefeller. In his *Report on the Americas*, presented to the US Congress at the conclusion of a fact-finding mission to Latin America, he argues that:

> What is needed now is a broadening division of labour among the nations of the Western hemisphere. At present, the US is producing, at high cost behind tariff walls and quotas, goods that could be produced more economically by other hemisphere nations. The US is short of skilled labour and, if anything, this shortage promises to get worse. The shortage of skilled labour is intensified when the US continues to keep workers in lines which are, by definition, inefficient, since production can only be carried on here behind tariff or quota barriers. National productivity would be enhanced by shifting workers and capital out of protected industries into industries where advanced technology and intensive capital investment permits the US to pay high wages and still remain competitive in world markets. The goods the US is now producing inefficiently would be imported, mainly

> from less developed countries. Consumers would gain through lower prices, workers would receive higher wages, and the return on capital would be higher.
>
> The less developed countries would also gain. With abundant supplies of labour and wage levels well below those in the US, they could export processed foods, textiles, apparel, footwear, and other light manufactures, as well as meat and other farm products. [In addition] such nations would become better customers for the high-technology products of the United States.

A combination of such strategic assessments and the strategic and tactical responses of the multinationals gave rise to a new structure of global production and what a decade later had all the appearance of a new international division of labour (Fröbel, Heinrichs and Kreye, 1980). The dynamics of this restructuring process had multiple dimensions, including a massive shift of FDI towards 'Third world' manufacturing – mostly resource-based and low-tech – and the persistence of a competitive inter-imperialist struggle, forming a trilateral structure of international economic relations. In the 1970s the world economy had a triadic structure, with its pillars in the US, Western Europe and Japan. The location of corporate headquarters provided clear evidence of this structure. However, two decades of economic restructuring brought about a very different and more variegated structure, neither triadic (US, Europe, Japan) nor polar (centre and periphery) or even easily viewed along a North-South dimension. Within this new structure of global production China and a group of newly industrializing countries in South-East Asia constitute the most dynamic centre of economic growth while the US struggles to regain its hegemony over the world capitalist system under conditions of inter-imperialist competition for the world market.

Although there are other considerations the evidence suggests that the US is engaged in a battle for the world market that it might possibly lose, in the long run if not the short term. A caveat: the US as a system of national production might be losing the battle of the world market, notwithstanding the dynamism and productivity growth in certain strategic export sectors, but many of its top corporations are not. For example, 50 per cent of Chinese exports to the US, the source of a major and steadily growing deficit on the country's current account – USD 174 million in 1995; 433 million in 2001, 4.3 per cent of GDP; currently USD 700 million, 6 per cent of the GDP – are in fact handled by US corporations in China.

A critical issue in the battle for the world market is productivity growth.[7] Indeed, the entire system has been struggling for decades to overcome a pronounced

7 The dynamics of productivity growth in the US and Europe is the subject of a considerable and as yet unsettled and ongoing debate, with a number of scholars (Lewis, 2004) pointing towards the greater capacity of the US economy, relative to that of the EU, to finally escape the decades-long systemic trend towards sluggish productivity growth. While a number of analysts have argued that EU manufacturing capital and labour has exhibited levels of growth equal or superior to the US, studies by the neoliberal Mckinsey Global Institute (Lewis, 2004), using a purchasing power parity (PPP) as opposed to market exchange rate approach, continue to argue that the EU has been losing ground to the US. In each critical industrial sector, Lewis (2004, 51) argues, US productivity (and productivity growth) is higher than in the EU – up to 30 per cent higher. However, other analysts have argued that this presumed productivity gap

sluggishness in the rate of productivity growth, a long-term trend that underlies the propensity towards crisis in the global economy. The major strategies used to halt and reverse this trend have included *technological conversion* – the application of new production, communication and transportation technologies and an associated new mode of regulation – post-Fordism (Lipietz, 1987). Another productivity-raising strategy was a direct assault on labour – on its capacity to organize and negotiate collective agreements for higher wages, improved work conditions and a share of productivity gains (Crouch, 1978; Davis, 1980). The outcome of this strategy is reflected in a trend towards compression in wage rates and a reduction in the share of labour in national income. In the US, for example, wages lost up to 10 per cent of its value from 1974 to 1983. A third crisis-management strategy was to relocate and globalize industry, seeking thereby to reduce production costs, particularly in regard to labour. Recent studies suggest that the combination of such strategies did indeed work. While the US economy has by no means escaped its propensity towards crisis, and its current account deficit has continued to climb, the US economy in the 1990s exhibited a certain dynamism in regard to overall production and productivity growth, outperforming its competitors in Japan and the EU and managing to attract the foreign capital needed to finance its rapidly growing expenditures and imports, and balance payments on its current account.[8]

Some of these changes in the global economy are reflected in a shift of FDI from natural resource extraction industries in the 'third world' towards manufacturing and subsequently 'services', which, in the 1990s attracted an increasingly disproportionate share of FDI–US$809bn in 1990 (versus US$770 n. in manufacturing and US$155bn in primary resources) and US$4,268 billion in 2002 (versus US$1,192bn. in manufacturing and US$260bn. in primary resources (UNCTAD, 2004: 303). Other dynamics of change included; a process of technological conversion and 'productive transformation'; the emergence of new dynamic sectors of the world economy, together with a recovery in the overall rate of productivity growth; and the emergence of a new 'growth pole' in this economy, constituted by a number of 'rapidly growing countries' in Asia, particularly China, which has posted an unprecedented rate of rapid GDP growth – up to an annualized average of 10 per cent – for over a decade.

---

is entirely accounted for in differences in the 'costs of doing business', that is, in the welfare state or the model of capitalist development (European versus American).

8 Alan Greenspan, President of the Federal Reserve (Central) Bank, in an address commemorating the 80 years since the founding of Mexico's Central Bank (*La Jornada*, November 15, 2005, 2005), observed that the deficit on the US current account is financed essentially through the purchase of treasury bonds by Asian, particularly Chinese, investors. The health of the world economy, as well as the US, he noted, is heavily dependent – too much so (the troubling level of the US deficit cannot be sustained in the long-term) – on the capacity of the US to continue to attract this investment as well as the continued use of the US dollar as the reserve currency for the world economy. Foreign investors will undoubtedly tire of the US market, and in fact, the US is already experiencing difficulties in maintaining the current level of foreign investment. So the only way of avoiding a meltdown of the US economy is to maintain and increase the productivity growth and the demonstrated flexibility of US enterprise.

Nayyar (1978, 59), in a study of these dynamics in the late 1970s, identified a trend towards foreign investments in manufacturing, and the exports of manufactures from a group of 'newly industrializing countries' (NICs) emerging in the 'developing world' to the industrialized countries of the Developed World, provided evidence of greater participation of foreign investment in this type of industrialization. For example, exports of manufactures from the 'developing countries' grew almost 500 per cent between 1966 and 1974, and in Latin America this growth was almost 600 per cent. Table 2.2 provides an indication of the base line trend in the sectoral distribution of foreign investment. Not only did investments in manufacturing continue to grow at double the average rate of economic growth but the dominant trend included a growing propensity towards exports. More recent studies confirm the persistence of these trends, notwithstanding an equally evident trend of investment-driven high-tech production and exports from the industrialized countries (UNCTAD, 2004).[9]

Table 2.2 World inward FDI (est.), average annual flows, by sector and region, 1989-1991, 2001-2002

	(US$bs.)			
	91-91		**2001-02**	
	DCs	LDCs	DCs	LDCs
Resource extraction	8.8	3.1	46.1	17.6
Manufacturing	51.0	17.1	90.2	76.6
Services	83.2	11.2	371.2	97.1

Source: UNCTAD, *World Investment Report*, 2004, p. 318.

In connection with an earlier sectoral and regional trend in regards to foreign investment and exports Nayar (1978, p. 59) noted that 'the past two decades … witnessed an increasing incidence of private foreign investment in the manufacturing sector of underdeveloped economies. 'In the beginning,' he continues, 'such investment was concentrated in import-substituting industries … but disenchantment with import substitution … led a few countries to adopt … *outward-looking policies*'. He added that 'the export expansion [fueled by these policies] has frequently been associated with a new type of foreign investment in manufacturing which is directed towards overseas sales rather than domestic markets.'

9 The 'service sector' is composed of the following activities, utilities and 'services': Electricity, gas and water; Construction; Trade; Hotels and restaurants; Transport, storage and communications; Finance; Business activities; Public administration and defence; Education; Health and social services; Community, social and personal service activities; and 'Other services'. Clearly not all of these 'services' are tradable and some of them rank very low on UNCTAD's 'Index of Internationalization'. Nevertheless, as UNCTAD (2004) analyzes in considerable detail, the dominant trend in world trade is towards an ever greater share of 'services' especially those with as 'high knowledge' or information content.

Nayyar also noted that the major determinant of this type of foreign investment was 'labour costs'. In fact, he noted, 'the absolute differences in wage rates between rich countries and poor, for workers engaged in the manufacturing sector, are phenomenal ... less than one-tenth the level prevalent in industrialized countries.' (Nayyar, 1978, p. 73.) Although many economists might dispute this point regarding world trade today (presumably more 'information-rich' and less dependent on direct labour costs) there is little doubt that in the late 1970s and 1980s the relative costs of labour in different countries was a major factor in corporate relocation decisions and the resulting international division of labour.

As for 'the timing of this phenomenon' (Third World Industrialization) it can be explained in terms of two basic factors: i) 'competition between advanced capitalist countries'; and ii) 'conflict between capital and labour within the industrial economies'.[10] What is more, Nayyar observed, trade unions had become more militant and therefore less willing to tolerate the demands of capital. On the other hand, workers in the world of poor and developing countries were frequently unorganized and more easily repressed 'so that transnational corporations [could] eliminate industrial disputes and need not worry about cutting back on employment in times of recession.'[11]

By the 1980s a new international division of labour and a global production system were in place, although very uneven in its dynamics and lacking the institution of what emerged as a 'new world order', supplying for the system appropriate rules of governance. These would eventually be supplied by the World Trade Organization (WTO), formed in 1994, some 50 years after its conception at Bretton Woods.

Within this new structure, manufacturing had become increasingly globalized and variegated in its spatial distribution, with a tendency to relocate technology- and capital-intensive operations to some parts of world economy and labour-intensive operations (maquiladores, for example) to other parts. However, notwithstanding the emergence of a new international division much of Latin America and virtually all of Sub-Saharan Africa, in terms of production and trade, were positioned outside this structure; they continued to export raw materials and minerals to the centre and import capital goods, industrial inputs and consumer manufactures. In effect, the world economy in the 1980s combined elements of the 'old imperialism' and the 'new imperialism'. After other forms of emerging market finance collapsed in the wreckage of the lending/debt financing mania of the 1970s, this new imperialism was fueled by the growth of FDI.

By 1990 the structure of the new imperialism, a global economy and a neoliberal world order based on what Williamson (1990) dubbed the 'Washington Consensus', was in place, brought about in a series of 'structural reforms' such as the privatization of public assets and enterprises, market deregulation and the liberalization of both trade and financial flows (see CEPAL, 2004).

---

10 On these political dynamics of inter-capitalist competition and class struggle in the European theatre of this class war see Davis (1980) and Crouch and Pizzorno (1978).

11 Nayyar quotes corporate CEOs to the effect that '[w]e won't go into that country until the government gets the union in line'; 'We need to be able to get goods, people and money in and out easily'; and 'We need political stability and labour docility'.

In the 1990s the economic structure of this new imperialism was consolidated, first through the investment and production operations of the MNCs, and then, through the diplomatic, economic, political and military operations of the imperial state. There is substantial evidence that these two forms of imperialism went hand in hand, notwithstanding the rather fanciful notion of Michael Hardt and Toni Negri (2002) that global capital had become disassociated from the imperial state (on this issue see the concluding section on the New Imperialism below).

In the early 1990s, 'private sector lenders and investors fell on the emerging market economies' – and the economies of Latin America, where the way for capital had been paved by sweeping economic reforms – 'as the Israelites once did on the promised land' (Wolf, 2003). The story unfolds in various reports on corporate structure of the global economy and on the changing pattern of 'international resource transfers' (capital flows) discussed in the next chapter.

Conclusion: The State and the New Imperialism

In this chapter the multinational corporation appears as the basic operating unit of the world capitalist system and key agents of US imperialism, a form of economic shock troops. However, this point needs to be argued, not merely asserted. For one thing, it raises questions that are by no means fully answered, surrounded as they are by several unresolved issues.

One of these issues is the fundamental nature of the new imperialism or its various contemporary forms. As a point of fact, the 'new imperialism' is actually most often identified with the projection of military rather than economic power, and it currently takes the form of war, rather than the globalization of capital or international cooperation for development (on development as a form of imperialism see Veltmeyer, 2005). In the form of war, the 'new imperialism' is widely viewed from both the left and the right as a 'return to the rougher methods of an earlier era – force, pre-emptive attack, deception, whatever is necessary to deal with those who still live in the nineteenth century world of every state for itself' (Cooper, 2000b, 7). From this perspective, widely shared among the neoconservatives that surround The White House, and in the words of Robert Cooper, Foreign Policy Advisor of Tony Blair, 'Among ourselves [post-modern states] we keep the law but … in the jungle we must also use the laws of the jungle' (2000b: 7).

Another unsettled issue has to do with the connection between the multinational corporations and the state, both in the 'global south', on the 'periphery' of the world system, and in the 'global north', at its centre. The critical issue here is that imperialism implies a strategic project or plan for world domination – to establish hegemony over the world system. To the degree that the CEOs of the multinational corporation typically do not pursue such a strategy; rather, they operate under the logic of capital accumulation, in terms of which their only concern is to operate with a profit and perhaps to maximize the return on the capital invested in the corporation. Thus, to view the world economy as Hardt and Negri do, as dominated by footloose forms of global capital operating in no national interest, allows them and others to conceive of a global 'empire', dominated by multinational corporations, without imperialism – without an imperial state and without a strategic project of world domination.

However, the world is different from the way these scholars see it. In fact, the multinational corporation works closely with the imperial state in the North, that is in the US and the EU. First, the MNCs have a home base, a headquarters; and most of the biggest and economically most powerful corporations are based in the US and the EU. The US remains the dominant power by far in terms of the number and percentage of MNCs among the top 500 with 227 (45 per cent), followed by Western Europe with 141 (28 per cent), Asia (mostly Japan, a pillar of the 1970s' triadic structure of the world economy and trilateral co-management of the system), with 92 (18 per cent). These three regional power blocs control 91 per cent of the biggest MNCs in the world (*Financial Times*, 2004).[12]

Secondly, the MNCs are dependent on their home state to pave the way for their overseas operations, to create the conditions (policy reforms) that allow them to penetrate local markets and set up shop, buying out lucrative but now privatized corporations. The US Government and its European allies in its imperialist project, both directly in the form of high level summits of Heads of State or Ministers of Finance and indirectly via its adjuncts in the UN system of international organizations (the World Bank and the IMF) were instrumental in forcing host governments in the developing countries of the global south in the 1980s and 1990s to reduce or eliminate barriers to the entry and operations of their MNCs.

Thirdly, it is evident that the political apparatus of the US state has imperialist designs for and over the world economy, and that it equates its imperialist project of world domination with the profitable operations of US-based corporations, i.e. the US state identifies the interests of corporate capital with the 'national interest' and is disposed to commit the state's resources and project its power to advance these interest, even to the point of war.

Finally, vis-à-vis the interests of corporate capital embodied in the operations of the MNCs, the state is hardly the powerless entity described by the globalization theorists. For one thing, these theorists do not distinguish clearly between the states in the global south, many, if not all, rendered powerless or by or subordinated to the forces of neoliberal globalization (and the imperial state, we might add). A number of these states, mostly in the EU are tied into the empire building and maintenance project of the US; they form and are part of a system of imperial states – the imperial state. Notwithstanding existing relations of inter-imperialist rivalry and competition for the world market, the states can be rallied in support of the system as a whole, and they are even prepared to concede US leadership if not domination and hegemony. The condition of this strategic alliance is a share in the proceeds of imperial rule

12 A closer examination of the 'peak' of the biggest MNCs illustrates even better the concentration of power of the US. Of the top 10 MNCs, 80 per cent are American and 20 per cent are European. Among the top 20 per cent, 75 per cent are American, 20 per cent are European and 5 per cent are Japanese. Of the top 50 MNCs, 60 per cent are US, 32 per cent are European, 6 per cent are Japanese and 5 per cent are other. The greatest concentration of US power is among the biggest MNCs while competition sets in as one moves to the lower tiers in the hierarchy of economic power.

and participation in high level strategic considerations, even if this participation in particular conjunctures is reduced to mere consultation.

Chapter 3

Foreign Investment at Work

As argued in the last chapter, MNCs are the basic operating units of the capitalist and imperialist system. Although they are fairly mobile, able to move into and operate in countries all over the world in search of profitable returns on their direct investments, this has not always been the case. Until the 1980s their investment and production operations were regulated by the central government of the host country. But under the rubric of the new economic model, and with the support and agency of the imperial state and its international financial institutions, the way was paved for these agents of 'private capital' to move almost at will. In the 1980s country after country liberalized their treatment of foreign investment and deregulated their operations, welcoming the multinationals as bearers of much needed capital and advanced production technologies, which, it was hoped, would be transferred.

However, notwithstanding ideas about the need of developing societies for external supplementary sources of capital ('development finance') and the benefits of FDI the presence of MNCs in host countries in many cases has been far from welcome. While some liberal governments sought to attract this investment, its entry was generally restricted; and the profit-seeking operations of the MNCs attracted opposition from diverse sectors concerned with the negative impacts of these operations on the environment, the economy, and society and the political system. In this opposition and resistance, it was understood that MNCs are concerned with profit-making and that in the process, if allowed to operate freely, they would tend to appropriate the benefits, leaving the local population to bear the environmental, economic, social and political costs. It was also understood that the effort of the UN and the international 'community' to rehabilitate the 'private sector', appealing to a sense of social responsibility in seeking to incorporate it into the development process, might mean sacrificing the public interest on the altar of private enterprise.

International Private Capital Flows

International capital flows are public and private. Public flows consist of financial resource transfers between governments in the form of 'foreign aid', which in theory (the rhetoric of international development associations and agencies) is made available to developing countries to assist them in accessing financial resources to compensate for a lack of 'capital'. Foreign aid can take a bilateral form, such as one government giving aid or lending money to another, or multilateral, lending from multilateral institutions such as the IMF and World Bank and the Inter-American Development Bank.

International private capital flows consist of three main types: foreign bank lending, portfolio investment (PI) and foreign direct investment (FDI).[1] Foreign bank lending refers to the loans extended by commercial banks or multilateral institutions (such as the IMF and the World Bank) to public- or private sector borrowers. In the 1970s there was a dramatic expansion of this form of capital flow, as the commercial banks such as Chase Manhattan began to operate overseas or increase these operations as a means of offsetting declining profit rates at home.

PI refers the purchase of stocks, bonds, derivatives and other financial instruments issued by the private sector (or the government, in the case of bonds) in a country other than that in which the purchaser resides. FDI refers to the purchase of a 'controlling interest' (at least 10 per cent of the assets) in a foreign business enterprise. FDI takes two basic forms: 'Greenfield', which involves the creation of a new facility – for example, construction of a factory by a foreign investor – or the incorporation of new production technologies; and 'Brownfield', namely mergers and acquisitions that involve the purchase of assets of existing domestic firms. In the 1990s much FDI took this form, taking advantage of the widespread private offerings of the stock of public companies under the widespread neoliberal policy of privatization, designed to revert the nationalization policy of earlier years under the model of state-led-and-directed development. Table 3.1 shows the connection between FDI and privatization in the Latin American context. It is estimated that for Latin America over one-half of FDI inflows in the 1990s took the form of 'acquisitions' (via privatization) and 'mergers', leaving less than 50 per cent for productive investment in new technologies, etc. In addition, much of the capital for this investment were raised on local markets or derived from profits on sales.

Table 3.1 Latin America and the Caribbean: value of privatization, 1990-1997

	(In US$ bs.)								
	1990	1991	1992	1993	1994	1995	1996	1997	Total
Argentina	2.1	1.9	5.3	4.6	1.4	1.3	1.0	9.7	27.3
Bolivia	-	-	.01	.01	-	.85	.87	-	1.7
Brazil	-	1.6	2.5	2.6	2.0	.9	3.8	17.4	30.8
Colombia	.12	.11	.03	.01	.68	.14	1.5	3.2	5.8
Chile	.03	.12	.02	-	.20	-	.58	.01	1.0
Mexico	3.6	10.7	6.8	2.5	.77	-	-	.08	24.5
Peru	-	-	.21	.32	2.6	.95	2.5	.42	7.0
Venezuela	.01	2.3	.03	.03	.02	.02	2.1	1.5	6.0
Others	-	.25	.03	.10	.87	.08	.07	.84	2.2
Total	5.9	17.8	14.9	10.2	8.5	4.2	12.4	33.2	106.3

Source: Cominetti (1996).

1 Another form of private financial resource transfers is remittances. We do not discuss this form of 'international resource transfers' because it generally does not take the form of 'capital', i.e. financial resources used to generate a profit (and expand production in the processes).

Debt Financing

Reasonable levels of external debt that help finance productive activity are expected by economists to enhance growth,[2] but even the IMF acknowledges that beyond a certain level 'additional indebtedness may reduce growth' (Pattillo and Ricci, 2002).

Over the past three decades, developing countries have borrowed large amounts, often at highly concessional interest rates. The hope was that these loans would put them on a faster development path. But as debt ratios reached very high levels in the 1980s, it became clear that for many of these countries, 'repayment would not just constrain economic performance but be virtually impossible' – Latin America's much studied but not so well understood 'debt crisis'. Thus, in the 1980s, several middle-income countries – particularly in Latin America (Argentina, Brazil, Mexico) – faced severe debt crises (that is, were unable to meet their obligations to creditors), leading the 'international financial community' to search for ways and to design specific measures to address the issue (and avoid radical proposals to default on a debt that was widely regarded as illegitimate): reduce the problem to manageable proportions ('bring the debt … to sustainable levels'). The aim was to obviate the need for debtor countries to default on their loans, allowing them to resume their debt payment obligations and thereby maintain creditworthiness (and thus access to more loans, foreign capital and 'aid'). Debt crisis alleviation or management measures included, first of all, a package of policy reforms (cut back on spending and imports, financial and trade liberalization, privatization, export promotion) designed (by the Bank and the Fund for the debtor countries) to promote fiscal discipline (balanced accounts), economic growth and export earnings. Secondly, the institution of the 'Brady Plan' (a formula concocted by US Secretary of State Brady) – to forgive a small part of the debt (discount its book value) and convert most of it into IOU bonds repayable in the long term, effectively reducing the debt balance and softening repayment terms.

The Plan worked. No heavily-indebted country defaulted on their debt obligations; they all swallowed the bitter medicine of fiscal discipline and structural adjustment; governments in Latin America assumed full responsibility for the debt obligations contracted by the private sector as well as previous governments; public spending, especially on social programs, was cut back, as were imports; and creditors receive full payment on their restructured loans. There was, however, a downside to these developments, viewed by World Bank and IMF economists as 'transitional costs': a 'decade lost to development' (zero economic growth), a drastic reduction of living standards for working people and producers, and an extension and deepening of social inequalities and bloated rates of poverty. At the beginning of the decade it was estimated that 36 per cent of the population was unable meet their 'basic needs'

2 'Economic theory' [i.e.that is neoliberalism], the IMF suggests, shows that 'reasonable levels of borrowing by a developing country are likely to enhance its economic growth' (*Finance & Development*, 39,2, June 2002). Countries 'at early stages of development' x continues, 'have small stocks of capital and are likely to have investment opportunities with rates of return higher than those in advanced economies.' Thus, '[a]s long as they use the borrowed funds for productive investment and do not suffer from macroeconomic instability, policies that distort economic incentives, or sizable adverse shocks, growth should increase and allow for timely debt repayments' (*Finance & Development*, 39, 2, June 2002).

– poor by then existing standards. By the end of the decade this figure had increased to 44 per cent.

Latin American Debt after the Asian Crisis

The 1990s saw the end of the Latin American debt crisis – or, more to the point, its 'manageability' – and the start of a broader financial crisis based on the uncontrolled and highly volatile flows of portfolio investments. In both cases of crisis current account balance of payment settlements were strangled due to the expiry of refinancing for original long-term loan schedules added to short-term loans. The only objective of lending funds is to recuperate the loans with profit. The magic solution for Latin America (re-establish debt repayment capacity) was a radical macroeconomic shift from interventionist to market-led economics and politics. Final agreements with private banks following the Brady Plan allowed debt balances to be reduced, IOUs to be used to effect privatizations and arrears to be converted into IOU bonds payable in 25 years.

As for debts owed to OECD governments they were reprogrammed in a set of final agreements made with the 'Paris Club' of OECD creditors, which gave the debtors 3 years' grace in rescheduling repayments over 25 years. The Brady Plan and the Paris Club agreements were in their essentials the same: designed to *restructure the debt in the long-term in return for debtors applying macroeconomic politics of stabilization and structural adjustment*, which, the theory went, would stabilize the economic system of their countries, provide a framework for resumed economic growth, and thus generate the financial resources needed to service their debt obligations.

These agreements were reached under the assumption that the stability of the international system would be guaranteed – that the conditions set for the debtors would prevent a major upset in the world economic order. The possibility of a collective cessation of debt repayment in the 1980s almost caused the international financial system to crash, but the 'performance of the IMF and the US Treasury' in playing off one country against the other prevented the formation of a Debtors' Club as well as a collective cessation of debt repayments. Thus, the international financial system suffered a big shake-up but did not collapse. But with the arrival of the Asian crisis in the mid-1997, the international situation changed dramatically. The international economic system was again stirred by shaky stock exchanges, commodity markets crashes and devalued exchange rates everywhere except in the US. International indices were weakened and current accounts deficits throughout the world, including the US, suffered. This did not mean that the system was on the verge of collapse. But it did mean that global GDP growth would – and did – slow down and a number of countries, both developed and developing, would (and did) suffer financial crises. In some Asian countries the financial crisis brought on a production crisis and the virtual collapse of the real economy. The financial crisis also meant that the economic balance of African and Latin American countries became increasingly vulnerable to a process designed to restructure the system – impose a level and form of capital control and design a set of institutions and mechanisms (financial architecture) that would re-establish order and good governance. Under the protective umbrella and favourable conditions created by these institutional mechanisms the TNCs moved in.

FDI and the Developing Countries

As for the MNCs, the shock troops of both the old and the new imperialism, they have come to dominate the global economy. Table 3.2 provides a snap shot of this 'development'. What the table shows is that the regional structure of international capital flows has changed dramatically. First, the developing countries overall, and Latin America in particular, have become an increasingly important destination for foreign investment. This is undoubtedly the result of a more investment-friendly climate and the more favourable conditions for foreign investment. Secondly, due in part to 'changing political sentiments', foreign aid flows stagnated relative to private capital flows in the form of FDI, bank loans and portfolio investments. Thirdly, there occurred a significant shift in the composition of this private capital. Historically, foreign lending by commercial banks was the most significant type of private capital flow to developing countries. But in the 1980s, commercial banks curtailed lending under conditions of an external debt crisis affecting all of Latin America, much of Africa and some of Asia. And the banks also found the speculative opportunities available in the liberalized financial environment of the 1990s more appealing than lending. The decline in both foreign lending and aid to developing countries in the 1990s increased the need to attract FDI and elevated the relative importance of both FDI and PI as sources of development finance. The flow of both types of capital has increased significantly.

Table 3.2 World distribution of net FDI, 1991-2003

	(US$ bs)							
	1992-06	1997	1998	1999	2000	2001	2002	2003
World	254	482	686	1079	1993	824	651	653
Developed countries	254	270	472	825	1121	589	460	467
EU	88	128	250	476	684	389	374	346
US	47	103	174	283	314	144	30	87
Japan	1	3	3	13	8	6	9	8
Developing Countries	92	193	191	229	246	209	162	156
Asia	59	109	100	109	142	107	95	99
China	26	44	44	40	41	47	53	57
Latin America	27	73	82	106	85	84	56	42
Africa	5	11	9	12	9	19	11	14

Source: Adapted from ECLAC, with data from (UNCTAD, 2003).

The fundamental changes in the composition of international capital flows to developing countries are illustrated in the following data (World Bank, various years). The new long-term bank lending (including bonds, and excluding IMF loans) to developing countries was US$7 billion in 1970, $65.3 billion in 1980, $43.1 in 1990, $5.1 billion in 2000 and -$9 billion in 2002 (Chan and Grabel, 2004; 107). FDI and PI flows to developing countries were scant until the 1990s but grew dramatically thereafter. For example, net FDI to developing countries was only $2.2 billion in 1970, $4.4 billion in 1980, $24.1 billion in 1990, $160.6 billion in 2000 and $143 billion in 2002. Net PI over the same period also grew dramatically. It was zero in 1970 and 1980, $3.7 billion in 1990, $26 billion in 2000 and $9.4B in 2002.

The shift from debt to equity financing is shown in Figure 3.1 in the cases of South Korea and Mexico. The table also shows a greater reliance of Mexico than South Korea on FDI, a pattern repeated for Latin America and Asia generally. What the table does not show, however, is the dramatic shift from debt to equity financing, with the banks in full retreat (albeit, with the help of the IMF and World Bank, not without collecting on their debts). In the 1990s FDI would became what the IMF termed the 'backbone' of the development financing process.

To understand the dynamics of these changing patterns, particularly in regard to the presumed role of these capital flows in financing and bringing about economic development, several facts about these flows need to be established.

First, developing countries actually receive but a small proportion of all global private flows. Since 1990, notwithstanding the ascendancy of FDI and PI in the North-South flows of private capital the developing country share of total PI flows has remained rather low – 9.7 per cent in 1991; 9.0 per cent in 1994; 6.2 per cent in 1998, a year into the 'Asian financial crisis'; and just 5.5 per cent in 2000.

Secondly, private capital flows are highly concentrated in a small number of middle-income, large developing countries such as Brazil and Mexico. The World Bank (2002) in this connection reports that over the last 13 years the top eight developing countries accounted for 84 per cent of total net flows to the South. As with FDI the largest net recipient of PI has been China, which has attracted 22 per cent of the developing country total since 1989 (Chang and Grabel, 2004: 188). China is followed by Mexico, Brazil, South Africa, India, Thailand, Malaysia. By contrast, the poorest countries receive very little of the PI flows that go to the developing countries. In 2002 South Asian countries other than India (which received 9.1 per cent of the developing world total PI) and countries in sub-saharan Africa other than South Africa received *no* net PI.

As for FDI the pattern is similar. From 1988 to 1998 world FDI flows more than tripled – from US$192 billion to US$610 billion, and the share of FDI to GDP was generally on the rise in both developed and developing countries (World Bank, 2000) although the developing countries received about a quarter of world FDI inflows (World Bank, 2000). In 1991, these countries received 22.5 per cent of global FDI and in 1994, the high point of these North-South flows, their share climbed to 35.2 per cent, with Asia and Latin America accounting for the bulk of this investment growth. In 1998, however, the developing country share of global FDI was reduced to 26 per cent in 1998 and only 16 per cent in 2000, reflecting the fact that the privatization program in many countries had exhausted their profit-making opportunities.

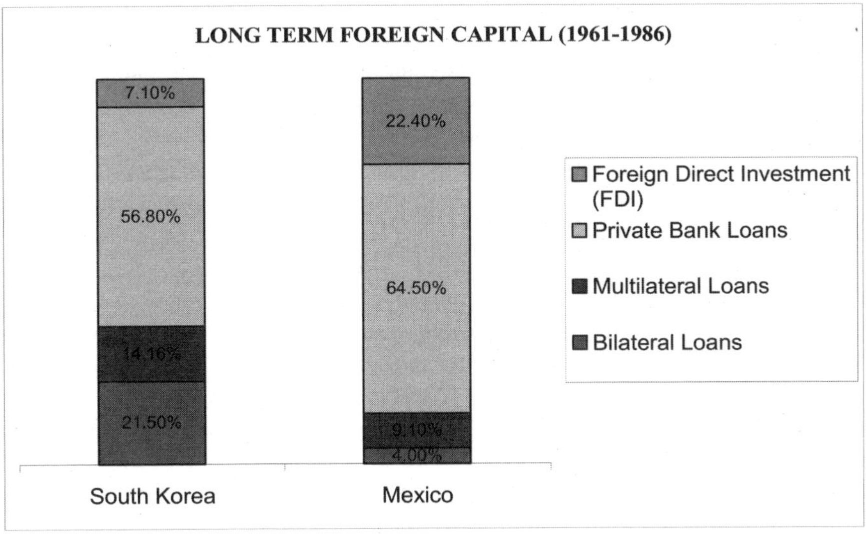

Figure 3.1 Long term foreign capital (1961-1986)
Source: IMF (various years), International Financial Statistics. Adapted from Gereffi and Wyman (1990: 61).

After falling for 3 years the worldwide flow of FDI resumed in 2004, bringing US$612 billion of capital into the developing countries, a 14 per cent jump on 2003 (*Fortune* 2004a, 2400b). However, most of this growth was accounted for by just two developing countries – China and India.

By 2004 the worldwide flow of FDI was US$612 billion, the first significant growth since 2000. Most of this growth in the volume and level of FDI, and the associated change in the macroeconomic panorama (prognostication of a recovery of the world economy), according to ECLAC reflected not so much the macroeconomic situation (increased openness and financial liberalization) as developments at the microeconomic level, specifically a six-fold increase in the level of profits on capital invested by the multinationals (540 per cent for US-based). This dramatic increase followed two years of negative growth, according to although ECLAC data show a steady increase in the mass, if not rate, of profits from 1990.

A partial explanation for the resurgence of FDI inflows in 2004 can be found in the recovery of various markets in the US and the Developing World. A second explanation is in an apparent recovery in the trend towards 'fusion and acquisition', which, together with the privatization program, absorbed much of the private capital flows in the 1990s. A third explanation can be found in the increased rate of return of profit on capitalism invested by the TNCs – up 540 per cent, according to ECLAC, in just 6 years (CEPAL). In this analysis, the increase in the volume of total profit, if not the actual rate of profitable returns – a micro-development, in ECLAC's optics – explains more of the resurgence in FDI than developments in the macroeconomic situation (increased openness and financial liberalization).

As for the sectoral distribution of this North-South flow of FDI in the last decade of the twentieth century and the first decade of the next, it would seem that manufacturing, especially in China and India but also Mexico, remains the chief destination point for FDI; and natural resources, particularly traditional sources of energy – oil, gas and hydroelectric, remains significant. However, the overall trend is towards increased investment in services, especially telecommunications (UNCTAD, 2004). As for 'industry', which still receives the largest share of North-South FDI flows, much of it, as in Mexico, takes the form of maquiladoras. The production operations of these maquillas, however, are closely integrated, via the TNCs, into the economies of the industrially advanced countries – the global production system. Indeed, they are more easily integrated into these economies than the domestic markets of the developing countries, a problem, according to Samir Amin of 'structural disarticulation' and 'unequal exchange'.

As for the global geodynamics of these capital flows Latin America and the Caribbean in recent years have been the only regions within the Developing World in which FDI has consistently declined. From 1990 to 1996, in response to sweeping structural reforms and a policy of privatization MNCs turned towards Latin America in a big way, stepping up new investments from $8.7 billion in 1990 to $61 billion in 1998 – a sixfold increase in FDI inflows. Latin America for a time led the world in attracting FDI, but this would not last. In 1997, as available opportunities provided by privatization were exhausted the flow of investment capital dropped and with it (temporarily anyway) any thoughts about a sustained economic recovery (ECLAC, 1998; UNCTAD, 1998, 256, 267–268, 362; 2002).

Private Capital Flows in Latin America

Even with the relatively poor performances of so many economies in Latin America in the 1990s huge profits were to made as evidenced by the large net outflow or transfers out of the region of money in the form of debt service payments and profit remittances, royalty and licence fees and interest payments throughout the 1990s. Calculations from data provided by ECLAC (2002a, 2000b) on profit and interest payments show that returns on the operations of US capital in Latin America in the 1990s averaged close to $60 billion a year – US$585 billion in total. And this is not the whole story. Saxe-Fernandez (2002) calculates that if one were to add to the ECLAC data revenues derived by capital from royalty payments, shipping, insurance and other service fees, and illegal transfers by the financial elite to overseas bank accounts, then the total transfer from Latin America to the North in the 1990s was in the order of US$100 billion.

This process of 'capital accumulation' (profit-making) and the associated resurgence of Euroamerican (and US-led) imperialism can be traced out with available statistics on capital flows, particularly in regard to investments undertaken by the multinationals. What these statistics show is a dramatic expansion in the flow of capital, particularly in the form of direct investments, towards parts of Asia and Latin America. In this process Latin America became the principal destination for new flows of FDI.

While the flow of FDI from 1990 to 1996 increased by 223 per cent, worldwide, FDI flows to Latin America increased 600 per cent. Over this same period Brazil received 2.5 per cent of all FDI flows to developing countries in 1990 and 8 per cent in 1998, at which point Brazil was second only to China in the volume of FDI flows absorbed by developing countries (Sobeet, 1999).[3] As for US-based outward investments, Latin America increased its share from 13 per cent in 1982 to over 20 per cent in 1998; from 1990 to 1997 43 per cent of FDI flows from the United States to developing countries were routed to Latin America, which, as a result, practically doubled its stock of US-based FDI – close to $900 billion (CEPAL, 1998, 196–197).

But as CEPAL researchers have discovered, the scale of these flows are not fully apparent in official statistics, given that as much as 43 per cent of US-based FDI to the region is channeled through a number of financial centres set up in the Caribbean islands (CEPAL, 1998, 199).[4] Nevertheless, the pattern is clear: over the course of the 1990s, Latin America significantly increased its stock and inflow of new FDI, in the process becoming the favored destination of US profit-seeking capital in the Developing World.[5]

---

3 From 1992 to 1997, Latin America absorbed US$ 185,4 billion in the form of FDI. This compares to $333.5 billion for the United States, the world's biggest recipient as well as provider of FDI. China over the same period absorbed 194.4 billion while the Asian Newly Industrializing Countries, China excepted, absorbed US$ 181.5 billion. The European Union was the recipient of US$ 553.7 billion, mostly from the US (SOBEET, 1999).

4 In 1997, 50 per cent of US FDI stock was in financial activities and 83 per cent of it was routed through financial centres in the Caribbean. In addition, investment flows to industries such as electrical and transport equipment also tends to be routed through these centres, especially Bermuda, the Netherlands Antilles, a number of other Caribbean Islands, and Panama. Because so much US-based FDI is channelled though these financial centres, the true scale of US FDI to Latin America is much larger than reflected in official statistics (CEPAL, 1998: 199-297). To get around the limitations of official data on FDI flows, and to pinpoint the final destination of the capital routed through the financial centres, CEPAL's Unit on Investment and Corporate Strategies supplements these data with data on the operations of the subsidiaries of US-based TNCs found in the US Dept. of Commerce's Benchmark Survey: U.S. Direct Investment Abroad. After its analysis of these two data sets, CEPAL (1998: 206) concludes that far from having declined, as the official data appear to suggest, the importance of Latin America's manufacturing sector for US-based TNCs has grown. The difference is that in recent years, manufacturing investment has been concentrated in activities catering to local markets (foodstuffs and chemicals) and in high-technology industries (electrical and transport equipment), whose exports have burgeoned.

5 Over the course of the decade, the flow of direct investment increased by 223 per cent world-wide but in Latin America the rate of increase has been close to 600 per cent, most of which (62 per cent) accounted for by Brazil, Mexico and Argentina, with Chile, Colombia, Peru and Venezuela accounting for another 26 per cent. The inflow of FDI to the region (see Table 2.2) is reflected in the rapid growth of the accumulated stock of FDI and an increase in the share of FDI in gross fixed capital formation – from an annual average of 4.2 per cent in the years 1984 to 1989, and 6.5 per cent in 1990 to 1993, 8.6 in 1993 and up to 11 per cent in subsequent years), a level that reflects the disproportionate weight of the TNCs in the regional economy.

Within the region, the major recipients of foreign direct and portfolio investments, have been Argentina, Mexico and Brazil, the most industrially advanced countries in the region and the largest 'emerging markets' for the integrated world production system set up over the past decades. Brazil, in particular, became the favoured destination for FDI and capitalist expansion.[6] Not only is Brazil the largest potential market in the region but under the Cardoso regime the government bent over backwards, and down it has to be said, in responding to the requirements of transnational capital – to create a favourable climate for their operations. The political dynamics of this process are complex but their tracings are evident in the available statistics on capital flows.

In Latin America, FDI inflows reached their height in the years 1997–2001. This was in response to the privatization programs at the time, especially in Cardoso's Brazil. In 2001, this program reached its limits, at least temporarily, blocked for political reasons from being extended to the generation of electrical power in Mexico and oil and gas production generally, the last major redoubts of state enterprise. In Mexico it was insulated and protected from government efforts to privatize the industry by a constitutional provision; in Bolivia and Ecuador plans to privatize the industry were blocked by the popular movement. With the exhaustion of the policy to privatize public assets and enterprises the inflow of FDI, at least 50 per cent of it absorbed by the privatization programs of the 1990s, subsided. While Latin America was the most important destination for FDI in the heyday of privatization, in 2002 the level of FDI in the region was eclipsed by emerging markets in Asia, especially China. It was not until 2004, when the region experienced an increase of 44 per cent in the inflow of FDI over 2003, that the region once again became a leading destination for FDI. Once again it was Brazil that absorbed the lion's share of this increase in FDI, with Mexico a close second.

The increase of FDI inflows in 2004 was the first since 1999, and like the inflows of FDI in the 1990s were influenced significantly by 'some enterprise acquisition operations' in the region (CEPAL, 36). Nevertheless, total FDI was well below levels from 1997 to 1983, when Latin America received 12 per cent of world inflows, or in the period 1994–1998 when FDI inflows were clearly driven by the privatization process. To put these figures in a broader perspective, in the 1970s – a period of rapid growth in the internationalization of capital as relates to both FDI and bank loans – Latin America received over 50 per cent of all FDI flows to developing countries while in 2004 it received only 22 per cent. Also, in 2004 FDI represented 2.6 of the regional GNP compared to a regional average of 3.6 per cent (up to 10 and even 15 per cent in some cases) in the preceding five-year period. Another pattern in the

6 Brazil, because of its belated but lucrative privatization program, was particularly favoured as a destination point for FDI. According to UNCTAD (1999) Brazil in 1990 received 0.7 per cent of the Developing World's share of worldwide FDI; in 1994, Brazil received 0.1 of total FDI, but this percentage share grew in subsequent years to 11.0 in 1995, 13.5 in 1996, 22.5 in 1997, and 43.5 in 1998 (ECLAC, 2000, 40ff.). According to CEPAL (2000, 40–41, Brazil received 33 per cent of all FDI directed towards Latin America from 1995 to 2000 and close to 45 per cent in 2000 despite the fact that the wave of privatization had ebbed to a trickle.

inflows of FDI in 2000–2004 compared to the 1990s has to do with the 'country of origin': it is increasingly concentrated in the US due, it would seem, to the effect of 'macroeconomic imbalance' in the region on EU investments as well as changed priorities of Spanish and other European investors (p. 38).

UNCTAD (2004) and CEPAL (2004) in their reports dedicated a lot of pages speculating on the motivations behind and the strategies involved in FDI. But whatever the destination of this investment (services for the most part) the explanation is not too hard to find. In 2004, the year of FDI recovery in the region and worldwide, Latin America experienced a net outflow of US$ 84 billion, including US$ 25 billion or so directly derived from FDI. This was more than double the outflow (US$ 34.4 billion) of profits on invested capital the year before, and well in excess of capital inflows. As for the level of profitable returns on FDI it has steadily increased.

The Spoils of Empire

The facts are startling. The imperial-centred neoliberal model has led to the long term, large-scale systematic pillage of every country in Latin America – or at least of those countries with resources to pillage. Calculations from data provided by ECLAC (2002b) on remittances for payments of profit and interest (Table 3.3) show that returns on the operations of US capital in Latin America averaged close to $60 billion a year in the 1990s. Over the decade $585 billion in interest payments and profits were remitted to the centre of the empire, the vast bulk of it to US home offices.

Table 3.3 Export earnings and remittances for payment of profit and interest, Latin America 1980-2001

	(US$ bs)											
	'80	'85	'90	'93	'94	'95	'96	'97	'98	'99	'00	'01
Export earnings	109	116	165	183	221	271	300	333	333	347	413	392
Profit remittances	32	47	43	45	48	54	60	66	72	71	82	78

Source: ECLAC, Balance Preliminar de Economias de América Latina, 2002a; *Statistical Yearbook*, 2002b.

This volume of returns to capital on investments and loans in Latin America is sufficient perhaps to explain by itself the 'sluggish growth' in the region and the failure of Latin America to meet the expectations of economic recovery and growth by the World Bank, the IMF and so many analysts throughout the 1990s. However, Table 3.3 provides only a part of this sordid story. Neither the UNCTAD study nor the data collected by ECLAC include the significant revenues drawn from royalty payments, shipping, insurance and other service fees; nor do they include the scores of billions of dollars illegally transferred by Latin American elites via US and European banks to overseas accounts.[7] Saxe-Fernandez (in Amador, 2003) estimates that with just the 'legal' transfers of financial resources the total pillage of Latin America for 2000 is closer to USD100bn than USD70bn. If we multiply this sum for the past decade we can estimate that Latin America made a net contribution to the empire of well over USD1tn. In fact, World Bank and IMF data show that if one were to combine the total transfer in the form of interest payments, capital flight and the price differential for the region's imports and exports (unequal exchange) then the outflow of financial resources is in the order of USD2.5tn, one and a half times the regional GDP (Saxe-Fernandez, 2005). Table 3.4 provides a snap shot of some of the mechanisms and capital flows involved in this 'resource transfer' from Latin America to the major centres of the empire. In five of the years in the 1990s outflows exceeded inflows.

What these data show is that the outflow of capital from the imperial centre – 'international resource transfers' in official lingo – serves as a means of capital drain, drawing out huge pools of accumulated and potential capital. In the late 1970s Latin America was the primary recipient of both FDI and international commercial bank loans placed in developing countries. The newly industrializing countries in East Asia were generally financing their own development. Governments in Latin America, however, a number of them under a military regime, were eager to attract FDI notwithstanding the regulations in place as well as borrow heavily at very low rates of interest offered by the banks anxious to hook foreign clients. As a result, these countries acquired a huge debt load pushing them into crisis when the US Federal Reserve (the Central Bank) hiked interest rates to an all-time high. In the late 1970s, the income received by the MNCs on their accumulated and new investments exceeded new outflows by a considerable margin – \$30 billion (on an accumulated stock of \$188 billion) from 1977 to 1979. Reported income on direct corporate investments represents an average profit rate of only 12 per cent on FDI as calculated by the US Department of Commerce but from 22 to 33 per cent as calculated by ECLAC (1998).

In just three years at the turn into the 1980s American MNCs made over \$15 billion in profits from their Latin American operations. Although this level of returns on invested capital might pale in comparison to the profits made by the commercial banks in the 1980s (some \$211.2 billion from 1985 to 1989 – \$300 billion over the decade) it was enough to stimulate another surge of new FDI in the 1990s, as government after another in the region was forced to liberalize their capital markets and remove the remaining barriers to their entry and free operations. The statistics on this are both revealing and startling.

Over the decade the multinationals turned towards Latin America in a big way, stepping up new investments from US\$8.7 billion in 1990 to \$61 billion in 1998 – a sevenfold increase in FDI inflows, twice the rate of growth experienced anywhere

7 According to the *World Investment Report* (2002) royalty payments of developing countries to the MNCs from 1986 to 1990 – crucial years in the 'decade lost to development' in which Latin America experienced a huge capital drain in the form of interest payments on external debts – increased by 22 per cent a year to a total of \$73 billion.

Table 3.4 Capital inflows and outflows (net), Latin America 1980-2002

($US billions)	1985-90	91-2	93	94	95	96	97	98	99	00	01	02
Capital Inflows	**-**	**105**	**124**	**126**	**67**	**99**	**104**	**109**	**97**	**97**	**83**	**50**
ODA	38	10	5	6	6	6	-9	11	2	11	20	13
Private Flows	95	118	120	61	93	112	98	95	85	63	37	-
FDI	43	29	17	29	32	44	66	73	88	76	69	42
Portfolio[b]	-	45	74	63	5	12	13	-2	-4	02	1	-
Loans	642	127	28	24	38	33	27	11	10	-9	-6	-
Returns to Capital	**142**	**74**	**73**	**79**	**79**	**83**	**99**	**108**	**91**	**100**	**97**	**-**
Profit on Assets	-	62	35	37	41	43	48	51	52	53	55	53
Interest[c]	211	76	38	35	36	35	33	46	54	35	43	42
Royalty fees[a]	5	2	1	2	2	1	2	2	2	2	2	2
Net Resource Transfer (on assets)	-150	31	32	10	19	23	32	27	-3	-0	-5	-39
Accumulated Capital Stock												
Debt	420	480	520	564	619	641	667	748	764	741	728	725
FDI	-	-	168	186	226	321	375	397	191	207	216	270

Sources: ECLAC, 1998; UNCTAD, 1998: 256, 267-268, 362; 2002; US Dept. of Commerce, (1994); World Bank (1997). FDI stock 1999-2001 for US only (US Census Bureau, *US Direct Investment Position Abroad on a Historical Cost Basis*) (2002); (a) as of 1995 – World Bank, *World Development Indicators*, 2002. (b) World Bank, *Global Development Finance, Statistical Appendix*, Table 20, 2002. (c) World Bank, *Global Development Finance*, 2000, 2002.

else (the worldwide average was 223 percent). Notwithstanding the enormous and rapidly growing capital and commodity markets emerging in China and elsewhere in the East, and the frenzied merger and acquisition activity elsewhere (especially in Europe and the US), Latin America experienced the highest rate of growth in directly invested capital. However, the bulk of this capital – some $400 billion over the decade (and another $160 billion from 2000 to 2002) – involved mergers and the acquisition of privatized firms rather than productive investments.[8] Even so the

8 At a global level North-South FDI inflows accounted for 60 per cent of all international resource flows in 2000 (versus 6 per cent in 1980 and 25 per cent in 1990) (*World Investment*

multinationals and IFIs managed to generate from this direct investment US$368 billion in profits and another US$18 billion in royalty charges.

The financial resources sucked out of the region in the 1990s were more than sufficient to explain the sluggish growth of the economies in the region over the decade – less than 3.0 per cent per annum and down to 0.3 in 2001 and – 0.9 in 2002 (on a per capita basis virtually zero growth over the decade).[9] UNCTAD (2003), in this context, has identified retrospectively the beginnings in the region of another 'decade lost to development'. If we take into account less obvious mechanisms of surplus transfer to the various centres of the empire then the pillage of the region's wealth reach truly gigantic proportions, a veritable haemorrhage of resources sucked out of the region's economy via (in the poetic language of Subcomandante Marcos (1994), 'the bloody jaws' of the 'wild beast' (imperialism)) whose teeth, he notes, have 'sunk deeply into the throat of south-Eastern Mexico, drawing out large pools of blood' [tribute in the form of 'petroleum, electrical energy, cattle, money, coffee, banana, honey, corn'] through '[as] many veins – oil and gas pipes, electrical lines, train-cars, bank accounts, trucks and vans, clandestine paths, gaps and forest trails'.

The financial mechanisms of resource transfers and capital flow are primary means of surplus extraction and transfer – 'exploitation' (extraction of surplus value or unpaid labour) to be more precise. But, as Marcos has suggested, the imperialist system can count on diverse agents and a number of different of mechanisms for pillaging the resources of dominated economies, some of them well hidden or disguised.

These other largely hidden mechanisms of surplus transfer ('net international resource outflows') can be put into two categories: 1) the structure of *international trade*, regarded by neoliberals as the 'engine of economic growth' (with the capitalist corporations as the driver of this engine); and 2) the structure of capital-labour relations as well as the organization of labour within this structure.

As for trade, an empire-building process is evident in the systematic takeover of production facilities within the region, the penetration of local markets and the push to dominate both inter- and intra-regional trade via policies designed to open up Latin America's economies and liberalize access to US-produced goods and services while limiting (and controlling) the access of Latin American competitors to the US market. According to a study by the Banco Bilbao Vizcaya Argentina (BBVA) headquartered in Spain, over one-third (56) of the 150 biggest enterprises in the country are now foreign owned, half are national private and almost 13 per cent (19)are national state firms.[10] However, the 75 national private firms only generate

Report, 2002: 24). UNCTAD estimates that from 1987 to 2000 up to US$4.6 trillion of FDI were deployed in mergers and acquisitions, which is to say, a large part of the capital assigned a productive function (by some accounts as little as 5 per cent of all the capital in circulation in world markets) is 'unproductive' – used to acquire already established firms rather than invest in new technology. This pattern holds for Latin America where, it is estimated, up to 70 per cent of all FDI is used in this unproductive fashion.

9 World Bank, *Global Development Finance, Statistical Appendix* (2003: Table 8).

10 Based on figures presented and analyzed by Gabetta, Calcagno and Calcagno (2002) 42 per cent of FDI in Argentina is European (25 per cent Spanish). As with US capital the bulk of this capital was used to buy up privatized enterprises rather than productive investment.

30 per cent of the total sales of this group of enterprises and 22 per cent of their exports. The foreign-owned firms, however, account for 63 per cent of the group's export earnings. Other studies indicate that American and European MNCs control a substantial share of Argentina's domestic market, while remaining public national firms are the major foreign exchange earners. In Brazil, we have shown, the pattern is all too similar (Petras and Veltmeyer, 2003).

American and European MNCs not only dominate inter-and intra-regional trade but dominate domestic markets in the region, largely displacing local producers in the process. The imperial formula for Latin America is to export capital so as to capture the domestic markets and to import raw materials from the publicly owned enterprises. In 2002, MNCs repatriated $22 billion in profits on direct investments of US$76 billion – almost a 35 percent rate of return.[11] Relevant data for the 1980s were presented above. Most of the net outflow of resources in this decade was in the form of interest payments on the external debt. In the 1990s, however, FDI or equity financing (mostly to purchase the assets of already existing or privatized enterprises) replaced debt as the principal source of capital.[12]

Although public or state enterprises accounted for US$245 billion in sales, of which 35 per cent represented exports, it is clear that the strategic goal of US empire building is to seize control of the assets and enterprises in this sector. In the 1980s this process was most advanced in Mexico, which, from 1982 to 1993 devolved almost all of its state enterprises, some 1152, to the 'private sector'. The crowning event in this process, which netted the government US$31.5 billion in revenues, was the sale from 1992 and 1993 of the country's 18 state banks, the largest of which have subsequently fallen into the hands (banks, rather) of the Euroamerican transnational capitalist class – Banamex to Citibank and Bancomer to Banco Bilbao Vizcaya. That the anticipated revenues from the sale of these state enterprises were not the primary object of the privatization agenda is evidenced by recent reports of Banco de Mexico and the Secretaría de Hacienda (*La Jornada*, 25 July 2003) that the total revenues derived from these privatizations in all economic sectors was only $31.5 billion, barely 28.8 per cent of the debt ($89.4 billion) subsequently assumed by the government in the process of bailing out the banks in the wake of the 1995 financial crisis. Amador (2003) estimates that the bailout of private capital in recent years has cost the country USD109.2bn.

---

11 As for financial corporations in Brazil, according to a Brazilian financial advisory firm, ABM Consulting, the 10 largest banks in Brazil, including Citibank and Bank Boston, earned returns of 22 per cent on their holdings in Brazil in 2001 compared to 12 per cent on a global level. This is one reason why George Soros, a forward-thinking international financier with significant holdings in Brazil, declares: 'The system has broken down' in that it 'does not provide an adequate flow of capital to countries [like Brazil] that need it and qualify for it'.

12 As for ODA, which also serves as a form of debt financing, overall flows in the region continue to lag well behind 'private international resource flows' although, given the retreat of the private commercial banks and the slump in FDI, the major multilateral lenders such as the World Bank did increase their lending to developing countries in 2002. However, even this 'inflow' of 'international resources' in one form served as a means of securing an 'outflow' in another. The relatively modest net IDS inflow of $418 million in the first half of the year can be compared to a net loan repayment to the World Bank of $260 million (IMF, 2002, 6).

In the 1990s, the privatization agenda was widely implemented as part of a second round of sweeping reforms mandated by the 'new economic model' of free market capitalism (Benhold-Thomas, 1996; Veltmeyer and Petras, 2000). The privatization policy, although pioneered in Chile by Agusto Pinochet in the 1970s and advanced in a spectacular fashion by Carlos Salinas Gortera in the late 1980s and early 1990s, achieved its paradigmatic form under the Carlos Menem regime in Argentina in the 1990s. The World Bank has portrayed the Argentina experience as a 'model' for other countries across the world as well as the region to follow, and Brazil, under Hernando Fernando Cardoso, did just that (Petras and Veltmeyer, 2003). Just as Argentina, Brazil and Mexico in 1983 accounted for 50 per cent of all Third World debt, in the next decade they represented some of the most important privatizations in the world.

The strategic focus of the privatization agenda and policy has shifted over the years. Currently, the strategic focus of the empire-builders in the region is on the state petroleum and gas companies of Mexico, Venezuela, Brazil, Ecuador, Colombia and Bolivia as well as the Chilean Copper Corporation (BBVA quoted in *La Jornada* June 15 2003). Saxe-Fernandez and Nuñez (2001) analyze in detail the machinations of the World Bank in this regard. They detail the systematic efforts of the Bank to bring about the de facto privatization of Pemex, Mexico's state oil company, and to facilitate thereby a massive expropriation of Mexico's denationalized natural and productive resources as well as transfer to the US centre of the empire of surplus value and capital sufficient to seriously undermine the Mexican economy and contribute substantially to the US economy. The devil, it is said, is in the details and Saxe-Fernandez and Nuñez certainly provides enough of them. They calculate (pp. 150–151) that in Mexico's turn towards the neoliberal model under IMF and World Bank conditionality in 1983 to 1997 an economic surplus of US$457 billion was sucked out of Mexico by various means into the US-EU centres of the empire. This calculation in regards to Mexico includes two forms of surplus transfer: 1) debt service; and 2) trade losses via the payment of rents, an unequal exchange of values and payment for franchises, concessions and patent rights.

At another level, the system of trade between the US and Mexico – and, for that matter, Latin America generally as well as other developing countries – is based on a structure that is highly skewed in terms of the distribution of economic benefits. However, at the level of world trade the US economy is not the behemoth that it would like to be – that it was, for example, in the immediate post world War II period when it commanded a lion's share of the world's productive and financial resources (up to 50 per cent in some estimates) and it had a commanding position in world industrial production and trade in both goods and services, accounting for 59 per cent of the world's developed oil reserves, 46 per cent of total energy production, over 80 per cent of total motor vehicle numbers and 50 per cent of the world's monetary gold and currency reserves (Lundestad, 1990).

However, over the years the US has steadily lost its market share in world trade, although this apparent trend reflects in part the growing share of this trade that is accounted for by affiliates of US MNCs whose output and sales are not included in the US trade account. These affiliates, according to UNCTAD (2002) by now account for at least 13 per cent of world trade today. Another half of this trade in goods and services takes the form of intra-firm transfers, which is to say, they do not enter the market at all. In any case, what can be said with more certainty is that the US national trade account has been in deficit since the late 1960s. At the time – in 1971 to be precise – the US administration began to institute a series of strategic measures, beginning with a unilateral abandonment of the Bretton Woods fixed rate regime for the US dollar, designed to improve its position in the world market vis-à-vis its major competitors (Aglietta, 1992).

Aglietta (1982) in his study of US strategic responses to the crisis in global capitalism, shows that the US's unilateral abandonment of the gold standard did not arrest a long-term trend towards ever larger deficits on the US's national trade account. The US continues to be in a substantial trade deficit situation, the deficit growing from $63.3 billion in 1991 (US$101 billion in 1990) to US$482.9 in 2002 (US$354.1 billion in 2003). The US continues to post a trade deficit with regard to economies in every major region in the world even in Latin America. For a time (most of the 1990s), Latin America helped the US Government reduce the deficit in its trade account. However, as of 1999 (as of 1995 in Mexico) this was no longer the case and the US had to rely even more on finance capital to cover its growing trade deficits. The changing situation in the US trade balance is represented in Table 3.5.

Table 3.5 US trade balance, 1990-2005

					(US$ billions)					
	'90	'92	'94	'96	'98	'00	'02	'03	'04	'05
World	-101.1	-84.5	-150.6	-170.2	-229.8	-436.1	-468.3	-354.1	-614.6	-716.7
Mexico	-1.9	5.4	1.4	-17.5	-15.9	-24.6	-37.1	-27.7	-45.1	-49.7
LA Other	-9.7	1.7	3.3	3.1	13.1	-14.1	-18.0	-17.7	-	-
EU	6.3	9.0	-1.0	-8.2	-16.8	-43.4	-61.3	-59.9	-109.3	-122.3

Source: US Census Bureau, US Trade balance. http://www.census.gov.foreign-trade/balance.

The US sustains these deficits by attracting from all over the world financial and investment capital seeking higher rates of stable returns secured by the strength of the US dollar as the dominant world currency. Nevetheless, the capacity of the US economy to ride out its propensity towards crisis, and to finance the enormous deficit on its trade account, depends on its capacity to capture new markets for its exports and to dominate existing markets where and when it can; Hence, the ongoing efforts of the US administration to establish a Free Trade Area for the Americas (*ALCA* in Spanish). It is clear to the US that Latin America has to make a greater contribution to the ailing US economy, notwithstanding its enormous contribution over the years, particularly in the 1990s. However, the precise nature and total of this contribution is not so easy to calculate. To do so would require a closer look at the diverse mechanisms of productive resource flow built into the structure of trade between the US and Latin America – and in this regard no country is as important as Mexico, the US's major trading partner in the region, absorbing up to 80 per cent of Mexico's exports.

Studies by UNCTAD (2002, 2003) and ECLAC (2000b) expose one of the hidden elements of this structure – deteriorating terms of trade between economies at the centre of the system and on its periphery. In this regard UNCTAD (2002, p. 42) estimates that Latin America (together with other areas of the Developing World) since the early 1980s has lost at least 10 per cent of the marketed value of the labour embodied in the production of its exported commodities – a 13 per cent decline just in 1998 and another 14 per cent in the following year.[13] The magnitude of this loss, via a 'downward pressure on export prices' is enormous. In the long run it might very well exceed the total value of the economic surplus sucked out by other means such as FDI. And this by no means is the end of the story – a story of resource pillage and rape. A series of built-in barriers erected against Latin American exports and the corresponding liberalization[14] of Latin America's capital and product markets vis-à-vis the US – dubbed by UNCTAD as a 'lack of balance in the liberalization process' (liberalization for the LCDs, protection and subsidies for the OECD countries)[15] – resulted in an outflow of 'productive resources' that compares with the total value of Latin America's 'capital flight' (investment capital deposited or marketed in the US), which, in itself, it has been estimated, approaches, if not exceeds, the total value of external debt payments over the years.[16] And these payments have been,

13 Using US export prices as a proxy, it has been found that even in the area of high-tech exports, exports from the developing countries are 'subject to a higher degree of volatility … [with] steeper falls in prices after 1998 than the exports … of the same products traded among the developed countries' (UNCTAD, 2002, 117). The evidence related to this issue of terms of trade for developing countries is reviewed in 197–199.

14 According to the *World Investment Report* (2002) from 1991 to 2001 a majority of countries in the developing world liberalized their trade regimes and financial markets and 'converg [ed] towards a more welcoming stance on FDI: in regard to 306 recorded regulatory changes all but 75 were more favourable to FDI.

15 UNCTAD (2002, 70) estimates that at least $700 billion in export earnings could be generated for the LCDs if protection for labour-intensive activities in the industrialized countries was removed. In this connection, even Horst Kohler, managing Director of the IMF, has said that 'the true test of the credibility of wealthy nations' efforts to combat poverty lies in their willingness to open up their markets and phase out trade-distorting subsidies in areas where the LCDs have a comparative advantage. Recent efforts at Doha in 2002 and Cancun in 2003 by the leading group of 21 developing countries to change this structure, and its unevenly applied rules of trade, to establish a 'fair and [free] market oriented trading system' on the basis of a 'program of fundamental reforms' have foundered on the reef of collective resistance by the US and the EU. The collapse of negotiations at Cancun between the OECD countries and the developing countries reflects a similar failure of a generalized call by and within the UN some three decades earlier for a 'new international economic order'. The imperial powers at these negotiations are willing to negotiate anything and everything except their own fundamental economic interests.

16 Not only is the existing structure of international trade tilted severely against the developing countries but these countries are expected to pay for reforms to this structure – reforms, such as TRIPS (trade related intellectual property rights), that clearly favour the developed countries. In this connection, UNCTAD (2002, p. 59) has identified 'significant

and continue to be, a significant factor in the expropriation of productive resources generated in the region. Joao Pedro Stedile (2003), leader of the landless Workers Movement in Brazil, estimates that in the case of Brazil up to US$480 billion in debt payments have been made by the Brazilian Government since its turn toward neoliberalism in 1991 but that over the course of these payments the accumulated debt has increased from US$6 billion to a staggering US$250 billion. These reforms have not only facilitated a process of globalization and asset appropriation but as a means of transferring to the centre of the empire a significant supply of resources.

Notwithstanding the disguised nature of these transfers as trade, and the difficulty of accurately measuring or estimating the outflows involved, the magnitude of surplus value probably exceeds the more visible outflow of financial resources. What is clear enough is that through the structure of its trade with the US in particular Latin America not only loses a large mass of surplus value extracted from its direct producers and workers but makes a substantial and significant contribution to the US economy. Indeed, trade with Latin America is one of the economic pillars of the US empire.

US-Latin American trade represents a major contribution of both different classes of producers and of workers to the US economy. As for labour, it is well established that it is a major factor in the production process, the principal source of added value and the major contributor to 'total factor productivity'. What is not so well known is how the organization and export of labour can be used – and is so used – as another means of pillaging a country's resources and transferring them to the imperial centre.

A study of transnational (Mexico-US) labour migration (Delgado Wise, 2003) is revealing on this point. He estimates that the direct and indirect contribution of Mexican labour to the US economy (the balance of payments) – and a corresponding loss to the Mexican economy – is in the order of $29 billion a year. This 'contribution' does not take into account the massive export of natural resources (oil, in the case of Mexico) and assets (in the acquisition by MNCs of the assets of privatized public companies at knock down prices).[17] What it does take into account is the

costs' incurred by the developing countries in implementing or securing these TRIPS. Finger and Schuller (2000, 60) estimate that the implementation costs of TRIPS would be, on average, $150 million, as much as the annual development budgets of some countries. Not only do these countries have to absorb the considerable administrative and implementation costs involved but the charges for the protected patent or intellectual property rights all go in one direction.

17 Nor does it take into account the indirect contribution of Mexican labour to capital formation via its depressant effect on the wages of employed workers in the sectors in which they tend to be employed. One of the major offensives of capital against labour over the past three decades has been to challenge and reduce the share of labour in national income and thereby increase the income available as capital. The first battle in this offensive was to break the social contract that guaranteed the participation of labour in productivity gains (on this see Davis, 1984 and Crouch and Pizzorno, 1978). In subsequent years capital has found diverse ways of increasing the share of capital and reducing that of labour in national income, including the use of unemployment as a lever for lowering wages and the importing

haemorrhage of potential capital, which leaks into the US economy through diverse conduits, including:

- the remuneration of labour in the maquilladoras that account for the bulk of Mexico's manufacturing exports (now 70 per cent of total exports) at a level that is well below the value of the labour-power employed and that generates an enormous reservoir of surplus value in the form of repatriated profits – at a rate of 35 per cent return on invested capital;[18]
- the direct export of agricultural and farm labour in the form of seasonal, controlled or 'illegal' migration of both documented and undocumented workers – accounting for, it is estimated, up to 80 per cent of the agricultural labour in the US, with a clearly depressive impact on the wages of employed wage-laborers in the sector; and
- migration into the US of educated and qualified forms of Mexican labour, estimated to constitute 40 per cent of all Mexican migrants, without the US having had to bear any of the reproduction costs of this labour.[19]

Although there are no studies into the magnitude of values involved in this transfer of labour-added value, the contribution to the US and the cost to Mexico in this regard are undoubtedly considerable. Delgado Wise (2003, 7) estimates the contribution of Mexican labour to the balance of trade with the US in 2002 to be in excess of \$28 billion.[20] Although the remittances of Mexican migrants are in the order of \$9.8 billion[21] – the country's third largest source of foreign exchange earnings (behind revenue from the exports of oil and manufacturing but ahead of tourism and agricultural exports, and comparable in volume to FDI) – these remittances are

---

of cheaper forms of labour as well as the international relocation of production in areas with abundant supplies of cheap labour.

18 In this connection Mexico essentially exports is its labour force – without it ever having to leave the country. The profitability of this labour process is reflected in the fact that US-based MNCs in the maquilladora sector account for a full third of all profits generated in the sector.

19 Delgado-Wise, *points out that in contrast to the stereotype of the Mexican migrant, 40.7 per cent* of the core group of temporary or 'circular' Mexican migrants have completed their secondary schooling or higher, a figure that rises to 55 per cent of all Mexican-born US residents (versus 51.8 per cent of the general population). In addition, over 250, 000 Mexican residents have a university degree or some postgraduate qualification (Delgado-Wise, 2003: 10).

20 To establish the dimensions of Mexican labour's contribution to the US economy Delgado-Wise (2003, 2, 9) calculates that: i) 8.5 million Mexicans, slightly more than one-third 'undocumented' (i.e, 'illegal') reside and work in the US; (ii) 'sojourners' (temporary migrants) account for between 800,000 and a million 'sojourns' a year; and iii) each year around 370,000 Mexicans 'settle' (establish a permanent residence) in the US, constituting a mass of 22.9 million (8.5 million immigrants born in Mexico – 27 per cent of all foreign-born immigrants in the US – and 14.4 Americans of Mexican descent).

21 Mexico is the world's 2nd largest recipient of migrant remittances after India. According to the IDB migrants in their remittances constitute the 6th largest economy in the world (125 million migrants with remittances to 500 million family members); Latin America and the Caribbean are a large part of this economy.

derived from economic activities by Mexican repatriates who, working *within* the US, are lost to Mexico and contribute substantially more to the US economy than to Mexico's, notwithstanding the economic importance of remittances.[22] Like trade (the export of natural resources and commodities), migration (the export of labour) constitutes a substantial net loss to Mexico and an equally substantial net benefit and boost to the US economy.[23]

If we add up these diverse mechanisms of surplus transfer, both overt and hidden, the contribution of the Mexican 'economy' (the labour of the 80 million or so who participate directly and directly in this economy) to the US and the corresponding capital drain from Mexico is staggering. If we further consider similar forms of capital drain from the other countries in the region, as well as the huge flows to the US of 'hot' or dirty money (from drugs, corrupt politicians, tax evasion, etc.), much of it channelled through or managed by US banks,[24] Latin America can be seen as a major economic pillar of the US empire, explaining the lengths that the US imperial state will go to ensure by political or military means the subservience of its client states in the region.

22 From a fiscal point of view, international migrants generally contribute more to the receiving economy than they receive in benefits and public services. Through their transfer of resources migrants contribute to the mass of social capital available to the US state. According to data from the National Migration Forum (Delgado-Wise, 2003, 14) in 1997 the migrant population in the US contributed US $80 billion more than they received in the form of benefits. In this and other ways migrants are a major force for dynamizing the receiving economy.

23 Delgado-Wise (2003, 14) points out that unlike labour that is exported indirectly (via the maquilladores), Mexican workers who emigrate and settle in the US consumed a significant part of their wages there, which means that the potential multiplying impact of their earnings is transferred to the US economy. This impact, he notes is considerable greater – over ten times greater – than the impact of remittances on foreign exchange earnings in Mexico and thus the balance of payments.

24 These illegal flows of 'financial resources' are difficult to measure and have not been systematically studied but US Senate hearings into the illegal management of hot money, much of it derived from the drug trade, by 'respectable' major US banks suggest that the volume of these flows are considerable, perhaps as much as the overt 'resource transfers' documented in this chapter (US Senate, 2001).

Chapter 4

The Social Dimension of Foreign Investment

Development economists have always argued that economic growth is based on a capital accumulation process, which is advanced via an increase in the rate of national savings and investment. The theory, articulated by Sir Arthur Lewis among others, a pioneer of development economics from the Caribbean, has been widely used to justify a policy of reducing the share of labour (wages) in national income. The idea is that workers and households have a low capacity to save and invest, and that they tend to spend all or most of their income. This spending keeps up demand for goods and services, and thus expands the domestic market, but it does nothing to generate economic growth. The rich generally, and capitalists more particularly to be more precise, have a higher propensity to 'save and invest' their savings. Thus, if the pool of income available to this class is increased (via wage compression) and a reduction in the share of labour in national income (via the reversion of progressive taxation and income redistribution social programs), then economic growth will result. And, of course, in this theoretical discourse of development economics no mention is made of the diverse mechanisms of international resource transfers discussed in Chapter 3.

The end result of this thinking, widely put into practice (applied as a matter of national policy) in the 1970s and 1980s as part of a protracted class war between labour and capital, was a reduction in the share of labour (and households) in national incomes and thus an increase in the inequitable distribution of this income as well as the growth of poverty in wealth. The impact of this pro-capital ('pro-growth') policy on the social distribution of national incomes will be discussed below but the most dramatic effect of the policy was wage compression – wages in many cases (the US, for example) losing at least 10 per cent of its average value from 1974 to 1984 and anywhere from 5 to 40 per cent in the following decades (even more in some of the developing countries in Sub-Saharan Africa and Latin America). In many Latin American countries, such as Argentina, average per capita income in 2000 was less than it was in 1970. And the share of wages (labour) in national income in many cases was reduced by as much and more than 50 per cent in the process – from around 40 per cent in the not atypical cases of Chile and Mexico to below 20 per cent. In East Asia – in South Korea, for example, or China in recent years – this trend is even more accentuated, with governments pursuing policies that result in a national savings and investment rate of over 30 and in some cases (Singapore, China) around 40 per cent. What this means is that workers in these countries work long hours for low wages, very low in the case of China, thus making a major contribution to national development (rapid economic growth). It also means that the capitalist class has appropriated virtually all of the new wealth generated over the course of this period, a well-documented fact in the case of the US.[1]

The capitalist class in these countries, whether or not they invested productively their share of national income, not only was in the driver's seat of the growth engine but have profited immensely. In Mexico, for example, one individual, Carlos Slim, a multi-billionaire and the richest man by far in Latin America (third on Forbes' list of the world's richest), after 12 years of 'market-friendly' neoliberal policies in Mexico, including the privatization of Telmex, has ended up with a personal fortune greater than the combined income of all the country's indigenous peoples, some 14 per cent of a population of 80 million. In one year alone (2003) it was reported that his personal income grew by 88 per cent. And Slim is not alone. *Forbes*' list of the world's richest, includes for Latin America 33 'men of business' who share a collective fortune of US$114 billion, double the total of FDI inflows in 2005 and equivalent to the annual combined income of the region's poor, 160 million forced to subsist on less than US$2 a day.

Economic Growth and Social Inequality: The Failure of Foreign Investment

The 'new economic model' of structural reform was widely implanted in the 1980s and the 1990s with the promise of new dawn – entry into the road to prosperity paved by foreign investment attracted by a market-friendly approach towards national development. By the end of the 1990s, however, after three rounds and two decades of experiments with neoliberal policy reforms the Promised Land was off into the receding horizon. Policies. First, neoliberalism failed utterly on its own terms – to deliver on the promised economic growth. Harvard University economist Dani Rodrik (2000), no radical political economist, cites dismal growth performance during the 1990s as the most damaging evidence of the failure of neoliberalism the facts are clear enough: two decades of neoliberalsm failed to generate the promised economic growth. Overall and system-wide an annually averaged per capita growth rate over the preceding period of state-led development and interventionism was reduced by half – from 3 to 1.5 per cent in the industrialized countries; in the developing countries (excluding China and India) the average rate of growth was

1 According to the latest Census Report (August 2005), the years 2000 to 2004 witnessed a marked deterioration in the distribution of income, with a corresponding growth of wealth at one extreme, and poverty on the other. The richest 10 per cent of households garnered almost all of the new wealth generated. As for the poor, their number has increased each year, growing from 35.9 million in 2003 to 37 million in 2004 (DPA, AFP Y Reuters, Washington DC, 31 August 2005). The Census Office also reports on the ethnic or racial dimension of poverty. Within the Hispanic population, now making up over a third of the population, the rate of poverty has remained relatively stable at 21.9 per cent, twice the rate of non-Hispanic whites. As for blacks, the poverty rate also remained about the same at 24.7 per cent or triple the poverty rate of non-Hispanic whites. Given the relatively stability of the poverty rates within the Hispanic and black population, the relative growth in the number of the poor over the past four years has been particularly pronounced within the dominant working class white population, a phenomenon with undoubted political implications.

reduced from an average of around 3.5 percent in the era of government intervention to 1.2 per cent during the neoliberal era (1980–2000); as for the poorest countries the rate of growth over the same period was reduced from a modest 1.9 per cent in GDP growth to a decline of 0.5 per cent per year (Chang and Grabel, 17).

Countries at every level of per capita GDP performed worse during the neoliberal era than in the two preceding decades. The only exceptions to this trend was in a group of Asian NICs (the World Bank's 'eight rapidly growing countries', notably China but also India) whose governments continued to pursue an essentially interventionist approach, eschewing neoliberal policies in their path towards national development and economic growth. Some economists have argued the existence of a trend towards convergence in the growth ratites of developed and developing countries trend. However ant such trend is accounted for entirely by the acceleration of growth in the two largest developing countries, namely China and India – countries that in no sense followed the neoliberal policy formula. As for Latin America per capita GDP for the entire region grew by 75 per cent from 1960 to 1980 but only 7 per cent in the subsequent neoliberal era (1980–2000; (ibid., p. 17). And the situation in Sub-Saharan Africa, where governments everywhere turned towards neoliberalism in the 1980s, an accumulated growth rate of 34 per cent turned into a decline of 15 per cent over the same period.

That neoliberalism has not delivered on its promise of economic growth is just the beginning of the problem. Even worse is the fact that the anaemic growth achievements of the neoliberal policy regime have been accompanied by numerous and onerous adverse consequences in other areas, particularly in regards to disparities in access to productive resources and the distribution of wealth and income. In this area neoliberalism has been indicted by a broad array of analysts, including erstwhile advocates. The dimensions of this problem can be analysed at various levels – along the North-south global divide, among countries across the world system, and within countries both north and south.

The Inequality Predicament: Disparities between Countries and Regions

When China and India are not factored into the analysis, available data show a rise in worldwide income inequality, owing to the combined effect of higher income disparities within countries and the adverse distributive effect of faster population growth in poorer countries. As shown in Table 4.1, the income gap between the richest and poorest countries has widened over the course of the neoliberal era of globalizing capital and neoimperialism. The table shows inequalities in the distribution of income among world regions, presenting the per capita income in each region as a percentage of per capita income in the rich OECD countries as a group, as well as the changes in these ratios over the past two decades.

The data in these and other studies (see Pochman, 2004) reveal a trend towards increasing international disparities in income distribution and a connection between this trend and the turn towards neoliberal policies. In the *Atlas of Social Exclusion* (Pochman et al., 2004) constructed by Pochman and colleagues over the past two decades 28 countries improved their standing on an index of social inequalities and exclusion; these countries, all found in the developed centre of the global economy, represent 14.4 per cent of world population but account for 52.1 per cent of world annual income (and, of course, a much larger percentage of wealth, most of which is neither earned nor measured in available statistics). Sixty countries, representing 35.5 per cent of world population, account for only 11.1 per cent of world income. Of the countries with the highest indices of poverty, social exclusion, and income inequality 41 are in Africa; 10 in Asia; and six in the Americas.

Table 4.1 GDP as percentage of aggregate GDP for 156 market economies

	1960	1970	1980	1990	1999
Industrialized countries (21)	83.2	83.2	78.4	83.3	84.3
Sub-Saharan Africa (50)	2.5	2.3	2.8	1.4	1.1
South Asia (8)	3.9	3.1	2.2	2.0	2.3
ME and Nth Africa (9)	1.8	2.6	5.5	3.1	1.8
LA & C (41)	6.7	6.8	7.7	5.9	6.7
East Asia and the Pacific (27)	2.0	2.1	3.3	4.4	3.8

Source: World Development Indicators and *World Development Report*, several years.

The figures in Table 4.1 indicate that per capita income in all developing regions except South Asia and East Asia and the Pacific has declined relative to the high-income OECD countries. Per capita income levels in Sub-Saharan Africa, the Middle East and North Africa, and Latin America and the Caribbean have been steadily declining relative to the average per capita income in the wealthier OECD countries. Between 1980 and 2001 these levels decreased from 3.3 to 1.9 per cent in Sub-Saharan Africa, from 9.7 to 6.7 per cent in the Middle East and North Africa, and from 18 to 12.8 per cent in Latin America and the Caribbean. The change in these ratios indicates not that per capita income in developing regions has decreased in absolute terms but that per capita income has grown faster in the richer regions than in the poorer ones, widening the inequality gap.

Table 4.2 points to a general trend towards increasing divergence and polarization under the new economic model and away from the convergence predicted by the advocates of free market policies. Neoliberalism has induced a rising inequality among countries, particularly along the North-South divide, partly as a result of a concentration of private capital flows and partly as a result of conditions generated by policies of structural adjustment designed as a means of attracting FI.

Notwithstanding the economic growth of recent years and evidence of a recovery from the production crisis of the early 1970s, what best defines neoliberalism in practice is a pattern of uneven development and the growth of social inequalities in the distribution of income. In this connection the UNDP finds that in 1960 the countries with the richest quintile of the world's population had aggregate income

30 times that of those countries with the poorest 20 per cent. By 1980, at the outset of the neoliberal era, the ratio had risen to 45 to 1; by 1989, it stood at 59 to 1; and by 1997, a full decade and a half into the neoliberal experience, it had risen to a staggering 70 to 1 (UNDP, 1999, 2001). In this context, the situation of people in the least developed or poorest countries worsened relative to those in the middle-income and higher income group. In 1960, for example, per capita income in Sub-Saharan Africa was about 11 per cent of per capita income in the industrialized countries. By 1998 it was only 4 per cent and in 2003 it was barely 3 per cent.

Table 4.2 Widening income gap among regions (GDP per capita)

	(1985 PPP US$)					
	1960	Dif. from OECD	1998	Dif. from OECD	2003	Dif. from OECD
OECD	6,200	-	17,000	-		
Latin America	2,000	4,200	4,900	12,100		
East Asia	500	5,700	2,500	14,500		
South Asia	800	5,400	1,400	15,600		
Sub-Saharan Africa	750	5,450	700	16,300		

Source: Human Development Report 2001, 2004.

Over the course of neoliberal policy implementation the inequality between the richest and poorest countries nearly doubled, reviving an earlier debate about the connection between economic growth and social inequality. This issue was at the centre of a theoretical and policy debate in the 1970s but in this new context the debate was re-opened and is ongoing, mostly involving economists at or associated with the World Bank (Christiaensen, Demery and Paternostro, 2002; Deininger, 1996; Dollar and Kraay, 2002; Forbes, 2000; Klasen, 2005; Ravallion, 2000).

As in bygone years, the key issue in this debate was whether social inequality inhibited or promoted economic growth. However, the focus in this new context of 'globalization' (i.e. imperialism) was on unequal access to society's productive resources and wealth rather than income distribution. And it was more or less understood that a minimal degree or greater equality in this regard was a precondition for growth and that an excessive inequality inhibits growth in its exclusion of a large number of group of individuals who are potentially productive. As for the policy of government interference in the redistribution of market-generated incomes, the issue was viewed differently. At this level, the old dogma was trotted out to the effect that an unequal distribution of income – or, what amounts to the same, increased participation of capital in national income, the acknowledged outcome of free market policies – was a good policy: it functioned as a motivating device, providing an incentive to produce – a catalyst of economic growth. Of course, this was the theory; the facts are quite otherwise. At issue here is the presumption of a built-in tendency towards a convergence of income levels after an initial income gap, which is needed as an incentive to capitalist entrepreneurs who have a higher propensity to invest than workers. The theory is that allowing market forces to operate freely without government interference will allow the poor to eventually participate in the fruits of economic growth. Once the seeds of economic growth have been sown a part of the enlarged national income will 'trickle down' to the poor, resulting in a sort of inverted income curve. With reference to this theory, which was initially advanced in the 1950s by Kuznets, World Bank economists have begun to write of their 'pro-growth' policies as 'pro-poor' (Dollar and Kraay, 2002; Kakwani and Pernia (2000).

The magnitude of the global income divide (see Table 4.2) and associated problems is staggering. The richest quintile of the world's people consume 86 per cent of all products while the poorest quintile consumes only 1.3 per cent – everything from meat to paper and automobiles. The OECD, with 19 per cent of the world's population, in 1998 accounted for 80 per cent of the world's GNP, 71 per cent of world trade, 58 per cent of foreign investment (UNDP, 1999, 3). And more recent data suggest that little has changed, except for the relative advance of China and India, admittedly a large part of the total picture, so much so that inclusion of these two most populous countries hides the growing development gap in the rest of the world. Within the structure of this gap, the three richest persons in the world have assets that exceed the combined GDP of the 48 poorest countries. In fact, if the poorest 47 per cent of the world (about 2.7 billion persons) were to pool their incomes they could barely purchase the assets of the world's wealthiest 225 individuals (UNDP, 1999, 3). A tax of 4 per cent on the wealth of these individuals would be enough to pay for basic and adequate health care, food, clean water and safe sewers for every person on earth.

Apart from the question of meeting the basic needs of the world's population – of lifting over 2.6 billion people, mostly in the developing countries, out of their poverty – these social inequalities, particularly in regard to the conditions of absolute poverty (associated, by the World Bank, with income of under $1 a day) that affect at least 1.5 billion, have severe damaging effects, including malnutrition, all sorts of illnesses that reduce both the quality and the length of life. It is estimated that hundreds of thousands of children a day die from these effects – from conditions that are structurally determined and quite remediable considering the idea of taxing the inordinate wealth of the rich. In this connection, it is estimated that a tax of four percent on the wealth of the richest 225 individuals in the world or a one percent tax on the speculative unproductive transactions in the world's capital markets, would generate enough income to abolish poverty altogether and meet the basic needs of the world's poor.

Mark Weisbrot, Dean Baker, Egor Kraev and Judy Chen at the CEPR (Center for Economic Policy Research) put the neoliberal hypothesis – that if the poor countries were to let their economies be dominated by private capital and the free market they would converge with the rich countries – to the test. They divided countries into five groups, from the poorest to the richest. Then they compared how these countries fared between 1960 and 1980 (before the introduction of neoliberal policies) and 1980 to 2000(when these policies were widely embraced). Their results are revealing of the impact of neoliberal policies, touted by the World Bank as 'pro-poor' ('What Have We Learnt?'), on economic growth and social inequality. They found that the 'performance' of the poorest countries got considerably worse relative to the rich countries. That is, there was no convergence either in regard to wealth or income. On the contrary, the rich got richer and the poor became poorer, a pattern that holds up for national distributions of income as well. Overall, social inequalities in the distribution of wealth and income, both within and among countries, and the social divide between the North and south, increased over the period of neoliberal structural reform.

Nevertheless, the issue has not been settled by the discovery of these facts and the arguments presented by the UNDP (1999, 36 and idem) in regard to the 'transition countries' and Asia and ECLAC (2002, 83) and idem) in regard to Latin America. The economists at the World Bank and the IMF continue to argue the need for neoliberal 'structural reforms', against all the evidence and arguments advanced by revisionists such as Joseph Stiglitz and Dani Rodrik. The argument is that governments should stay the course and extend these reforms. The medicine prescribed by the IMF and World Bank as far back as 1983, it is argued, is the best way to bring about prosperity for all and ultimately benefit the poor. The failure in economic performance of so many developing countries in this regard, and the lack of a global income convergence, can be attributed to the failure of governments to fully implement the recommended reforms.

Income Disparities Within: The Predicament of Neoliberal Capitalism

The neoliberal revolution has deepened their global income and wealth divide but, as shown in the UN's most recent Social Development Report – the *Inequality Predicament* (UNDP, 2005), it has also deepened inequalities within countries both North and South. Table 4.2 above reflects a general trend towards increasing income divergence and polarization at the global level. But the UN study also points towards a growth of social inequalities within most countries, both North and South. In addition it shows that income inequality has grow comparably faster in countries such as the US and the UK that have thoroughly embraced the neoliberal doctrine than in countries that have not (UNDP, 2001, p8). In these countries, particularly in the US, analysts have documented the growing gap between the very rich and the very poor with a rapidly shrinking middle class (Chang and Grabel; 21).

This pattern of a growing income gap within countries both North and South, and the connection between this pattern and the turn towards neoliberalism, also shows up in other studies. For example, data provided by the *World Income Inequality Database* (WIID) shows that within-country income inequality decreased during the 1950s, 1960s and 1970s in most developed, developing and centrally planned economies but that since the 1980s this decline has slowed or levelled off, and that within many countries income inequality has risen and is on the rise, in some cases dramatically so. Under the conditions of this rise in income inequality, and as the direct result of the dismantling of the socialist state, Cornia and Kiiski (2001) discovered that in the countries that once constituted the socialist bloc income inequality from

1989 to 1996 rose by an average of 10–20 Gini points, and the number of people living in poverty jumped from 14 million in 1989 to 147 million.

The Gini index of income inequality is the most commonly used summary measure of national income distribution. In most countries has increased over the past two decades of neoliberalism and imperialism. In the US, for example, it is 17 per cent higher than in 1980. In Latin America, the region showing the greatest disparities in national income distribution, income disparities have increased dramatically over the past two decades and a half. In the 1950s and 1960s and into the 1970s the structured inequalities in income distribution were on the decline, the result of an economic model and a developmental state that slowly incorporated workers a, producers and the middle class into the economic development process, providing various improvements in their access to society's productive resources and in regard to governmental social and development programs.

In the 1980s, within the framework of a conservative (neoliberal) counterrevolution and sweeping reforms in national policy that restructured the economies in the region, and facilitated their integration into the world economy, this process was halted and reversed. The outcome, marked by a process of privatization, financial liberalization, market deregulation and downsizing, was visible some years later in an extension of structured inequalities in income distribution, with a consequent deepening of the conditions of poverty and wealth at the extremes of this distribution.

Over the course of the 1980s and 1990s, the share of labour (wages and salaries) in national income was reduced in many cases by half – from plus in Chile, for example, to below. A clear reflection of these developments and their outcomes is in the ratio of incomes received by the poorest quintile of households, a useful and revealing unit of analysis, to those received by the richest 20 per cent. In most countries this ratio was comparatively high to begin with – up to 18 to one in the case of Brazil – but increased over the course of the 1980s and 1990s in every case except perhaps Chile.

According to ECLAC (2002, p. 83), at the turn towards the new millennium, 83.8 per cent of the population in Latin America live in countries with worsening inequality. As for Chile, the government's apparent 'success' in avoiding the economic contraction and increased social inequalities that accompanied the structural adjustment process in other countries it turns out is the direct result of its imposition, in 1998, of a regime of 'capital control' – a reserve requirement tax of 30 per cent on FDI, a 1-year residence requirement on both PI and FDI, and a severe restriction on the freedom of pension fund managers to invest their assets abroad (Chang and Grabel, 2004, 132).[2] As a direct result of its restrictive approach to foreign investment and an expansion of its social investment policy, Chile began to experience a significant reduction in private capital inflows in August 1998. The upside of this trend was macroeconomic stability and an improvement in the distribution of national income – Chile and Colombia (which also imposed

2 This restrictive policy on capital outflows bears comparison to the draconian controls imposed by the Government of South Korea on domestic investors in the mid-1990s. According to Chang and Grabel (2004, 133) it was this policy that saved South Korea from a debt crisis despite its having become at the time the fourth largest foreign debtor in the world.

capital controls) being virtually the only countries in the region able to escape the devastating after-effects of the Mexican and Asian financial crises.

Recent studies show a persistence of a pattern of growing social inequalities associated with 'structural reform' in macroeconomic policy. In the case of Mexico, a recent study by the Instituto Nacional de Estadística, Geografía e Informática (INEGI, 2004) showed that from 2000 to 2004 the only part of the population that increased its share of national income (from 35.6 in 2000 to 36.5 in 2004) and improved its situation was the richest quintile of households (*La Jornada*, June 14 2005). The bottom quintile's share of national income remains unchanged at 1.6 per cent. This 1.6 per cent corresponds to the income share of the poorest fifth of Latin America's population – some 220 million, 44 per cent of the region's total population are classified by the bank as 'poor' (earning less than $2 per day) while 96 million arte 'extremely poor'; as for the richest quintile, their average share of total regional income is , while in Mexico, according to INEGI, it is 52.7 per cent, up 1.3 per cent in just two years of a deepening of neoliberal policies under the Presidency of Vicente Fox. Thirty-nine per cent of the extremely poor, those who have to survive with less than a dollar a day, are found in Mexico and Brazil, both regional champions of neoliberalism – and of an opening of the national economy to FDI.

The statistics are an eloquent testimony to neoliberalism's social legacy: to build the prosperity of the few – such as Mexico's 11 billionaires, whose combined incomes exceeds that of the country's total poor, some 40 million people – on the exploitation, degradation and misery of the many, on low wages and shattered dreams. It is about foreign investment, which works like a suction pump, leading to a massive unregulated outflow of financial and productive resources, both financial and 'human', and, as a result, social conditions of banking, currency and financial crises; super-exploitation and exclusion – an increase in inequality, poverty and immiseration (Weller and Hersch, 2002). It is about 'freedom', the banner of which is waved about so much by the ideologues of neoliberalism. But how many of the world's poor – over 2.5 billion who cannot meet their basic needs – are free to choose, free to make decisions that might improve the quality of their lives, free from exploitation and oppression, from the operations of capital freed from all constraints an 'interference'.

The Inequality Predicament: The Case of Argentina

A recent report entitled *La dueda interna se acebtua*: *ingresos, salarios y convenios colectivos en Argentina 2006*, by a research team and commission headed by Claudio Lozana, Congressional Deputy in Argentina's parliament, provides a close look at a microcosm of what the United Nations has described as 'the inequality predicament'. The report also proves a revealing window on this chapter's topic: FDI in its social dimension. What the Congressional Commission discovered was that the recent post crisis spurt of economic growth, averaging over 7 per cent a year since 2003, is associated with a notable increase of social inequality in the distribution of incomes generated in this period. After years into one of the worst economic crisis of the

20th century, the country has experienced the highest rate of economic growth in the entire region.

By several accounts this growth was stimulated by government policy, particularly the decision to suspend payments on the foreign debt and to productively invest the resulting savings, and by an economic reactivation process led by the investments of the largest corporations, many of which are foreign-owned. However, what Lozano and his team found was that the contribution of labour to productivity growth was not duly remunerated, far from it.

While in the largest 1,000 corporations, the contribution of labour to annual production was valued at around $120,000 per worker, the average wage received by the workers at the end of 2005 was only $722, an exceedingly and excessively high rate of exploitation that, the Report concluded, represented only 32.7 per cent of the cost of the basket of goods and services needed by households to cover the essentials of life. And the situation was even worse for the 100 largest corporations, close to one-half of which are foreign-owned. Each worker added $200,000 to the value of production, but was remunerated on average with a wage of $2379. The report concludes that given the productivity of labour wages could easily be increased fourfold and needs to be increased minimally by 45 per cent – to the level of the *canasta básica*.

Lozana and his team drew a number of conclusions that have a direct bearing on the relation of FDI (reflected in the operations of the largest corporations) to economic growth and its impact on the distribution of household income. In general, the Report notes, assuming two workers per household earning on average $722 each, and receiving an additional $60 in the form of family welfare, average household income at the end of 2005 was $1.564, 30 per cent less than the cost of a basket of basic goods and services. As for those working 'on their own account' in the informal sector, accounting an estimated 43 per cent of the labour force, average income ($632) is below the household poverty line ($860), and for households composed of informal sector workers average income represents only 57.3 per cent of the *canasta básica*. Thus, even where households are composed of two income earners, difficult enough in a situation of high unemployment, household income is insufficient to lift the average household out of poverty. The poor, as a result, today encompasses close to one-half of households and an even higher percentage of the total population, reaching well into what used to be one of the strongest middle classes in Latin America. By official government estimates one-half of this class today is now poor, constituting a large part of the 'new poor'.

The Lozano Report clearly connects this inequality predicament not only to government policy but to the operations of capital on the free market and the capital-labour relation. In this connection, the authors show that while productivity in the industrial sector from 2001 to 2005 grew by 12.4 per cent (representing a reduction of 35.9 per cent in labour costs) real wages grew only 0.4 per cent. This deterioration in the capital-labour relation, and in the share of labour in national in come and value added, is clearly reflected in the abysmally low level of average wages, which at the end of 2005 barely reached a level achieved in 1970, three decades earlier. In this situation, total wages represent only 25.6 per cent of value added to production by the 1,000 largest companies. For the 100 largest wages are only 19.9 per cent of value added (Table 4.3).

Table 4.3 Economic variables, 1,000 and 100 biggest firms, Argentina 2003

	1,000	100
Wages (millions pesos)	18,839	8,503
Value added (millions pesos)	73,496	47,592
Profit	54,657	39,089
Wages/value added	25.6%	17.9%
No. of workers	609,243	245,019
Value added/workers (pesos/mth.)	120,635	194,239
Average wage (pesos/mth.)	2,379	2,669
Productivity per worker (pesos/mth.)	9,290	14,941
Profits per firm (pesos/mth.)	,4,564,750	32,574,417
Profits per month/wages	1,915	12,203

Source: Lozano (2006). Elaborated with data from INDEC, Censo nacional Económico de 2004.

Blanco (2006), a columnist for *La Jornada* notes, with reference to Mexico, where income distribution is similar to Argentina's, if not worse, points out that 'inequality is not poverty' (25 April, 2006). The point made here is that the increased disparities in income distribution found across Latin America, and that is clearly connected to (the result of) government policies of financial and trade liberalization, and privatization (and foreignization) of assets and enterprises, does not necessarily translate into more poverty. And indeed several studies and reports by CEPAL and the World Bank seem to bear this out. Despite the stark inequality predicament documented for Argentina – and notwithstanding the fact that household incomes and wages in a context of rapid economic growth keep many working class households immersed in poverty – these studies have determined that the poverty rate in recent years has declined somewhat both in Argentina and elsewhere in the region, even in countries such as Mexico and Peru, where social inequalities have worsened. Presumably this amelioration in the number of people in dire straits, i.e. those earning by the World Bank's standard of poverty less than $1 a day, is the result of corrective action taken by governments and intergovernmental organizations in their 'war against poverty'. But as we see below the issue is by no means so simple.

Living the Washington Consensus: The Social Face of Neoliberalism

From Stagnation to Class Crisis

To sustain their profits under conditions of chronic stagnation, the Latin American capitalist class has periodically engaged in a direct assault on the working class, attacking its organizational and negotiating capacity. It has also engaged in an indirect assault (via the state) on state-legislated social benefits, reversing the social legislation of the previous period to undermine the capacity of labour to participate in productivity gains. Very little of the capital attracted to the region has been invested productively. Over the course of the 1980s and 1990s the rate of participation of capital in productivity gains has been negative or marginal. Labour has participated substantially in productivity growth, but it has done so without a corresponding increase in its level of participation. In fact, the share of labour in the value-added to production and national income (Table 4.4) has been drastically reduced by labour restructuring. Thus, the working class has undoubtedly borne the brunt of the 'structural adjustment' generated by efforts to insert the Latin American economy into the 'globalization' process.

Table 4.4 Wages as a percentage of national income

	1970	1980	1985	1989	1992
Argentina	40.9	31.5	31. 2	-	24.9
Chile	-	47.7	43.4	37.8	-
Ecuador	34.4	34.8	23.6	16.0	15.8
Mexico	37.5	39.0	31.6	28.4	27.3
Peru	40.0	32.8	30.5	25.5	16.8

Source: CEPAL, several years.

The basis of this 'adjustment' is the restructuring of labour in its forms of employment (creating more precariousness), its conditions of work (causing more irregularity and informality) and in its relation to capital. The process can be seen at two levels. It is reflected first of all in conditions that have resulted in a significant reduction of the share of labour in national incomes (and value added). For example, under the Allende regime, Chilean labour received well over one-half of the national income. By 1980, however, after five years of crisis and draconian anti-labour measures, this share was reduced to 43 per cent and by 1989, after seventeen years of military dictatorship and free market reforms, to 19 per cent. In other countries can be found variations on the same theme. On average, the share of labour (wages) in national income has been reduced from around 40 per cent at the beginning of the adjustment process to less than 20 per cent, and this development has been paralleled by an even greater reduction in the share of labour in the value added to the social product. Other structural changes can be seen in the reduction of jobs in the formal sector of production and in an associated decline and disappearance of the industrial proletariat.

Structural change vis-à-vis the working class, particularly in regard to the growth of the informal sector of street work, has also been evident in the fall in the value of wages and the worsening of wide disparities in the distribution of earned incomes among households. In many cases, wage levels in the early 1990s were still well below levels reached by 1980 and, in the case of Argentina and Venezuela, by 1970. The Bank of Mexico estimates that at the end of 1994, that is, before the later outbreak of crisis, wages had maintained barely 40 per cent of their 1980 value. In Venezuela and Argentina workers have not yet recovered wage levels achieved in 1970.

As for the pattern of developments that relate to the distribution of income and the compression of wages, Argentina provides the exemplar: in 1975 the ratio of income received by the top and bottom quintiles of income earners was eight to one, but by 1991 this gap had doubled and by 1997 it was a staggering 25 to one. In the extreme but not atypical case of Brazil, the top 10 per cent of income earners receive 44 times more income than the bottom. And in other countries we witness the same growing social inequalities in the distribution of wealth and income – at one extreme, the sprouting of a handful of huge fortunes and an associated process of capital accumulation, and, at the other, the spread and deepening of grinding poverty. ECLAC estimates that over the period of structural reforms implemented in the 1980s the rate of poverty in the region increased from 35 per cent to 41 per cent of the population (or, using the World Bank's more conservative and very problematic measure of $2 a day, from 27 to 28 per cent). But according to ECLAC in the 1990s (from 1993 to 1996 actually) the incidence and rate of poverty was reduced in eight of the 12 countries it examined, a trend reversed later in the decade when an emerging pattern of low growth led ECLAC to see the beginnings of another 'decade lost to development'. A closer look at the statistics provided by the World Bank and used by ECLAC suggests that the observed reduction in the rate of poverty (see Table 4.5) involved either sleight of hand or outright obfuscation and lies: the rate of poverty was reduced by redefining the poverty line according to the World Bank's base measure of $2 a day ($1 for the rate of absolute poverty or indigence). By the earlier, more reasonable measure related to the capacity of the population to meet its basic needs, the rate of poverty has continued to climb – up to a half of all households by some estimates, at least 40 per cent according to the latest ECLAC study (Cepal, 2005). In any case, the minimal progress identified for Latin America in the mid-1990s disappeared soon thereafter. In Sub-Saharan Africa, North Africa and the Middle East, South Asia and the countries 'in transition', even when using the World Bank's conservative measure of the poverty line, the number of the poor increased by 195 million from 1993 to 2001. In the countries 'in transition' from socialism to capitalism (East Europe/Central Asia) from socialism to capitalism the absolute number of the poor increased dramatically in the immediate aftermath of the collapse of the socialist regime, not the result of statistical fiat but an abrupt change in government policy. In just 3 years, from 1990 to 1993, the percentage of the poor jumped from five to 17 per cent.

Table 4.5 Poverty rates by major regions, and India and China, 1981-2001

	Number of people living on less than US$2 per day (millions)							
	1981	1984	1987	1990	1993	1996	1999	2001
Sub-Sahara Africa	288	326	355	382	410	447	489	516
Middle East/Nth Africa	52	50	53	51	52	61	70	70
Latin America/ Caribbean	99	119	115	125	136	117	127	128
Europe/Central Asia	20	18	15	23	81	98	113	93
South Asia	821	859	911	958	1005	1029	1039	1064
East Asia	1170	1109	1028	1116	1079	922	900	864
China	876	814	731	825	803	650	627	594
India	630	662	697	731	770	807	805	826
World	2450	2480	2478	2654	2764	2674	2739	2735
	People living on less than US$2 per day (%)							
	1981	1984	1987	1990	1993	1996	1999	2001
Sub-Sahara Africa	73	76	76	75	75	75	75	76
Middle East/Nth Africa	29	25	24	21	20	22	24	23
Latin America/ Caribbean	27	30	28	28	30	24	25	25
Europe/Central Asia	5	4	3	5	17	21	24	20
South Asia	89	87	87	86	85	82	78	77
East Asia	85	77	68	70	65	53	50	47
China	88	79	67	73	68	53	50	47
India	90	88	87	86	86	85	81	80

Source: UN, The Inequality Predicament, 2005, pp. 52-53.

On the political level, the adjustment of workers to the demands of imperialism is reflected in the destruction of their class organizations and in a generalized weakening of their capacity to negotiate collective agreements with capital. These developments, as well as the notable failure or incapacity everywhere of the working class to resist the imperial imposition of neoliberalism, reflect a new correlation of class forces in the region. In the 1970s, workers confronted a concentration of armed force and repression, as well as a direct assault by capital on their organizational capacities and conditions of social existence. In the 1980s the major mechanism of adjustment was the restructuring of the capital-labour relation based on forces released during the change in economic policy.

In the 1990s, within the same institutional and policy framework, the working class also confronted a major campaign by organizations such as the World Bank for labour market reform. The aim of this campaign was to create political conditions for a new and more flexible regime of capital accumulation and mode of labour regulation: to give capital, in its management function, more freedom to hire, fire and use labour as needed; and to render labour more flexible, that is, disposed to accept wages offered under free market conditions and to submit to the new management model of its relation to capital and the organization of production. As the World Bank constructs it, widespread government interference in the labour market and workplace (minimum wage legislation), as well as excessive (monopoly) union power, have distorted the workings of the market, leading capital to withdraw from the production process, and thereby generating the problems of unemployment, poverty and informality that plague the region.

To resolve these 'problems', labour legislation protecting employment have been replaced by laws that enhance the arbitrary power of employers to fire workers, reduce compensation for firings and hire temporary and casual labour. Such deregulation of the labour and other markets has led to new rules that facilitate new investments and the transfer of profits, but also result in massive decimation of stable jobs for workers, increased marginality for and within many communities, and sharply polarized national economies.

Disparities in income distribution and access to productive resources are reflected, at one extreme, in a concentration of income within the capitalist class and the spawning of a number of huge fortunes – *Fortune*'s richest billionaires. Worse, much of the income available to this class is undeclared. For example, revenues from narcotrafficking by capitalists in Mexico, the proceeds of which are distributed among crony politicians, bankers and others and exceed revenues from Mexico's principal export (oil), are grossly under-reported.

The poorest households dispose of a reduced share of income that, in any case, is growing little or not at all in real terms. One result is the generation of new forms and conditions of poverty and social exclusion that have even reached well into the middle classes. In fact, a striking characteristic of imperial-induced inequality is the growth of the urban poor and the changing class composition of the poor: the new poverty is urban rather than rural and extends well beyond the working and producing classes into the once proud but now decimated middle class.

While rural poverty continues to be the rule, the fastest growing number of poor today is found in the cities. The new urban poor are not simply 'rural migrants' but include socially excluded and downwardly mobile workers and the lower middle class individuals who have been fired from their jobs and have found employment in the burgeoning informal sector. The growing armies of urban poor in Latin America now constitutes a second and third generation of workers many of whom live in slums or shantytowns, unable to follow the earlier generations' occupational ladder towards incremental improvement. One consequence of this class situation has been the skyrocketing growth of crime directly linked to family disintegration and concentrated among young people who earlier would have channelled their grievances through trade unions or the factory system.

Pillars of Social Exclusion

It has become fashionable to write of the urban poor as 'socially excluded' rather than as poor. Not only is this new language more acceptable to the poor who do not like to see themselves as such but it is more convenient for the development agencies that have sprung up all over the urban landscape. The reason is that the term 'socially excluded' draws attention away from social relations of capitalist exploitation and oppression that are associated with or dictate more organized forms of class action. For whatever reason, the conditions of social exclusion, which certainly includes low income and poverty, are more amenable to redress and less violent political responses than relations and conditions of economic exploitation. A probable reason for this is that it is politically more feasible to design more socially inclusive strategies of poverty reduction/alleviation than to directly challenge the existing highly concentrated structure of economic power.

In fact, it is possible, if not necessary or politically expedient, to conceive of the poor as both economically exploited and socially excluded. Needless to say or write, the social conditions of exploitation derive from the capital-labour relation, which, despite the transformative change in associated conditions of work and forms of employment – in the growth of the so-called 'informal sector' over the 1980s and 1990s – still defines the class situation of many if not most urban dwellers. First, urban workers in the so-called 'informal sector' of economically marginal enterprises (street work 'on one's own account' – to use the language of statisticians) are by no means disconnected from the capitalist system. In effect, they, like the unemployed and rural-to-urban migrants more generally, constitute an enormous reservoir of surplus labour for capital – what Marx in a different historic context termed an 'industrial reserve army'. This reserve army helps keep down the wages of workers in the formal sector of capitalist enterprise and foreign investment. And it also servers to weaken labour in its capacity to negotiate collective agreements and organize.

As for 'social exclusion', six major 'pillars' or structural conditions have been identified (Ghai, 1991; Paugam, 1996; IFAD, 2001):[3]

1. Dispossession of the means of social production, reflected in the widespread condition of landlessness, near-landlessness and a process of rural outmigration;
2. lack of access to urban and rural labour markets and opportunities for wage employment, reflected in the low rate of labour force participation and the high rate of unemployment in the rural sector;

3 In its 1992 report, IFAD (Jazairy, 1992) identified up to 20 sources of rural poverty, including the structural sources or pillars identified below. As for the social conditions of this social exclusion and poverty, the associated literature, most of it generated in the past decade, is voluminous, as reflected in the ILO's 1994 compilation of studies. Given the array of international organizations and research institutions, both within the UN system and the international development community, involved in the war against poverty and the broader conditions of social exclusion it is clear that the problem has not only reached critical proportions but that it is global in scope. One of many organizations set up in the search for solutions to the problem of social exclusion is Research Centre for Analysis of Social Exclusion (CASE) was established in October 1997 at the London School of Economics and Political Science (LSE) with funding from the UK Economic and Social Research Council.

3. lack of access to 'good quality or decent jobs', reflected most clearly in evidence of increased rates of super-and under-employment, and in the growth and prevalence of jobs that are contingent in form (seasonal, involuntary part-time, short-term, and so on) with a high degree of informality and inordinately low wages and other forms of remuneration;
4. reduced access to government social services in areas of social development such as education, health and social security;
5. lack of access to stable forms of adequate income, reflected in the incapacity of many households to meet their basic needs and indicators of relative and absolute poverty;[4] and, above all,
6. exclusion from the apparatus of decision-making or 'political power', reflected in the centralized nature of this power structure, elite control of this structure, the prevalence of client-patron relations in the political arena and frequent recourse to political organization and action in the form of anti-systemic social movements.

A New Dualism

Presidents Carlos Menem, Fernando Cardoso, Ernesto Zedillo and Eduardo Frei at one time or another all announced the entrance of their respective countries (Argentina, Brazil, Mexico, Chile) into the Developed World. They showcased modern shopping malls, the boom in cellular phones, supermarkets loaded with imported foods, streets choked with cars, and stock markets that attract big overseas speculators. Today, 15–20 per cent of Latin Americans share a 'First World' lifestyle: they send their kids to private schools; belong to private country clubs where they swim, play tennis and do aerobic exercises; get facelifts at private clinics; travel in luxury cars on private toll roads; and communicate via computer, fax and private courier service. They live in gated communities protected by private police. They frequently vacation and shop in New York, Miami, London or Paris. Their children attend overseas universities. They enjoy easy access to influential politicians, media moguls, celebrities and business consultants. They are usually fluent in English and have most of their savings in overseas accounts or in dollar-denominated local paper. They form part of the international circuit of the new imperial system. They are the audience to which presidents address their grandiloquent Developed World discourse of a new wave of global prosperity based on an adjustment to the requirements of the new world economic order. Despite the ups and downs of the economy they benefit from the imperial system.

4 A poverty-oriented Basic Needs approach dominated the study of international development in the 1970s. Originating in the 1973 discovery of the World Bank that upwards of 2/5 of the world's population was in a state of relative deprivation, unable to meet its basic needs. According to Amartya Sen a household without sufficient income to meet the basic needs of its members is poor, a condition that can be measured in terms of a head count, that is, the number and percentage of the population that falls below a defined income poverty line; or, according to Sen, by an index of disparity in income distribution, viz. income gap ratio multiplied by the number of the poor, which provides a coefficient of specific poverty.

The rest of the population, however, lives in a totally different world. Cuts in social spending and the elimination of basic food subsidies have pushed peasants towards malnutrition and hunger. Large-scale redundancy of factory workers and their entry into the 'informed sector' means a subsistence existence and dependence on the 'extended family', community-based charities and 'solidarity [soup kitchens] for survival'. Slashed public health and education budgets result in increasing payments and deteriorating services. Cuts in funds for maintenance of water, sewage and other public services have resulted in a resurgence of infectious diseases. Declining living standards measured in income and living conditions is the reality for two-thirds or more of the population. There has been a decline from Third World welfarism to Fourth World immiseration.

As the crisis of the system as a whole deepens, the elite classes intensify the exploitation of wage labour. As the costs of associating with Developed World powers increases, the elite diverts a greater percentage of state revenues towards subsidizing their partnerships at the expense of social programs for working families.

As debt payments accumulate, and interest, royalty and profits move outward, declining incomes shrink the domestic market. Bankruptcies multiply and competition for declining overseas markets intensifies. The crises become systemic and economies totter on the verge of collapse. Stagnation turns into depression, and major banks and financial institutions go bankrupt, fuse or are bought by overseas financial groups. Overseas speculators threaten a fast exit. International bailouts put in place to prevent imminent collapse become larger and more frequent.

The Economics of Poverty and the Poverty of Economics

Already by the end of the 1980s it was apparent that the neoliberal agenda of policy reform and structural adjustment was very problematic – dysfunctional in economic terms and politically unsustainable or 'ungovernable'. The problem, as diagnosed early on by Kapstein (1985), Director at the time of the US Council on Foreign relations (CFR), was that the social inequalities generated and exacerbated by the World Bank's 'pro-growth' policies generates forces of resistance that tend to destabilize the regimes that pressured by the World Bank and the IMF to toe the line of 'structural reform'.

The response of the architects of the new world order was threefold: 1) to give the structural adjustment program a 'human face' in the form of a 'New Social Policy' (NSP) that targeted then poor and alleviated the worst of the social conditions of the poverty generated in the adjustment process; 2) the arranged marriage between the forces of economic and political liberalization – democracy (free elections) and capitalism (the free market); 3) a good governance regime in the form of a social consensus constructed on the basis of the participation of 'civil society' in the implementation of public policy via the decentralization of decision-making and responsibilities …; and 4) a local development strategy based on the accumulation of the poor's 'social capital' – capital embedded and invested in relations of reciprocal exchange and social solidarity (the 'new paradigm'). This local development strategy, implemented with the assistance of NGOs, strategic partner in a program of 'assistance', was designed to turn social organizations in the popular sector of civil society away from a confrontational approach – direct actions against the government's neoliberal policies – and seek improvements in their lives on the basis of 'self-development' via support of their micro-enterprises within the local spaces available within the power structure (Harris, 2001; Petras and Veltmeyer, 2005).

Poverty As Global: The Social Dimensions of an Economic and Political Problem

The World Bank discovered the existence of world poverty under the Presidency of Robert McNamara, who had just been reassigned by President Johnson from prosecuting the Vietnam War to engage the war on world poverty. By the calculations of the Bank at least one fifth of the world population at the time was poor, i.e. unable to meet their basic needs; and about one-half of these were desperately poor, deprived of their basic needs to the point of seriously affecting their health and survival and certainly reducing life expectation and increasing child and infant mortality, cutting off at the very outset the possibility for the human development of a large part of the world's poor.

In 1982, at the onset of the debt crisis in Latin America and Sub-Saharan Africa, close to 40 per cent of the population in Latin America, which had experienced several decades of economic growth and social development was deemed to be poor, with the highest incidence and worst conditions found in rural society (IFAD, 1992). By the end of the decade, however, after several years of experience with the 'new economic model' of free market structural reforms, the rate of poverty, as calculated by ECLAC as defined by a basic subsistence income (poverty line), had increased to 44 per cent – a rate if anything higher than in 1973 when the problem was first diagnosed by World Bank economists. Fifteen years later, in 2005, after two decades of what the World Bank describes as 'pro-poor policies'; the problem of poverty is a visible as ever, notwithstanding the Bank's efforts at reducing the rate of poverty by definition. Even by the World Bank's highly conservative and very problematic new measure (the number of households subsisting on less than $2 a day), the world's poor had dramatically increased in number if not as a percentage of the total population. If one were to use a more conventional and valid measure of poverty (the income needed by individuals or households to access an adequate 'basket of goods and services' constructed to meet their 'basic needs') then the poor as a percentage of the population and social group would be considerably larger.[5]

This number represented virtually the same rate (percentage of the total population) as 1989 when the World Bank began in earnest its anti-poverty campaign. Indeed the evidence suggest that not only has the international development community failed to reduce the incidence of poverty or even to substantially alleviate its worst effects, but the World Bank's pro-poor policies actually generated new forms of poverty, extending it from the countryside into the urban centres and cities. In the 1980s the bulk of the poor were found in the rural areas of society, victims of an economic and social structure that was entrenched in hundreds of years of exploitation, social exclusion, oppression and discrimination.

---

5 On this issue see the discussion on Chapter 4.

Towards the end of the next decade, however, as a fairly direct result of neoliberal policies, as well as a massive process of rural-to-urban migration, poverty increasingly assumed an urban form. In the case of Argentina, it has been estimated by government officials, that up to one-half of the /new poor' originated not in the countryside but in a hitherto powerful and sizeable 'middle class' decimated by a decade of neoliberal policies. The other half of the poor originated in the low income sectors of the working class – the working poor, the self-employed, the un- and under-employed, the vast mass of street workers that make up the so-called 'informal sector' (ILO, Tokman, PREALC).

The World Bank on Growth and Poverty Reduction: Distribution Matters

Economists at and associated with the World Bank have carried on with little respite and no fundamental change in policy a three-decades long war on poverty, and with it an equally protracted debate on the relation of economic growth to social inequality – —and more recently on the effect of the World bank's structural adjustment program (neoliberal program of macroeconomic policy reforms) on social inequalities in income distribution (and the generation of poverty). In the 1970s the orthodoxy of development economics was that a growth-only-or-first approach that relied on the market (and a presumed tendency for the fruits of economic growth to 'trickle down' to other social sectors and the poor) for the distribution of income, could not resolve the problem of poverty – reducing its incidence and alleviating its worst effects. The dominant theory at the time was that the reduction/alleviation of poverty would require the efforts of an active developmental state in redistributing market-generated inequalities in income distribution – i.e. a growth-with-equity (income redistribution) approach.

However, this social welfare approach was seriously contested by economists armed with a neoclassical (neoliberal) theory of economic growth. In this view, which came into its own in the 1980s in the context of a conservative reaction and neoliberal revolution ('structural adjustment'), the market, 'liberated' from government constraint (the regulatory apparatus of the developmental state), was the most efficient mechanism for an optimum allocation of resources across the world system. From this neoliberal perspective, government income-redistribution programs, via progressive taxation, at best were ineffectual and at worst they seriously interfered with the proper functioning of the free market.

This view would prevail throughout the 1980s until widespread evidence that a growth-only approach (free market policy reforms) and a process of structural adjustment were socially and politically unsustainable, generating as they did destabilizing forms of social discontent; even worse these policies proved to be economically dysfunctional, failing to deliver on the expectation of economic growth. With the evidence in, and after an exceedingly long process of transition, a number of economists once again began to rethink the link between growth (and pro-growth policies) and social inequality (and poverty). The evidence in this reassessment appears to be mixed and there certainly is no new consensus. But a number of economist, even those at the World bank, established as an indisputable fact that a free market, pro-growth approach (and corresponding policies) seriously exacerbated existing social inequalities without any appreciable economic or social benefits. On the contrary. The reluctant conclusion drawn from unavoidable and pressing facts was that improved access by the poor to society's productive resources (such as land, capital and technology) and greater 'equity' in the distribution of income, were needed to allow for and promote a process of economic and social development (Birdsall, 1997).

It was further argued by these revisionist economists that the market by itself could not be counted on for creating these preconditions ('growth' – and 'structural adjustment' – with 'equity'); that it required corrective action by 'the state' – in effect, restoring (at least in theory) a policy of mixed support for the market and an active state. This view was adopted by an increasing number of economists at the Bank (for example, Stiglitz) without, of course, affecting the Bank's fundamental commitment to macroeconomic (structural) and political reform – to its 'pro-growth' 'pro-poor' policies (Eastwood and Lipton, 2001; Kakwani and Pernia, 2000).[6]

The War on Poverty

No problem describes so well international development as a project taken on by the world community of developed nations as poverty. The problem that is defined most often in socioeconomic terms as the inability of a given population to meet its basic needs. The World Bank in particular has taken on this project, taking it on in the early 1970s – in 1973, to be exact, when under Robert McNamara's presidency, it 'discovered' that at a minimum 2/5 of the world's population was unable to meet its basic needs and this because of a fundamental lack of income – a problem of what it would come to define as 'low income countries'. Over the years the bank has periodically reaffirmed its commitment in this regard, declaring war against it in the late 1988 in the context of Sub-Saharan Africa and more generally in its 1980 *World Development Report*, and then again most recently in the late 1990s when the Bank defined its mission in terms of the on-going (for some decades by then) war against poverty.

So where do we (i.e., the world and the Bank) stand today after so many battles staged and fought, so many diverse strategies pursued with funds and vigour, so much effort targeted at the problem of poverty?

In a word: exactly where we were in the 1970s and in a number of way further back. Not only have the numbers of the poor increased, with no change in the percentage of the population affected by poverty in its various dimensions and perverse effects, but it has taken on new forms, reaching even into the households of what had hitherto been 'the middle class' in terms of income. In 1973, the poor were some 40 per cent of the total population; in 1983 after a decade of liberal reforms aimed, by governments, at redistributing market-generated incomes, the

6 The tortuous efforts of the World Bank economists to square this circle – to place the peg of 'pro-poor' policies in the square of /'pro-growth' policies of market-led or -friendly 'structural reform') can be traced out in the various websites and electronic 'discussion groups' on 'pro-poor' policies (poverty reduction/alleviation) set up by the Bank (http://www.worldbank.org; povertynet@worldbank.org).

rate of poverty if anything had increased. By 1993, a decade into a regional- and world-wide debt crisis and widespread implementation of a neoliberal approach towards development (globalization and structural adjustment), most people in the world's poor countries were in as bad a situation or worse off. Three decades of a concerted war, with countless battles waged at the national and local levels, and no development whatsoever – no change and no improvement.

This fact begs several questions. One is about the strategy and tactics that have been used to wage this war – its weapons? Perhaps the weapons were faulty or inadequate? Or not well targeted? Or, more likely, used in a faulty campaign, marred by misguided strategy and inappropriate ineffective tactics? Even more likely is that the war was fought with faulty intelligence – misguided ideas as to the causes of the problem? Practice, as we now know, closely follows theory, being guided by it in essential aspects. The question thus is: i) what strategies have been pursued in the war against poverty? And what explanations or theories lie behind these strategies?

The World Bank's first anti-poverty strategy was based on the notion that every individual had certain definable basic needs that had to be met in order for the individual to reach a minimally acceptable level of what would later be dubbed 'human development'. This minimum condition obviously included access to a minimum quota of nutrition and food security, access to potable water, adequate shelter, protection from disease, a minimum level of schooling, some level of personal security and decency. Beyond these basic needs, theorists (mostly economists), in their consultations with and advice to the World bank and governments, varied in their advice and prescription, with lists of needs that included political participation and in one important case up to 22 needs' (conditions needed for human to realize their potential) and corresponding 'satisfiers'. These same economists devised various strategies based on this conception of poverty as relative or absolute deprivation, low income and the lack of access to essential 'services'. The most common strategies were income redistribution (growth with redistribution) – advising governments to implement social programs (education, health, social welfare and security), and programs of integrated rural development (subsidized credit, etc.), funded via mechanisms, such as progressive taxation on earned and investment income. These development and social programs were more or less implemented within the framework of macroeconomic policies of a state-led model of economic development.

By 1983, however, this strategy had failed to close the income gap and many liberal reformers lost confidence in their ideas and policy prescriptions, creating a space that a new generation of policy advisors (many connected to the World Bank and the IMF) soon filled with contrary ideas and prescriptions based on a neoclassical theory of economic development and corresponding 'new economic model' of free market capitalism globalization and structural adjustment of national policy to the requirements of the new world economic order. Within this new policy framework, the World Bank's war on poverty was recommenced on the basis of a 'structural adjustment program', a program of 'market-friendly' structural reforms in macroeconomic policy. These polices, as per the Washington Consensus, were (and still are) deemed to be absolutely minimum conditions for reactivating the economy – preconditions of economic growth and thus attacking the problem of poverty – with 'pro-growth' and thus 'pro-poor' policies (World Bank, 'What Have We Learnt from Theory and Practice?'). These 'pro-growth' policies, implemented at the national level by the governments of the day, were described by the Bank as the minimum policy and institutional framework for attacking the problem at the sub-national and local levels via a program of 'self-help' projects – engaging the poor in the process (the project cycle) as 'participants' and enlisting the help of 'third sector' NGOs (neither governmental nor profit-oriented) as intermediaries and strategic partners.

In the 1990s, the intractability of the poverty problem, proving as it did resistant to all efforts, led the Bank (and its strategic partners, particularly in the UN) to enlist the help of the private sector (profit-oriented enterprises as well as business associations) and to modify its approach towards poverty eradication / reduction / alleviation. Globalization was retained as the fundamental means of entering the path towards 'general prosperity' and the new economic model of structural reform was retained as the fundamental macroeconomic policy framework (pro-growth = pro-poor). But within this institutional and policy framework, adjusted and tweaked for greater functionality and sustainability (adding to it a 'new social policy' that protected the most vulnerable, providing them a minimal level of economic and social security), the war against poverty was prosecuted with a much greater reliance on 'self-help', full participation of the poor themselves – enhancing their capacity for economic and social development, empowering them to find their own solutions to the problem of poverty (with development assistance from the Bank and other Overseas development Associations).

Within this reformulated institutional and policy framework ('pro-poor' institutions and policies) various 'poverty reduction / alleviation' strategies were formulated and designed. The most popular, perhaps, in regard to rural poor and their communities, was the 'sustainable Livelihoods Approach' – a school of development thought and practice that emphasizes the critical role of social capital, building on assets that the poor are deemed to have 'in abundance'. Hitherto, development theory and practice had always emphasized financial and physical forms of capital as the critical ingredients of the development process – the fundamental 'factors of production', the driving forces of 'development'. However, improving access to the 'resources' had proven to be intractable – too many obstacles that could not be overcome because of political opposition from the proprietors of land and capital, owners of the means of production, whose rights of ownership were protected by private property legal regimes ('law').

The theoretical and political advantage of the 'social capital' approach towards economic and social development – in alleviating, if not eradicating or reducing poverty – was that it did not require or entail fundamental economic change and state-led social reform. It only required the full participation of the poor themselves, with minimum technical and financial assistance from the outside. It did not presume a structural source of widespread poverty (lack of access to productive resources – financial and physical capital, land, etc.). Nor did it view the World Bank's macroeconomic policies as a major contributing factor to poverty, a major structural obstacle.

Poverty here was viewed fundamentally as a matter of social exclusion (a problem that could be remedied without fundamental structural change), lukewarm support of needed structural reforms (level of political will to stay the course in national policy), failure to take full advantage of existing opportunities for development in the world economy, and various deficiencies in the local society and economies (corrupt officials, rentierism, lack of entrepreneurship, ineffective policy framework, inappropriate politics, orientation towards traditional non-modern values, etc.), could be implemented under prevailing political conditions, without provoking destabilizing demands for fundamental social change and within the existing policy and institutional framework of 'pro-growth'/'pro-poor' policies and a political framework of democratic institutions, making maximum use of readily available resources. Above all the approach was sustainable both in terms of livelihoods and in social and political terms.

Within the framework of the Bank's own 'pro-poor' macroeconomic policies, a partnership approach towards local community-based development and wide support for a 'social capital' approach, and support for the forces of economic and political freedom (capitalism and democracy) the World Bank added its own twist to what it regarded as 'best practice' vis-à-vis the battle against poverty. In the late 1990s economists at the Bank (and the IMF) conceived of a program of 'poverty Reduction Strategy Papers' in which in exchange for future development assistance governments in the Developing World of poor countries would sign on the Bank's latest campaign against poverty – a coalition of the willing, able and desperate (Ames, Bhatt, and Plant, 2002).

The Social and Political Dynamics of a Distributional Crisis

Critical features of any state are their regimes of (capital) accumulation and distribution, and their effective articulation. In the post world II context, regimes of distribution were constituted by the Keynesian state in the 'First World' of Western Europe and North America; the socialist state in the 'Second World' of the Soviet Union and Eastern Europe; and the developmental state of the 'third world'. However, toward the end of the 1970s, a worldwide accumulation crisis crated conditions and paved the way for a new neoliberal regime of accumulation based on foreign investment: the state, in effect, withdrew from its responsibility to secure an effective form of social distribution, leaving this responsibility to 'civil society', in effect, leaving people to fend for themselves (in adjusting to, managing and resisting the forces of 'globalization') but also, as an unintended but inescapable consequence, generating the conditions of a distributional crisis. This crisis, as Rapley (2004) argues and documents, is bringing about the demise of neoliberalism and its foreign investment regime.

Rapley's argument, supported with considerable evidence, is as follows.

Systemic responses to the distributional crisis have included various attempts, at times successful and mostly ineffective, to manage the explosive forces of political resistance. Another response has been to redesign the structural adjustment program of structural reform, providing for a new social policy targeted at the poor, so as to give the whole reform process a 'human face'. A third systemic response, another element of a post-Washington Consensus, has been to establish a new more ostensibly 'democratic' form of governance – self-management of the distributional crisis. The end result: an emerging political crisis: an explosion of local, regional and sub-national conflicts over society's productive resources that have exceeded the capacity of a decentralized state to control or manage.

Conclusion

An incontrovertible fact provided by the available evidence is that both social inequality and poverty are intricately, if indirectly, linked to the 'pro-growth', 'pro-poor' imperialist policies of the World Bank. A second incontrovertible fact is that a foreign investment regime, promoted by policies of financial liberalization, privatization and market deregulation, exacerbates these inequalities, and, in the process generates a wide array of disabling social problems, conditions of low income and impoverishment, such as disease, malnutrition, high levels of child mortality and widespread social disorganization. In fact, foreign investment provides the link between neoliberalism and structural adjustment on the other hand, and social inequality and poverty on the other.

The link is found in an outflow of capital – the transfer to the centre of the world capitalist system of resources (surplus value) generated on its periphery: a siphoning off of resource that constitute a potential source of capital, which instead of being invested productively is siphoned off. In effect, foreign investment, via the operations of TNCs, create a paradoxical situation of capital shortage, so working to sustain the myth that peripheral economies are 'underdeveloped' because of a shortage of financial resources and the lack of an institutional capacity to exploit and develop these scarce resources in the form of productive investment in modern technology, and to access foreign capital. Foreign investors and TNCs, parading as white knights bearing much-needed capital, technological and managerial know-how, and jobs, in reality serve as a mechanism of imperial domination, capitalist underdevelopment, technological dependence, and capital drain – an enormous economic cost relative to the meagre economic benefits provided by FI.

Another conclusion that we draw from the pattern of developments associated with the North-South transfer of financial resources is that the economic costs of foreign investment, substantial as they are, pale in significance compared to the heavy and widespread social costs and the negative impact of FI on the livelihoods and the social existence of people living and working in the popular sector of developing societies. Widespread poverty and a deepening of social inequalities in access to world society's productive resources and the distribution of income are the indirect result of foreign investment – of the policies and conditions created as means of facilitating the entry of foreign investment.

Our final conclusion is that neither the politics of adjustment nor that of resistance have been able to bring about any substantive change in the workings of neoliberalism on economies and people across the world. Nor has politics in one form or another been able to stave off the political conditions of a fundamental distributional crisis, which, as argued by Rapley (2004), is in the process of bringing about the demise of neoliberalism, the victim of its own built-in contradictions. As for the response of the system itself – the war on poverty – it is designed as a palliative (program of poverty alleviation) to advance the neoliberal agenda of 'pro-poor' policies while reorienting the popular movement away from a confrontational politics – the 'old politics' of class struggle and state power. As for the forces of resistance and opposition they are taking diverse forms, having been mobilized in three directions: 1) *a postmodern identity politics* and associated struggles for subnational autonomy; 2) *mass mobilization* against government policies; and 3) *local development*. The dynamics of the responses are beyond the scope of this book but it is clear enough that although to date they have failed to bring about any substantive social change capitalist development in its neoliberal form is clearly on its last legs.

Chapter 5

Policy Dynamics of Foreign Investment

Foreign investment is not just a matter of capital flows in and out of different markets in search of profitable returns. For one thing markets are not necessarily or rarely free. They are generally regulated by the control mechanisms of national governments or an assemblage of international financial institutions, that in a spirit of self-regulation have established a 'financial architecture' for global capital flows. But in the 1980s financial markets all over the world were deregulated and the financial transactions and capital flows were 'liberated' from control. Profit-seeking capital in its diverse forms became increasingly free to move around the world, and, with the advances in communication technologies, at a dazzlingly fast rate, with deals worth hundreds of billions of dollars made in a matter of seconds. By the end of the 1980s these global flows of mobile capital (the money economy) had reached such gigantic proportions as to outstrip by a factor of anywhere from 50 to 100 the productive operations in the 'real' economy of global and national production. It has been estimated that the value of one day's trade in money (financial transactions) in just one money market (London) was 25 times greater than the value of global production over a year. It has also been estimated that as little as 5 per cent of total 'international financial resource transfers' (capital flows or foreign investment) has any productive function, that is rather than serving to expand production, the theoretical function assigned to capital, financial transactions on these capital markets were non-productive or speculative, resulting in enormous sums of money and private fortunes, feeding parasitically off the global mass of producers and workers in the real economy.

Of course, the entire edifice was bound to come tumbling down sooner or later and it did, in the mid-1990s, in a financial crash that almost brought the entire system down. The collapse of the system, and of several economies most directly affected by the crash, was averted only by the rear guard defensive capital control measures taken by governments such as Malaysia and Thailand, and by the expedient action taken by the 'international financial community' to re-establish a measure of regulatory control over global capital via a functional institutional architecture.

Development in Theory and practice: A Question of Two Models

The theory of economic development from the outset identified the accumulation of capital as the basic ingredient in a menu of economic growth. In this theory, it was also assumed that developing countries suffered from a shortage of capital and would require international assistance and cooperation in the provision of supplementary forms of development finance. In these 'international resource transfers' foreign aid dispensed by Northern multilateral organizations and governments in a program of 'international cooperation' (for economic development) was assigned a role to play but the major presumed channels of capital were not 'official' or 'public' but private – basically the multinational commercial and investment banks, and the multinational corporations (via FDI).

Capital provides the fuel for economic growth and national development while international trade is one of its driving forces, the 'motor' of the process. However, these forces do not operate in a vacuum: they require a supportive institutional framework and facilitating conditions created by appropriate national policies. As to what might be an appropriate institutional and policy framework is a matter of debate but over the years development economists have constructed two basic models (theoretically simplified representations of the key variables) to guide a process of policy reform and institutional development. One model assigned an active role to the 'state' vis-à-vis enterprise ownership, substituting the state for a weak or absent capitalist class that in theory was assigned the 'functions of capital' (ownership, investment, entrepreneurship, management and commercialization) dominated thinking and practice for some three decades – from the late 1940s to the late 1970s (the so-called 'golden age of capitalism'). By the end of the 1970s this model was subject to attack from the perspective of a 'conservative reaction' to the economic development project. In its place was put a 'new economic model' predicated on the free world market and the construction of a new world economic order in which the private sector and 'forces of economic freedom' were in command. This 'new economic model' (neoliberalism) was more or less implemented in the 1980s, achieving dominance – ideological hegemony, as it were – by 1990s, a hegemony that was reflected in what would become known as the 'Washington Consensus' (on correct policy and needed 'structural reforms').

State-led Development: The Role of Foreign Investment

In the geopolitical post-war context, and within the institutional framework of a new world economic order established at Bretton Woods by the victorious capitalist powers, 'international development' was conceived of as *progress* in per capita *economic growth* based on a process of *industrialization, modernization and capitalist development*. Development, so conceived, had eight conditions:

1. an *increase in the rate of savings and investment* – the accumulation of physical and financial capital;
2. productive investment of this capital in industry, i.e. technological conversion of production;
3. in the absence or weakness of an endogenous capitalist class, the assumption by the state of the theoretically defined 'functions of capital' – *public ownership* of the means of production, control over investment, entrepreneurship (combining factors of production) and enterprise management;
4. *nationalization* of economic enterprises in strategic industries and sectors;[1]

1 Not all development economists at the time, whose thinking was generally based on theories of economic growth and modernization, shared this nationalist concern for the

5. *industrialization* in the form of import substitution, protecting domestic enterprises from the forces of global competition;
6. an *inward orientation* to economic production, which, together with a secular increase in wages and salaries, was designed to expand the domestic product market;
7. *regulation* of this and other markets (labour, capital) and the protection (subsidized support) of the firms producing for the market, insulating them from the competitive pressures of the world economy; and
8. *modernization* of the production apparatus (capitalist development, productive transformation and technological conversion), the state and social institutions, reorienting them towards values and norms functional for economic growth.

Together, these ideas constituted a theoretical model that was used to direct analysis and inform government policy for three decades of 'development' (the 1950s – 1970s).

In the changed context of a system-wide crisis that put an end to the period of rapid economic growth (1948–1973), and a decade of reforms with negligible results if not a total failure in closing the North-South development gap, the Keynesian reformers that dominated the field of development lost confidence in their analysis and prescriptions. They abandoned the field, providing space for a counter-revolution in development thinking and practice. The constraints of wages (too high a share of national income for capital accumulation) and consumption (a crisis of production or under-consumption), and the excessive fiscal costs of social and development, induced capital to turn towards the exports on the world market and the government to reduce social benefits, to increase thereby the national rate of savings (and thus rates of profit, productive investment and productive investment). The underlying concern for the fall in the rate of corporate profit, sluggish productivity and stagnant economic growth, and an incipient fiscal crisis, undermined Keynesianism and in effect 'converted' many Keysenian economists and policy makers towards neoliberalism.

In political terms this counter-revolution in economic thought was supported by a neoconservative ideology and associated political regimes – Reaganism and Thatcherism, for example. In economic terms, it was based on a neoliberal conception of the 'world market' as the fundamental engine of economic growth, with the 'private sector' (multinational corporations) as its driver and 'freedom' – the untrammelled freedom of individuals to pursue their self-interest, accumulate capital and profit from their investments – as the fuel and catalyst of the development process. In fact, this theory returned to ideas that prevailed before the 1930s – before the glaring failure of the market under conditions of untrammelled freedom, and the near collapse of the capitalist system gave way to 'the new deal' and a state-led model.

developmental state in the absence or weakness of an indigenous capitalist class. Some mainstream thinkers on this tradition such as Sir Arthur Lewis and Walt Rostow continued to pin their hopes and expectations in regard to 'an expansion of the capitalist nucleus' on the 'private sector'.

The economists at the World Bank assumed primary responsibility for designing a new model to promote capitalist development on the basis of this theory. This 'new economic model' (Bulmer-Thomas, 1996) was based not so much on the idea of development as 'globalization' – the integration of all national economies into the 'new world economic order' (Ostry, 1990). In these terms, the World Bank economists designed a series of structural reforms (dubbed 'structural adjustment') to facilitate integration into the new [neoliberal] world order of free market capitalism. This model, like the model it displaced, also had eight major components:

1. a *realistic* rate of currency exchange (that is, devaluation) together with policy measures to *stabilize* the economy – tight fiscal and monetary discipline;
2. *privatization* of the means of production and state enterprises, reverting the nationalization of strategic industry;
3. *liberalization* of capital markets and trade, reversing the policy of state protection and opening up domestic firms to free competition and market prices;
4. *deregulation* of private economic activity, reducing the scope and impact of government regulations on the operation of market forces;
5. *labour market reform* – reduced regulation and employment protection, erosion of minimum wages, restrictions on collective bargaining and reduced public expenditures;
6. *downsizing* of the state in regard to social and development programs, restricting its role to the provision of basic infrastructure and security matters;
7. *decentralizion of policy formulation and* decision-making to provincial and local levels of government, allowing for a more democratic and participatory form of top-down development as well as good governance; and
8. a *free market* in both capital and tradable goods and services – the last of various 'steps to hell' – to quote no less than Stiglitz (2002), former chief economist at the World Bank but now a major critic of the IMF's neoliberal policies.

As in earlier decades, in the 1980s there was a strong link between development theory and policy practice. In short order, the World Bank's Structural Adjustment Programme (SAP) was implemented throughout the Developing World, most often as a conditionality of foreign aid or access to global capital. The first experiments with neoliberal policies were conducted in the 1970s, by the military regimes in the Southern Cone of South America (principally in Chile and Argentina) but these crashed and burned in the debt crisis of the early 1980s. By the end of the decade, however, only four countries in Latin America – Argentina, Brazil, Peru and Venezuela – had managed to resist the pressures to conform to the 'Washington Consensus'. 'newly industrializing countries' of East and south East Asia, pursuing the old model of state-led development, managed to escape the strictures of World Bank policy (structural adjustment to the new world order) and IMF fiscal discipline.

The ensuing economic dislocations and hardships in structurally adjusted economies, suffered particularly by the poor, led to widespread denunciations of these neoliberal policies. This was particularly the case in Latin America where by the late 1980s the region had already experienced two cycles of neoliberal experiments (Veltmeyer and Petras, 1997, 2000). At this point a number of economists at the World Bank began to recognize that the SAP needed to be not just tinkered with but fundamentally redesigned. Not only were the transitional costs not as short-term as anticipated but they were disproportionately borne by the poor who were particularly vulnerable to the forces of change unleashed by the reform process (Cornia, Jolly and Stewart, 1987; Levitt, 1990; Morley, 1995). The 'Washington Consensus' on the correctness of neoliberal policy (Williamson, 1990) began to unravel and the World Bank, under pressure from other organizations in the UN system – and a growing 'global civil society' of NGOs and grassroots community-based organizations (Hulme and Edwards, 1997) – began to rethink both its theory and its practice. Although still a matter of debate, with the orthodox economists at the IMF holding firm, the need for a redesigned 'Structural Adjustment Program' with a 'human face' was becoming all too evident (Stahl, 1996; Salop, 1992).

It would take another decade to bring about the realization that the neoliberal model of capitalist development was unsustainable, both economically dysfunctional and politically destabilizing.

Foreign Investment and the State in South Korea, 1965–2006

Together with Taiwan in East Asia and Brazil and, to some extent, Mexico in Latin America, the priorities of relatively autonomous and strong state is a key element of the development model followed by South Korea in the years of its emergence as a 'newly industrializing country'. According to Chibber (2002, p. 960), it was the investment selectivity of the sectors targeted by the government what eventually led to South Korea's industrial development. Industrial development planning was based on allocating not only foreign but domestic investment in strategically targeted sectors.[2]

To shape investment and economic decisions, South Korea established the Economic Planning Board (EPB), along the lines of Japan's Ministry of International

2 The notion of the 'developmental state' was introduced by Chalmers Johnson in his study of the Japanese Ministry of International Trade and Industry (MITI). In this study Johnson described the importance of the state in Japan's post-War II development and its achievement of what became known as an 'economic miracle', the first of several in East and South-East Asia (Johnson, 1982). The role of the Miti was described as essential for managing Japan's 'industrial rationalization' – the specific ability of the state for setting policies and implementing investment plans to encourage the rapid process of industrialization (Johnson, 1982, p. 27).

At the same time (the early 1980s) Robert Wade and his colleagues at the institute of development studies at Sussex dubbed Taiwan and South Korea as 'developmental states' (Evans, 1995). As they saw it, the experience of South Korea and Taiwan researchers reflected state directive intervention in the economy strategically aimed at encouraging a process of industrial capitalist development. In the mid-1980s the arguments advanced by Evans in *Bringing the State Back in* (Evans et al., 1985) and Wade in *How to Govern the Market* (1990) gave rise to the notion of a developmental state.

Trade and Industry (MITI). The idea was to develop a 'super ministry able to control investment' – to allocate investment according to the developmental goal of industrial development (Gereffi and Wyman, 1990; Kim and Nugget, 1994; Evans, 1995; Hayami, 1998; Hayami, 1998). The main objective of this 'super ministry' was to boost productivity by increasing investment and technological transformation. Control over investment as a means of closing the technological gap with the industrialized countries, was viewed as the critical factor in the economic development process. To this end, FDI was subjected to special and specific regulations designed to protect domestic industry while acquiring the knowledge and the technology necessary to upgrade it. In fact, the government encouraged the formation of joint ventures with foreign enterprises but always under domestic majority ownership. The strategic objective was to ensure, or at least facilitate, the transfer of technology and administrative skills (Clark and Jung, 2002, p. 31).

State control over the sources of capital and credit was not the only development strategy pursued by the government. Nor was FDI a particularly critical factor in Korea's economic development. On the contrary. From 1961 to 1986, years in which the South Korean Government actively pursued and acted on its strategic plan, FDI was but a small part (7.10 per cent) of the foreign capital inflow to South Korea (Amsden, 1989, p. 76). This compares to 22.40 per cent for Mexico over the same period (Gereffi and Wyman, 1990, p. 61). The government itself looked for money from several sources, preferring to borrow money over attracting foreign investments and to redistribute this money through its own banks (Chul-Lee and Macnulty, 2003, p. 34). When the government turned to foreign enterprises for investment capital it did so under a regulatory regime that ensured that direct investments were allocated to designated sectors and used to transfer needed technology and managerial know-how.

South Korea's subsequent transformation into an industrialized country with a relatively high level of economic and social development provide a clear testament to the state-led model of economic development, despite efforts of neoliberal ideologues to paint economic development in South Korea and East Asia – 'the Asian Economic Miracle', the 'East Asia model' – in different terms; to construct it somehow as an exemplar of neoliberal policy: an 'economic miracle' (World Bank, 2003). As Bienefeld (1988), among others have shown, nothing could be further from the truth. South Korea's vaunted 'economic success' had little to do with free market or free trade policies and a lot to do with centralized state planning and thorough state economic control.

The South Korea Model: No Panacea

South Korea's rapid transformation from a relatively backward agrarian society into an industrialized society with a relatively advanced level of economic and social development validated the importance of a strong and competent state – directive state intervention – in the development process (Evans et al.; Wade, 1990; Leftwich, 1995, 1985; Weiss, 2000). However, the state is no panacea; nor is Korea's development path a model for other developing countries to follow. For one thing, in its political form the state was profoundly undemocratic, authoritarian and repressive, a veritable dictatorship of capital based on a synergistic alliance between 'the private sector' (*chaebols* – large economic groups of capitalist enterprises) and state officials and government bureaucrats.[3] Secondly, the advances achieved in a process of rapid industrialization between the state and the *chaeobols*, clusters of state-supported capitalist corporations, were at the expense of workers, who as a class bore the heavy social costs of capitalist development.

Working class repression was as characteristic a feature of Korea's development path as directive state intervention based on a strategic partnership with capital (the *chaebols*) and benevolent welfarism. The dynamics of this repression have been well documented (inter alia, Johnson, 1982; Prestowitz, 1988; Amsden, 1989; Wade, 1990; Fallows, 1994; and Woo, 1991). These dynamics, which were manifest in a the brutal suppression of labour activism and union organization, served as a fundamental lever of capital accumulation, regulating and holding down the cost of labour in the capitalist development process – reducing the share of labour (wages) in national income and thereby increasing the pool of capital available for productive investment. The size of this pool, and the 'contributions' of labour to it, is reflected in the 'extremely high proportion of gross fixed capital formation', which has tended to average above 30–28.7 per cent in 2004 (Economy Watch.com. accessed 25/08/05). Despite a relatively equitable distribution of national income achieved through state redistributive social programs of health, education and welfare – for example, a Gini Index of 32, compared to 53 for Mexico; a ranking of 28th on the UNDP's HDI versus 53rd for Mexico – the 'economic situation' of most Korean workers remains rather dismal. Despite a relative equitable distribution of national income, under South Korea's benevolent dictatorship, the share of labour (wages) in national income and the value added to national production each year remains relatively low (below 20 per cent) and for most workers a nine hour a day, six-day working week is the norm.

It was not until 1987 that, along with a dormant but emergent democracy movement, workers finally managed to escape the iron fist of an authoritarian state and to demand a greater share in the proceeds of rapid industrialization and capitalist development. This political development of a popular and working class struggle for change – democracy and socialism – is reflected in a dramatic increase in labour activism and militancy shown in Table 5.1.

Notwithstanding a decade and more of renewed labour activism, South Korea's working class continues to heavily underwrite and subsidize the participation of capital and a substantial middle class and consumer society, has profited from its subservience to capital and the niche that Korean capital found in the world market for the social product. Analysts and the government itself refer to these dynamics as 'a strong labour effort' (Economy Watch.com). This 'effort' (coerced for the most

---

3 Evans (1995) argues that South Korea's economic development model, like that of Brazil at the time (the 1960s and 1970s) was based on a triple strategic alliance that also included foreign capital. Lie (1998) in his review of Korea's economic development also uses the 'triple alliance' model that Evans used to explain Brazil's economic development, focusing on the precarious yet crucial developmental alliance among the state, foreign capital and local capital, as the theoretical framework for his analysis.

part) is one reason why South Korea today ranks among the largest and strongest 'high-income' countries in the world – 28th by size and level of per capita income.

Table 5.1 Number of Strikes in Korea, 1984-2001

	No. Strikes/ Lockouts	Workdays Lost to Strikes/ Lockouts		No. Strikes/ Lockouts	Days Lost to Strikes/ Lockouts
1984	114	20	**1993**	144	1308
1985	265	64	**1994**	121	1484
1986	276	72	**1995**	88	393
1987	3749	6847	**1996**	65	893
1988	1873	5401	**1997**	78	445
1989	1616	6351	**1998**	129	1452
1990	322	4487	**1999**	198	1366
1991	234	3271	**2000**	250	1894
1992	235	1528	**2001**	235	1083

Source: South Korean Ministry of Labour (2002), Adapted from Chul-Lee and McNulty (2003: 58).

South Korea's Neoliberal Turn: From State-led Development to a Managed 'Free' Market

In 1987, South Korean voters elected ROH Tae-woo to the presidency, ending 26 years of military dictatorship and inaugurating what the CIA (in its *World Factbook*) dubs 'a fully functioning modern democracy'. Korea's political opening in the 1980s paralleled the opening of its economy to the forces of economic freedom operating in the world market, thus consummating a marriage of convenience and strategic import between political and economic liberalism (Dominguez and Lowenthal, 1996). This double opening was the price that South Korea was forced to pay for its integration into the new world economic order ('the high-tech modern world economy') and eventually, in 1996, admission into the club of rich nations – the OECD. The process included dropping the strong hand of the state on capital and removing restrictions against foreign investment, with results that were all too manifest in the Asian crisis of 1997, which led to a negative growth rate of 6.6 per cent in 1998 and a 40 per cent fall in the per capita GNP – from USD5,000 in 1996 to USD3,000 in 1998 (Bank of Korea, 2004). The economy since then has received some of its former dynamism, as has the labour movement, but the fix appears to be in. Foreign investors and global capital in the form of multinational banks and industrial corporations have made significant inroads into Korea's economy, resulting in an extraordinarily high debt/equity ratio, massive foreign borrowing, increased dependence on foreign investment and 'an undisciplined financial sector'. The *Korean Times* in its Anniversary Special edition might well write of South Korea as having 'outgrown its economic model' (even though in the same breath the *Korean Times* attributes the nation's plunge into the abyss of low economic growth in the 2000–2002 period) and 'clear signs that the Korean economy is heading into a low growth stage' – to its having 'adhered to the old economic model despite a rapidly-changing environment'.

The results of this 'development' are evident in a deteriorating economic situation, growing dependence on foreign investment and debt financing, a huge external debt – and the relative quiescence of the working class, chastened and disciplined by a deteriorating economic situation and rise in the rate of unemployment.

South Korea Today

South Korea today is at a crossroads between a state development past and a neoliberal present, between the dictatorship of an authoritarian (and relatively autonomous) capitalist state and the dictatorship of the free market, between fully realized capitalism and an unrealized future, between barbarism and socialism. At these crossroads the only forward for South Korea is to step backwards towards a strong state with a development agenda and forwards towards socialism and democracy. And the only way back towards the future is to build a popular working class base for a socialist transformation of the state and the economy.

Mexico, 1980–2005: The Makings of a Neoliberal Revolution[4]

In the 1960s and 1970s the Mexican Government, as the other governments in the region, assumed primary responsibility for promoting economic development and it did so on the basis of a state-directed model. To finance national development the government had been reliant on bank loans and somewhat on official resource transfers to make up a perceived shortfall in capital. From 1976 to 1982 the government, as well as companies in the private sector, had borrowed so much from the commercial banks that, with the high interest policy of the US and under changed and very unfavourable conditions for its exports, it fell victim to a scissors-squeeze of what would become known as the 'debt crisis'.

The complex dynamics of this crisis has been the subject of many studies and commentaries. They include a decade 'lost to development' and the abandonment of the economic model that had guided economic policy for decades and that was associated with rates of economic growth exceeding 5 per cent per annum. Under pressure from the World Bank and the IMF, which assumed the responsibility of ensuring that debtor governments did not default on their obligations to the private creditors who had advanced them capital in the form of bank loans. Under pressure from the Bank and the Fund to restructure their debt and to adopt what would become known as the 'new economic model' (NEM) the Mexican Government, together with

4 The following review of neoliberalism in Mexico relies on data collected and points made by Lau Zayago (2005).

others in the region, discarded the model that had served it so well but now deemed to have exhausted its productive capacity. They turned to a model constructed by economists at the Bank on the basis of the 'sweeping economic reforms' instituted by the Pinochet regime in Chile. In the context of Mexico's debt crisis these institutions were able to lever the adoption of a program of policy reforms, although under duress and not without resistance.

The prescribed policy reforms were predicated on ideas advanced by von Hayek and Milton Friedman to the point that the free market is the basic engine of economic growth and the private sector of capitalist corporations the best driver of this engine. These reforms were designed to foster market expansion as well as adjusting all national economies to the requirements of the new world economic order. Another aim of these policy reforms was to increase the efficiency of both the government and the market, thereby helping bring about productivity growth, which was seriously lagging in Mexico as elsewhere. Economic and productivity growth, facilitated by these policy reforms, would be unleashed (so went 'economic theory') in a process of capital accumulation and productive investment of this capital by the 'private sector' – i.e. the foreign enterprises attracted by the improved conditions created by the policy reforms.

Economists at the Bank and the other financial institutions of the new world order, offered a radical but at the time appealing solution for solving the problems of the capitalist world, particularly lagging productivity and stagnant growth but also fiscal and national account imbalances, etc. With a shift in emphasis from 'development' (international cooperation for) – the impetus for which had dissipated and would almost disappear with the collapse of the socialist bloc – towards 'globalization' the World Bank launched its war on poverty in an entirely new context, proclaiming that the 'pro-growth' policies of the 'new economic model' were 'pro-poor' (see discussion in Chapter 4). Over the next two decades this war was fought on various fronts, with diverse strategies designed to reduce world poverty, eradicating its most extreme forms and alleviating the pain and discomfort accompanying the transition from backwardness and poverty towards modernity and prosperity.

Throughout the 1980s the process (and associated discourse) of 'economic development' was dominated by reference to market-led economic growth, austerity, monetary and fiscal discipline; budget equilibrium, deregulation, privatization and downsizing of the state; globalization and structural reforms. These terms became part of the economic jargon in both official and academic discourse, key elements of the 'Washington consensus' and the discourse on globalization (Levitt, 2004). The reforms and policies that they entailed were portrayed as universal remedies for particular problems such as sluggish productivity growth, stagnant production and the fiscal crisis experienced by many governments both north and south – problems attributed to the failure of government and state-led development. One single expression embodied these policies: *neoliberalism*.

The neoliberal path towards economic growth under the Washington Consensus has subsequently been taken by many, if not all, countries but none so diligently as in Latin America, where regime after regime abandoned the state-led model of capitalist development – supposedly 'exhausted' and having failed – in favour of neoliberalism. The turn towards this model can be traced out in virtually every country in Latin America but for our purposes we will take the case of Mexico, reviewing briefly Mexico's experience under a succession of s regimes constituted by the *sexenios* (six-year term) of Miguel de la Madrid (1982–1988), Carlos Salinas De Gortari (1988–1994), Ernesto Zedillo (1994–2000) and Vicente Fox Quesada (2000–2004).

Miguel La Madrid (1982–88): On the Horns of a Neoliberal Dilemma

De La Madrid was put charge of undoing the state-led approach towards national development, and dismantling related government programs, because of the apparent 'failure' of this model. Starting his career at Mexico's central bank, he taught law at UNAM and then, from 1970 to 1972, he worked for PEMEX, the state oil company. His political career took off with an appointment, in 1976, as Secretary of Budget and Planning in José López Portillo's cabinet. He was later selected by Portillo (given the 'dedo' as was the presidential prerogative and custom) to be PRI's presidential candidate for the next elections. It meant that he would win these elections and become President of the country and indeed he did in 1982, initiating his *sexenio* under a particularly 'difficult economic situation' arising out of the debt crisis. Mexico's turn, under De La Madrid, away from an inwardly oriented process of economic development, predicated on the protection of national capital and the expansion of the domestic market, took place under conditions that included negative growth (0.2 per cent) of the GDP – 2.4 per cent in the manufacturing sector – inflation up to 100 per cent and a net external debt exceeding US $80 billion (Story, 1986). Under these conditions, the government easily succumbed to pressures exerted by the World Bank and IMF to comply with their requirements of the new world economic order.

In this situation the government abandoned the state-led model of Import Substitution for Industrialization (ISI) and drastically reduced its intervention in the market, dismantling its regulatory apparatus and its discriminatory regime against FDI (Hoshino, 1996). Adopting the IMF's rescue package or reform measures and policy prescriptions, the government devalued the peso and changed the law governing FDI, liberalizing the inflow of foreign capital, providing a major impetus to the inflow of FDI. The National Commission for Foreign Investment (Comisión Nacional de Inversión Extranjera CNIE) deregulated the operations of multinational capital (foreign investment) in both its financial and industrial forms.

In February 1982 the peso's value in relation to the US dollar shot up from 26 to 45 but after De La Madrid took office it shot up to 150 pesos per US dollar (Soederberg, 2001). The aim of the government's devaluation measure was to adopt a more 'realistic' exchange rate so as to encourage exports and attract foreign investment. Other measures included fiscal discipline (cutting public expenditures on social and development programs), adopted as a means of bringing national accounts and the operational budget into balance as well as bringing inflation under control, a measure of critical importance to foreign investors concerned with protecting the value of their investments. This measure (fiscal discipline – reduction of the public budget), initiated by de la Madrid has continued over several presidential periods, resulting in a dramatic decline in the share of the government (the 'public sector') in the GNP – from 41.4 per cent of the GDP under De la Madrid to 26.6 per cent under Zedillo (SHCP, in Guillen, 1997, p. 101).

Another neoliberal measure taken was privatization. Toeing the line imposed by the IMF and the World Bank the government implemented a policy of dismantling public enterprises, a policy also maintained by subsequent presidents, most notably de Gortieri (1988–94). The main objective of this policy was to increase economic efficiency. To this end, Mexico's version of the *Chicago boys* (Chile's students of neoliberal economics) began to dismantle public enterprises, both profitable and unprofitable. In addition, De La Madrid started a program designed to privatize (and, in the process, denationalize) Mexico's banking system, reversing Lopez Portillo's nationalization policy. This policy instituted by De la Madrid was extended under the *sexenio* of Zedillo (1994–2000) who responded to the financial crisis of 1994–1995 by restructuring the banking system via a program of privatization and denationalization, putting all but one bank in the hands (banks) of foreign investors. The policy (see more detailed discussion below) included a massive bailout of the remaining banks, resulting in a public debt on which the government in 2005 is still paying interest – USD 3-4 billion a year.

From Portillo's perspective the banks were responsible for the massive capital flight exacerbating the government's balance of payments difficulties in 1982. Thus, in a move to regain the confidence of 'the private sector' (capitalists inside and outside Mexico) his government nationalized and took over 58 of the 60 banks in the private sector (Haluk, 1999).

Privatization was the main neoliberal policy implemented during the De La Madrid tenure in office. As Teichman (1996, 4) has noted: 'Dismantling the state and its withdrawal from a wide variety of activities hitherto considered the legitimate arena of the state was the cornerstone of the new program.' She adds that 'divestitures of state companies (their sale liquidation or transfer) have probably been the most publicized aspect of that policy thrust.' From well over a thousand companies in 1983, when De la Madrid took power, the number of companies in the hands of the federal government was reduced to only 209 by the end of the Salinas regime.

Under the 1973 Investment Law, foreign investment was restricted to 49 per cent of business shares. But this requirement was entirely dropped in the 1984 Investment law in regard to the export sector, high technology industry and the maquilladoras that were deemed to generate short-term employment (CNIE, 1984, 1988). The outcome of this measure was reflected in a dramatic increase in the flow of FDI from USD$362.2 million in 1974 to USD5.6bn in 1993 (SECOFI, 1994).

Most of the increase in FDI was absorbed by enterprises in the manufacturing sector, particularly the maquilas. De la Madrid's policy was designed by Mexico's version of the *Chicago boys* – Pedro Aspé, Jose Cordoba and Jose Angel Gurria – who designed and engineered the National Law of FDI, with changes that went into effect in 1989 under Salinas de Gortieri, who eliminated the remaining regulatory controls over FDI. Thus, foreign investors free to move their capital into and out of the country (Guillen, 1997, p. 125). The response of foreign investors to this liberalization regime was almost immediate. In 1989, alone the foreign capital invested in Mexico exceeded total investment over the entire decade of the 1970s (Guillen, 1997, p. 125).

The government's neoliberal approach in terms of privatization, deregulation and financial liberalization – opening up the economy to the world market – included trade reform measures designed to integrate the economy into the global economy and the new order governing it. The first step taken by the De La Madrid government in this connection was in 1986 with the admission of Mexico to the General Agreement on Tariffs and Trade (GATT). Once Mexico adopted GATT, the elimination of import licenses and the reduction of trade tariffs became part of the trade reform. While in 1983 all imports were subjected to special licenses, by the end of 1991 only 9.1 per cent of imports required pre-authorization (SECOFI, cited in Guillén, 1997, p. 108). Almost all of the country's trade was liberalized in six years.

Between 1982 and 1988 the government's protectionist policies were dismantled, public enterprises were privatized, the peso was devalued, real wages were allowed to plummet and public spending was cut back dramatically, including social spending in the areas of health, education, food subsidies and rural development. Nevertheless, despite these cutbacks, the traditional welfare system was maintained. It took Carlos Salinas de Gortari, a devout advocate of the neoliberal model to dismantle this system in the context of a 'new social policy' that was oriented towards – 'targeted at' – the poor. This policy was programmed in the form of *Solidaridad.*

Carlos Salinas de Gortari (1988–94): Taking the Bull by the Horns

At the end of his term De La Madrid elected his former student, Carlos Salinas de Gortari, as the next presidential candidate, charging him with the responsibility of advancing the neoliberal model of Mexico's economic development to ensure conditions for financing this development by means of foreign investment rather than relying on surpluses generated in the oil industry and agriculture (Trevino, 1994). The centrality of FDI to the government's economic growth strategy is reflected in the increase in the flow of FDI – from 28 per cent under De La Madrid to 34.5 per cent under Salinas (SECOFI, 1994). Under Salinas the Foreign Investment Law was changed to allow FDI flows into the cities, including Mexico City, Guadalajara and Monterrey, hitherto off limits to foreign investors.

When Salinas assumed power, macroeconomic stability was temporarily restored. But he was immediately faced with a legitimacy crisis, in part due to deteriorating social conditions and in part because of the clear evidence of electoral fraud. In his attempt to head off the crisis, Salinas promised to democratize Mexico's political system and maintain macroeconomic stability as well as reducing poverty. The path taken in this direction was paved by a second round of structural reforms, including liberalization of the financial and agricultural sectors and the privatization of more state enterprises. To combat poverty, social spending was marginally increased but *focalizado* – 'targeted' at the poor and their communities via the *Programa Nacional de Solidaridad* (National Solidarity Program, PRONASOL). This program focused on the population living in extreme poverty and encouraged the participation of its intended beneficiaries – 'participatory development' as it would be termed by the international development community. At the same time, Salinas revamped the traditional welfare system via application of the principles of decentralization, fiscal balance and privatization to the areas of health, education, social security and housing.

In addition, neoliberal reforms, such as budget austerity, foreign trade liberalization; budget cuts to social programs and the privatization of state-owned enterprises, were both extended and deepened. But the central element of the government's strategy for national development was the liberalization of foreign direct investment.

To advance this agenda the government liberalized banking and other forms of finance, and deregulated capital markets. The mechanism used was the Foreign Investment Law of 1989. To that point the government had closely regulated the Mexican financial system, using diverse mechanisms operated by the Ministry of Public Credit and Taxes (SHCP) and the Central Bank to maintain some control over the financial sector, much as the South Korean Government had. But with his Minister of Finance, Pedro Aspe,[5] the Salinas government took an entirely different tack, initiating a policy of radical financial liberalization. To this purpose Aspe configured an open market strategy for the Mexican stock system. Several public debt instruments, such as the CETE, Petrodolares, Ajustabonos and Tesobonos, were created to the purpose of encouraging the development of a private capital market. By the end of 1991, the Mexican stock exchange became one of the most important developing country capital markets in the world, just behind those of Taiwanese and Hong Kong (Guillén, 1997).

De La Madrid liberalized Mexico's economy, opening and integrating it into the emerging world economy vis-à-vis manufacturing. But under Salinas, the agricultural sector was opened to foreign investment, primarily by means of removing the fixed prices and subsidies to producers. In this context, state-owned companies belonging to CONASUPO (Compania Nacional de Subsistencias Populares), the main support institution for agricultural producers, were privatized. In addition, half way through his term (1992), Salinas pushed through congress new legislation designed to modernize agriculture, that is privatize ownership of land and the means of production, leading to a process of economic concentration and productive transformation. The main object of this agricultural modernization law was the *ejido*, a socioeconomic unit (and way of life) encompassing much of the peasantry and the country's economically marginal indigenous communities. The government, through reform of Article 27 of the Constitution, which gave protection to social ownership, encouraged private ownership via land titling, subjecting what had been the social property of the indigenous community to the market, allowing individuals within the community to buy and sell land. The process was designed, and in fact led, to the privatization, a concentration of land ownership and a drastic fall in productivity because the *ejidatarios* were unable to compete with the highly subsidized US farmers (Teichman, 1996). The end result: a drastic deterioration of the situation of most *ejiditarios* and the further marginalization and impoverishment of their communities.

As the government moved to 'modernize' agriculture it restructured the system of rural credit available to peasant producers via BANRURAL. This bank had been

5 In Mexico, he was Secretary of the Treasury (1988–94), of Programming and Budget (1987-1988) and President and founder of the INEGI (1982-1985). He has a B.A. in Economics from the Instituto Tecnológico Autónomo de México (ITAM) and a Ph.D. in Economics from the Massachusetts Institute of Technology (MIT).

the main source of credit for the peasantry but after it was restructured the bank only provided funding to producers at commercial rates and with a high possibility of solvency and commercial success. The system of credit and integrated rural development, designed primarily to incorporate the marginalized peasantry into the economic development process, but also available to independent farmers, was dismantled. The end result: large-scale bankruptcies and the indebtedness of the bulk of Mexico's middle class independent farmers, now organized in the form of El Barzon, an association of several hundred thousand indebted agricultural producers.

Salinas privatized the most important state-owned enterprises – over 1,000 of them – including the state telephone company (TELMEX), Mexicana de Cobre, Red Nacional de Televisión, Siderúrgica Lázaro Cárdenas, CONASUPO, Aeronaves de México, Altos Hornos de México, Grupo DINA, Constructora Nacional de Carros de Ferrocarril, Compañía operadora de Extracción y de Serviciós de PEMEX, Hules Mexicanos and the banks that were statified and nationalized under Lopez Portillo, including Banco Nacional de México (BANAMEX) and Banco Nacional de Comercio (BANCOMER). The government also privatized the remaining state steel companies and a variety of functions carried out by state enterprises in areas such as oil, basic petrochemicals and certain areas of mining, reserved exclusively to the state by the constitution (Teichman, 1996, p. 4).

His extension of De la Madrid's neoliberal agenda earned Salinas enthusiastic praise from the international financial community, who not only applauded his 'bold economic reforms' but as a reward promised and eventually provided Mexico entry into the club of rich nations – the Organization for Economic Cooperation and Development (OECD). But not all was a bed of roses for Salinas' Mexico. The year 1994 opened with the eruption of the Zapatista Movement of National Liberation (EZLN), which put an end to the illusion of political stability and broad support for the neoliberal transformation of Mexico. The 'party was over' for the ruling class, as the country lurched from one political 'disturbance' (the irruption of the EZLN onto the political stage) to others (the assassination of Luis Donald Colosio Murrieta, PRI's candidate for the 1994 elections, and José Francisco Ruiz Massie). By the end of the year and the end of Salinas' term in office, and his reputation seriously tarnished if not in tatters, the economy crashed, converting another 'free market' miracle into a major financial crisis.

Ernesto Zedillo Ponce de Leon 1994-2000:[6] *Consolidating the Model*

In December of 1994, just after Zedillo assumed office, the Mexican economy went into crisis. The immediate causes of this crisis have been the subject of much debate. Some Mexican analysts pointed to the loss of investor confidence brought on by political events such as the Zapatista uprising and the assasination of presidential

6 Notwithstanding his rhetoric about 'social liberalism' while in office Ernesto Zedillo Ponce de Leon is a truly neoclassical economist. At a public meeting of the World Economic Forum he coined the term 'globaphobic' to refer to the detractors of globalization. The term became widely used in Mexico and Worldwide.

candidate Donaldo Colosio, and by the Zedillo administration's mishandling of the peso's devaluation. Others emphasized the way in which structural reforms were carried out during Salinas' term, particularly the speed at which the financial sector was liberalized and the way in which tariffs were reduced (unilaterally and indiscriminately). And almost every analyst mentions the magnitude of the monetary policy and the current account deficit in the months leading up to the crisis (liquidity, exchange rate, interest rates) (Griffith-Jones, 1996; González-Gómez, 1999; Lustig, 2002; Laos and Roa, 2003). But whatever the immediate causes of the crisis, the consequences were severe, especially for the middle class and the lower strata of the population. In the first half of 1995, the peso was devalued by 43 per cent, inflation rose 52 per cent, thousands of businesses were forced to close, real wages dropped 25 per cent and two million people lost their jobs (Manning, 1996).

In confronting the crisis Zedillo responded with a stabilization program that included deep social spending cuts. And thanks to this program, a USD52bn bailout package from the 'international community' (basically the US) and high export earnings, a measure of macroeconomic stability was restored as was economic growth (from 1996 to 2000 the economy grew at an average rate of 5.5 per cent per annum, a rate of growth not seen since the 1970s).

During Zedillo's term in office, the structural reforms undertaken by the previous two administrations were maintained and consolidated. Once the crisis was overcome, social spending was restored but within the framework of new program – the *Programa para la Educación, la Salud y la Alimentación* (Program for Education, Health and Food, PROGRESA), which focused exclusively on families living in extreme poverty in marginalized rural communities, transferring money and food supplements directly to them. At the same time, having abolished Salinas' *Solidaridad*, the government remodelled the traditional welfare system on the basis of decentralization, privatization and fiscal discipline.

Zedillo was as supportive of FDI as previous PRI regimes had been, if not more so. The main mechanism of this support was the North American Free Trade Agreement (NAFTA), which became operational on January 1, 1994, at the outset of Zedillo's term in office. NAFTA, it turns out, provided a major impetus to imports from and exports to the US. It was also a major stimulus to FDI inflows – once the EZLN scare (working on investors for several years) was over. At the point of Mexico entry into NAFTA the US accounted for close to 80 per cent of total exports; by 2002, however, 90 per cent of Mexican exports went to the US market, much of it fuelled by US investments (Economia, 2004).

On Zedillo's election to the presidency socioeconomic conditions in Mexico were 'difficult' to say the least. The neoliberal engine had run out of steam and the economy, fuelled by market deregulation and financial liberalization, lurched towards crisis. But the neoliberal agenda was well under way. All of the strategically important policies under this agenda were in place and fully operational. They included market liberalization, privatization, budget austerity, monetary and fiscal discipline; budgetary equilibrium, market deregulation, financial liberalization and currency devaluation.

But 1994, Zedillo's first year in the Presidency, was not a good year for Mexico's neoliberals and neoliberalism. The year started with the Zapatista uprising and it ended in what would emerge as Mexico's worst financial crisis for decade. The precipitating event of the crisis appeared to be the assassination of Luis Donaldo Colosio Murrieta, the PRI's presidential candidate, but there were numerous economic social and political conditions that came together to expose the seamy underside of the neoliberal revolution and Mexico's vaunted 'economic miracle'. With the assassination, conditions of political instability spread to the economic system. With a seriously over-valued peso, investors began to pull their money out of the country, inducing a capital flight of critical proportions. On December 21 1994 the capital that decamped reached almost USD2.5 billion, contributing to a crisis-level fiscal deficit and national account imbalance (Guillen, 1997, p. 189). In less than a month Mexico lost US$11 billion of its reserves due to the speculative attack on the peso (Guillen, 1997, p. 189). In an attempt to avert the crisis – to 'overcome the economic emergency' – Zedillo called in the IMF for 'technical assistance' and, as part of an 'adjustment policy package', devaluated the currency to a more 'realistic' level so as to promote exports, supposedly control inflation and relieve the pressure of speculative attacks on the currency, which lost almost 80 per cent of its value against the dollar. But it was too little too late, or rather, too much too soon. The IMF reform package (AUSEE) included US$17 billion from the IMF and another USD $3 billion contributed by the commercial banks (Guillen, 1997, p. 191).

After the crisis, Zedillo took the Mexican economy even further along the path of neoliberal reform, exceeding even Salinas in his commitments to global capitalism. He extended the privatization of public utilities and services, including ports, railroads, airports and telecommunications, and, most notably, social security and pensions (Kaufman and Rubio, 1998, p. 58). All of these policies were already in place with the De La Madrid and Salinas but it seems that Zedillo used the crisis as an opportunity to consolidate the neoliberal agenda. To this end he privatized the pension fund system with the idea of encouraging private savings, but the only beneficiaries were those already working since the unemployed had no access to any social security plan. This policy is still in place today. The unemployed, including millions of 'self' and near-employed, have no access to any social security programs because they were dismantled by a succession of neoliberal governments and replaced by a very restricted program targeted at and limited to what the government defines as 'the poor'.

Zedillo continued to advance the neoliberal agenda by negotiating several free trade agreements in addition to NAFTA, which took effect at the outset of Zedillo's administration – and the emergence of the EZLN on the political stage. To attract investors and encourage an increased flow of FDI, the Zedillo regime prepared a supportive ('foreign investor friendly') legal and regulatory framework, including several changes to the Foreign Investment Law legislated in 1993 and modified in 1996 (DOF, 1996). The 1993 Foreign Investment Law, introduced on December 27, anticipated NAFTA by a few days (DOF, 1993).

The 1998 Foreign Investment Law homogenized regulations regarding intellectual property rights, providing legal security to foreign investors, and allowing foreigners to invest in sectors that had reserved to nationals – telecommunications and the railroad among others. This policy was facilitated by special permits extended by the Ministry of Foreign Relations to a maximum of 50 years (DOF, 1993, 94; DOF, 1996, 28).

The US has always been the main source of FDI flows into the Mexican manufacturing sector but the volume and investment share of US firms dramatically increased as of NAFTA. In 1992, US FDI flows to Mexico were US$1.3 billion but by 1997 it had more than doubled to USD$5.6 billion and in 2003, although overall foreign investments declined significantly, the volume of US investment actually increased as did the US share of total foreign investment – from 55.5 to 70 per cent (DC-EU, 1999; Dussel, 2000). Most of this FDI was directed towards the manufacturing sector, which saw increased exports as a result of the 'maquila' program or PITEX (Programa Temporal de Importación para productos de Exportación). In fact, the trend has been maintained. With most FDI directed towards manufacturing and the maquiladoras the trend if anything has been consolidated. Manufacturing absorbs the bulk of foreign investment, even with the abnormally high price of oil on the world market, second only to oil, a sector that has managed to attract foreign investment notwithstanding constitutional restrictions on ownership. As Saxe-Fernandez (2002) has shown, the profits to be had were simply too great to ignore.

Since 1995, sectors such as electronics and transport vehicles have had a higher than 70 per cent participation rate of US FDI. In fact, the most important exporting companies in Mexico in this sector remain Ford, General Motors and Chrysler, which also have the highest propensity towards exports of all companies in Latin America (Expansion, 1999). But there is also a significant presence of Asian and European capital in the sector of automobile manufacturing – mostly assembly operations but also complete production lines. Thus, automobile makes such as Honda, Hyundai, Toyota and Nissan as well as Peugeot, Renault, BMW, Volkswagen, Mercedes-Benz, Volvo and Audi are not uncommon on the streets or in the registry of exports. Within the framework of NAFTA, a number of US-based enterprises in the automobile industry invested heavily and relocated most of their manufacturing processes in Mexico. This strategy was implemented to expand the automobile industry through NAFTA's member countries and other international markets (CEPAL, 2000). By 1998 up to 93 per cent of Mexico's total automobile exports, originating in the maquilas, were destined for the US market (SIC-M, 1999).

The electronic industry followed the automobile industry in its relocation to Mexico under NAFTA. Most enterprises in the sector are foreign, and the Mexican subsidiaries of US electronic companies have contributed almost 20 per cent of overall US electronic imports. In 1990, there were only 19 foreign enterprises in the electronics industry but after just four years of NAFTA there were 52 (Dussel, 2000, p. 44). In fact, Mexico became a place where US and Asian enterprises would compete for spaces in order to establish subsidiaries. Cities such as Tijuana and Ciudad Juárez became major centres of assembly and sub-assembly manufacturing operations, even though the growth of the maquilladoras, and foreign investment, has since fallen off as a result of increased foreign competition from even cheaper locations of labour (Expansion, 1998; Dussel, 2000).

Another industry that expanded after NAFTA is the manufacture of computers and semiconductors, a sector that attracted a large chunk of FDI inflows in the 1990s. This sector is dominated by Asian companies such as NEC, Hitachi, Fujitsu, Sony,

Seiko, Epson, Mitsubishi, Toshiba, Sanyo and Matsushita, Samsung, LG Electronics and Hyundai. The only US companies with an important presence in this sector are Intel, Microsoft, IBM, Dell and Hewlett Packard (Expansion, 1998).

Under NAFTA, FDI inflows dramatically increased, particularly in 1997 by which time foreign investors had recovered from their nervous reaction to the EZLN uprising. With the aim of attracting more foreign investment Zedillo negotiated another eight free trade agreements (FTAs), including one with the European Union that has become the second largest source of FDI in Mexico.

In addition, Zedillo advanced the privatization agenda, opening up remaining state-owned enterprises to private investors, both national and foreign. This process included the banks which today as a sector is 92 per cent owned by four foreign financial groups. In the 1980s there were no foreign banks in Mexico but after NAFTA the number of banks dramatically decreased in a process of acquisition and fusion. In 1982, all of Mexico's banks, some 60, were re-privatized; in 1991 Salinas initiated a policy of re-privatizing the remaining eight major banks, all but one of which (Banorte) falling under foreign control in the context of the 1994–1995 financial crisis. In descending order of size Mexico's banking system today is constituted by five major groups, four of them under foreign control: BBVA-Bancomer (Spain), Banamex-Citibank (US), Santander (Spain), Banorte (Mexico) and Scotia Bank-Inverlat (Canada). The Honk Kong and Shangai Banking Corporation (HSBC) are minor foreign players in this highly lucrative field.

The privatization and denationalization of the banking system was facilitated by the largest bailout of private investors in Latin America's sordid history of bank bailouts, a history that can be traced back to 1983 when Pinochet's neoliberal regime crashed and almost burned – a bailout so massive that it equated with 3.5 per cent of Chile's GNP at the time. In Mexico's case the Zedillo government created a special fund *FOBAPROA* (Fondo Bancario de Protección al Ahorro) to provide a rescue package ('assistance') to all of the 14 remaining private banks with financial problems during the 1994 crisis – to prevent them from going broke.[7] This fund, through which the government insured 100 per cent of bank deposits, in effect turned

7 In addition to assuming responsibility for the liabilities of the bank sector and interest payments to the international financial groups organized around the four restructured banks, the government gave away ('sold' at bargain prices) to the latter the assets of the 14 failed banks. In effect none of these banks were dissolved or ceased to operate; they were simply absorbed by the 4 financial groups that emerged out of the crisis by a virtual government grant of their assets and assumption of their liabilities. While Citigroup acquired one of Mexico's most profitable and biggest banks, Banamex for a song (and an as yet secret 'deal' with Fobaproa under the direction of Medina *Mora*, Banco, Spain's Bilbao Vizcaya absorbed Multibanco Probarsa, Banca Cremi, Banco Unión, Banco de Oriente, Banca Promix and Bancomer, under whose name the group still operates a major bank in Mexico. British-owned HSBC absorbed Banco Internacional (Bital), which had acquired Banco de Atlantico. Canada's Scotia Bank took over Inverlat while Banco Santander Central Hispano 'bought' Banco Mexicano (Somex) and Banco Serfin, whose 'saneamiento' (healthification) was the most costly on a world scale in the long history of bank bailouts. Banorte, the only bank that managed to remain under control of Mexican capital, absorbed Bancen, Banpaís and Bancrecer, which had only just taken over Banoro.

a private debt into a public debt – privatizing ownership of the banks' assets but socializing their liabilities. This bailout of the bank's private investors was so large that in 2005, 10 years later, the accumulated public debt had grown to USD60bn, requiring annual interest payments to these same banks (but mostly to new owners) in the order of USD2–3bn a year, constituting a significant drain on the public purse (and a huge scandal, for which the new owners, and the official responsible for this give away, have managed to avert any and all responsibility).[8]

Since 2000, the financial sector received USD25.3bn of FDI, nearly 40 per cent of total FDI inflows into the country (Steinfeld, 2004, 3). As a result of these flows the country's financial sector and banking system has been 'transformed', according to the Carnegie Endowment for International Peace (Steinfeld, 2004), making it the region's second largest (with assets of USD165bn in 2003) and with the highest ratio of foreign ownership (90 versus 60 per cent for Argentina and Chile) in Latin America. The system, the Carnegie Foundation adds, 'has been extremely profitable' and this because the industry remains 'relatively uncompetitive' and because of 'improved microeconomic efficiency' not to speak of (and the Foundation does not) recapitalization (absorption of the sector's liabilities). With the new foreign (and some of the old) owners of the banks assuming the accumulated assets of the privatized banks and the government absorbing all of their liabilities – at a staggering social cost (USD2–3bn a year) – 'better management' and 'micro-efficiencies' (reducing the number of employees), according to Steinfeld, led to 'soaring profits'.

Another source of soaring profits for the foreign-controlled banks has been exceptionally large flows of migrant remittances, which, like the privatized pension funds (AFORE), are channelled through the private banks. Fees charged for these and other banking operations by all accounts is a lucrative business and a major supplement to the increased rents collected by the banks on extended loans.[9] As noted by Steinfeld (2004, p. 25) 'foreign participation in Mexico's banking sector

8 The sheer enormity of the bailout, in the context of enormous profits made by the new bank owners and continuing interest payments to the very same albeit restructured and denationalized banks, has kept the scandal alive, periodically breaking out as it did in March 2005. At this point (*La Jornada*, March 5, 2005) it was noted by Lopez Obregón, Mexico City's former mayor and PRD candidate for the presidency, that the size of the annual interest payments constituted a drain on the public purse larger than the budget for UNAM, a public university of more than 120,000 faulty/employees and 250,000 students.

9 According to a report by the Organization for Economic Cooperation and Development (OECD, 2003), the fees for transferring money from the United States to Mexico decreased significantly from 1999 to 2003. The OECD report finds that, in 1999, a $300 transfer could cost up to $60, or 20 per cent of the total amount. By 2003, this figure decreased to a range of $10–$18. An Inter-American Development Bank-Pew Hispanic Center survey found that the share of Mexicans using banks to collect remittances was twice that of other Latin American countries (43 per cent in Mexico, 20 per cent in Central America, and 19 per cent in Ecuador). In 2004, according to the IDB, remittances from the United States to Latin America comprise more than 100 million separate transactions every year, which, Steinfeld (2004, 11) notes, 'provides a significant opportunity for foreign banks to capture a steady flow of revenues from an expanding market, while continuing to lower costs for the benefit of senders and receivers of remittances'.

has benefited foreign banks tremendously'. Elaborating on this point Steinfeld observes that 'the low level of industry competitiveness and the increasing market share and concentration of foreign banks have allowed banks to charge high fees and maintain wide spreads between lending and deposit rates.' In addition, he notes, 'the banks … capture of some of the growing remittance market have contributed to revenue growth, thus producing high profits.'

To place these migrant remittances in perspective they are Mexico's second most important source of income. In fact, since 2001 they exceed FDI flows, generating revenues greater than generated by the tourist industry and equivalent to two-thirds of petroleum exports and 180 per cent of agricultural exports.

In line with his predecessors Zedillo avidly pursued the privatization policy. At the time, a combination of worldwide stagnation, a fall in oil prices and growing fiscal pressures pushed the government towards privatizing the last public enterprises of the energy sector as a means of obtaining capital – attracting FDI. The declared purpose was to increase economic efficiency, encourage the economic growth and foster foreign investment (Baker and Blume, 1999). However, the process was obstructed, if not halted, by opposition in some political circles and parts of the civil society who consider these enterprises as sacred cows. And indeed public ownership in these strategic sectors is still protected by the constitution. Three public enterprises have been at issue in this struggle: the *Comisión Federal de Electricidad* (*CFE*); *Luz y Fuerza del Centro (LFC)*; and *Petroleos Mexicanos* (PEMEX), all enterprises whose 'public' character is protected by the Constitution.

Zedillo's offer to privatize CFE and LFC was immediately rejected by the unions – the *Sindicato Unico de Trabajadores Electricistas de la Republica Mexicana* (SUTERM) and the *Sindicato Unico de Electricistas* (*SME*). In addition, political instability and a profound crisis in the social sector due to the levels of poverty discouraged the privatization processes. Even so, in February 1999, Zedillo sent a proposal to the congress outlining the implications of privatizing the power industry. Its main objectives were to:

- Guarantee electricity supply to cover the growing demands of the Mexican people;
- Provide a reliable, high quality service at competitive prices to encourage further growth of the nation's economy;
- Attract more investment from all sectors in order to strengthen the development of the electricity industry;
- Expand the coverage of electricity and subsidize the sectors of the population with the highest necessity;
- Create new and better jobs for the labour force of both the electricity industry and the country;
- Devote resources to high priority programs such as education, health and combating poverty, and;
- Strengthen the regulatory function of the government within the electricity sector (Baker and Blume, 1999, pp. 28–29.

According to Zedillo, the privatization of the energy sector would bring about several benefits – a line maintained and enunciated *ad nausem* if periodically by his successor, Vicente Fox, as well as a chorus of voices from the World Bank, the IMF and related institutions. However, the social and political dynamics of opposition thus far have foiled all efforts to bring about the privatization of these enterprises. For one thing, the neoliberal discourse about increasing efficiency and incrementing profits was widely rejected in the civil society. As a result, the discourse used to justify privatization was modified. Luis Tellez, former Minister of Energy, for one, argued that the reason for privatizing CFE and LFC was to increase benefits for the social sector. In addition, he argued that this privatization would help advance the struggle against poverty and inequality. In his own words:

> Mexico cannot afford to miss opportunities to attain the levels of efficiency and low costs reached by the electricity industries of other countries were barriers to competition have been eliminated. Nor can Mexico afford to waste the opportunity to devote resources to remedying poverty, inequality and lack of capital. The energy sector must be at the forefront in supporting the international competitiveness of the nation's industries and the welfare of all Mexicans (in Baker and Blume, 1999, 29).

This quote epitomizes official discourse in Zedillo's last years in office. On the one hand, there was an increased focus on the social dimension of government policy – on its orientation towards poverty alleviation (social liberalism). On the other hand, a continuation of neoliberal economic policy was seen as a vital means to this end – a view that would be accentuated by Zedillo's successor in the presidency: Vicente Fox.

Vicente Fox Quesada (2000-2006)[10] *The Neoliberal Debacle*

Taking advantage of the neoliberal crisis, Vicente Fox Quesada, former manager of Coca-Cola Mexico and presidential candidate of the National Action Party (PAN), assumed the presidency after nearly 72 years of PRI rule. In the Mexican context Pan represents a turn to the right relative to the centrist politics of the PRI, which has both a left-of-centre nationalist wing (Bartlett, etc.) and a right-wing faction oriented towards political conservatism and economic liberalism, a formula at work in the politics of so many countries in the 'new world order'. In the context of this conservative counter-revolution, under the ideological influence if not control of a behind-the-scene and extreme right-wing secret religious organization, 'los yunques', the Pan promoted a combination of fiscal conservatism and free market economics, including financial liberalization, privatization and other 'structural reforms'. In this regard, despite an electoral discourse to the contrary, Fox and the *Pan* regime did

10 His education included a stint at the Universidad Iberoamericana and seminars imparted by lecturers from the Business School of Harvard University. After the end of his education he went to work for the Coca-Cola Company, starting off as a route supervisor and driving a delivery truck. He rose in the company to become supervisor of Coca-Cola's operations in Mexico, and then in all of Latin America. Notwithstanding not having graduated from university he became PAN's presidential candidate in 2000.

not in any way modify the neoliberal agenda of the previous PRI-regimes. On the contrary, most observers are of the opinion that what defined the Fox regime was a fundamental *continuismo* vis-à-vis the policies of the preceding regimes, most particularly those of Zedillo. For example, Fox signed and negotiated a Free Trade Agreement with Japan (going into effect in 2005) that parallels NAFTA and like NAFTA was expected to boost FDI inflows.

Despite the government's efforts in support of foreign investors, FDI inflows generally declined over the course of Fox's sexenio and the economy failed to rebound. A few months after Fox assumed the presidency, the economy entered into a recession, growing at an average rate of only 0.64 per cent per annum from 2001 to 2003. The volume of foreign investment in 2003 relative to 2002 dropped USD3.1bn. Lower than any year since 1998. However, the government not only maintained but consolidated the structural reforms of his predecessors. In fact, he even tried to extend economic liberalization to the energy sector, but without success because of widespread opposition in Congress and from the unions.

The failure of the economy to rebound from a close-to-crisis level of growth has been attributed by the political opposition to his strict adherence to orthodoxy. Others have argued that these market (and foreign investment)-friendly 'pro-growth' policies failed to deliver on their expected outcomes because of unfavourable conditions in the global economy, namely stagnation of the US economy (and thus reduced demand for Mexican exports) and increased competition from China and the turn of foreign investors towards greener pastures. In any case, notwithstanding a recent upsurge in FDI (as of mid-2004) foreign investment in the Mexican economy over the course of Fox's *sexenio* generally declined from an exceptionally high point in 2001, and in some sectors such as agriculture the decline has been dramatic.

Despite the admittedly unfavourable conditions the Fox regime continued his predecessors' neoliberal policies of privatization and financial and trade liberalization. However, since these predecessors had implemented so much of the neoliberal agenda, Fox was not able to do much more than 'hold the line', except for moving ahead on certain issues such as labour reform and extending the privatization agenda to the last redoubts of state enterprise – oil production and electricity generation in the energy sector, higher education (universities) in the social sector and, according to Gonzalez Amador (*Public citizen* July 3, 2005) water.[11] In these areas Fox continued to vigorously pursue the neoliberal agenda, albeit with many difficulties and growing resistance from diverse sectors, both political and social. Well into his *sexenio*, on February 27, 2004 he announced a new initiative in the area of reforms in the energy sector that would 'preserve (the country's) sovereignty' as well as advancing the 'economic model' used by the government to guide national policy and that his government would maintain to the end (of his presidential term).

---

11 Despite growing pressures from civil society and social movements against the privatization of water provision – and without regard to the accumulated record of high social costs of privatizing water (higher prices, reduced access an increased incidence of disease, etc, in Argentina, Chile and Uruguay, and mass resistance in Bolivia and Ecuador) – the government gave significant concessions to operate in this area to MNCs such as Suez, RWE, Aguas de Barcelona y Vivendi.

Not surprisingly, this initiative was met with widespread opposition. At issue in this resistance, which the government found more difficult to deal with than the resistance structural reform in the agricultural sector some years earlier, was constitutional protection of public enterprise (and employment) in the strategic sectors of the economy. Nevertheless, despite widespread opposition the government managed to institute what in the oil sector amounts to de facto privatization and denationalization – privatizing a number of critical functions hitherto under the exclusive control of state enterprise (Saxe-Fernandxez, 2004) and turning over the booty to foreign investors.

Ironically, as it turns out, Fox came to power precisely because of his discourse, directed at the electorate, regarding the privatization of Pemex – to prevent it from happening. As the country's largest enterprise, with over 130,000 employees and sales up to USD40bn (Pemex, 2004), Pemex continues to play a critically important role in the economy, particularly as regards the national budget and the balance of payments. As for the Balance of Payments oil exports remain the largest source of governments revenues, particularly in the context of a dramatic rise in the price of oil.

Notwithstanding the centrality of oil to Mexico's national development, and the major contribution of Pemex to this development, the company continues to be the object of continuous and persistent government efforts to bring about fundamental 'structural reforms' (i.e. privatization), and, according to the Pemex's chairman Munoz *Leos* 'the government is [engaged in an] ambitious program to improve [its] operation and efficiency' (Webb, 2001, 27). Needless to say, behind the neoliberal discourse on 'efficiency and competitiveness' is a program to restructure Pemex, i.e. fire a good part of its workforce, as many (or as few) as 30,000 workers, in the name of 'efficiency' and the 'structural reforms' required by the World bank and the IMF in the interest of foreign investors.

To advance his neoliberal agenda, Fox created a management board incorporating the country's 'most successful' businessmen: among others, Carlos Slim Helu, the richest individual in Latin America (Number 17 on Forbes' Global List); Lorenzo Zambrano, the owner of the world's third largest cement maker (CEMEX); Rogelio Rebolledo, the CEO of Frito lay Latin America; and the Minister of Finance Francisco Gil Diaz. The official discourse is that the board only promotes the 'modernization of industry'. Needless to say, this 'management board' has pushed privatization and other elements of the neoliberal agenda, notwithstanding Slim's personal view that neoliberalism is 'economically dysfunctional' (and, more to the point, politically destabilizing).

Most analysts remember share Fox's term in office for following rather closely the steps of previous governments regarding neoliberalism. Indeed, most of the important 'structural reforms' advanced and passed by Congress in Fox's regime were initially proposed by the PRI in previous *sexenios* (and, at the time, rejected by Fox and PAN). His economic policy was a continuation of Zedillo's. This was particularly evident in the Fox regime's persistence in proposing to privatize CFE and LFC. From the beginning and to the end Fox assiduously sought to advance the privatization of the oil and electric power industries but so far without success, notwithstanding the intermittent but persistent campaign launched from the president's office as well as from within the IFIs (the WB and IMF, etc.). Opposition to this agenda, including a sector of PRI (Fox did manage to engineer a PAN-PRI congressional alliance on this point), has simply been too strong. The *Sindicato Mexicano de Electricistas* (*SME*) and other independent unions (the FTM is in the government's pocket) have to date mounted a successful campaign in support of the constitution and resisting the Fox agenda in regard to both labour reform and reform (privatization) of the public sector in the production of electric power and oil.

While the government's agenda was stymied in this strategic area the regime managed to give a new twist to its neoliberal agenda, if not advance it, in regards to social policy. In this connection Fox steered the same general course as his predecessors but implemented several strategic changes. The most significant of these changes include: (i) modifying PROGRESA (now called 'Oportunidades') by extending the program to semi-urban communities; ii) promulgation of the Social Development Law, which makes it illegal to make cuts to social spending; and iii) a direct attack on the level of public funding of the universities, encouraging their privatization. In regard to this issue of public education the regime launched a frontal attack against what is widely regarded as the most important institution of higher education in Latin America – UNAM (Autonomous National University of Mexico), a publicly-funded university with an enrolment of over 200,000 and a staff/faculty complement of over 140,000, constituting a city-size campus (la ciudad universitaria) in the capital district. However, as in other attempts to extend and deepen the neoliberal agenda in this policy the government encountered vociferous opposition. It turned out that the Fox regime ran its course without being able to significantly advance its agenda, stymied as it was by widespread opposition.

Conclusion

Vicente Fox's period in office brought an end to a cycle of neoliberal policies, exposing fundamental flaws and internal contradictions of a free market approach towards economic development fuelled by a dependence on foreign investment. The failure of the Fox regime to bring about a sustainable process of economic growth and associated developments demonstrates that even with windfall revenues measured in billions of pesos (record oil prices) and record low interest rates the neoliberal model is economically dysfunctional and has exhausted its economic limits. The failure of the Fox regime to privatize the generation of electric power and the production of oil, both of them priorities of the regime, demonstrates that the neoliberal has also reached its political limits.

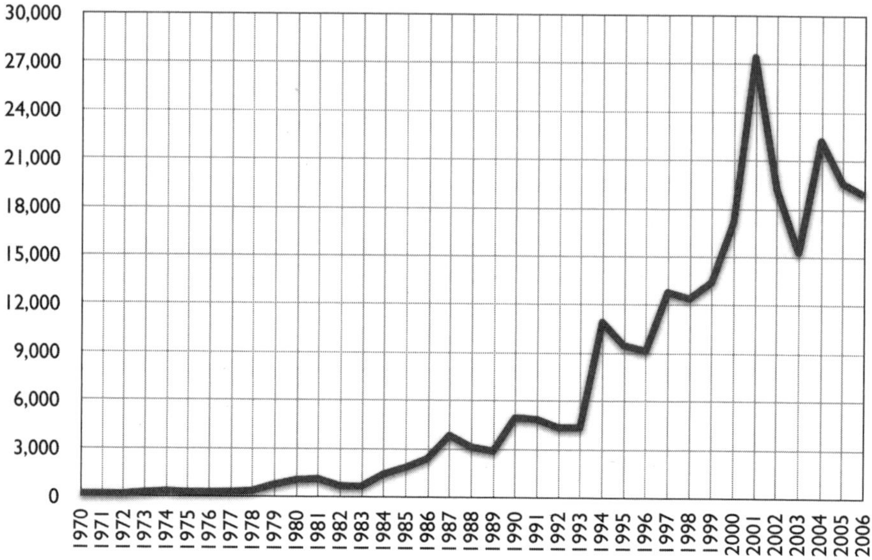

Figure 5.1 Foreign Direct Investment Flow, Mexico 1970-2006

Chapter 6

Foreign Investment and the State

Foreign investment tends to be prejudicial to most Third World countries because of the non-market incentives that it demands. Much of what passes as favourable 'market conditions' are in large part political decisions that maximize benefits to the MNC at the cost of the local economy, its tax payers, consumers and workers. The meaning is clear: investments are not merely market transactions in which MNCs justify their profits on the basis of the risks they run, the innovations they introduce, the capital they invest. Abundant evidence is available to demonstrate that most foreign investment is subsidized and risk-free, and relies on securing monopoly profits based on the appropriation of existing national (state) enterprises and control of strategic markets.

Privatizing Lucrative Public Enterprises

A great deal of foreign investment adds little to new productive or distributive systems since it is directed at purchasing existing privatized public enterprises directly or via the takeover of the same from original private national capitalists. The transfer of ownership from state to private/foreign capital increases the outflow of profits, which previously accrued to the national treasury or were reinvested in the local economy. Privatization is part of the structural adjustment policies imposed by the IMF and World Bank as conditions for refinancing debt payments. The sale of national assets more often than not is hardly transparent and the sales take place far below market value, let alone their value to the indigenous population. In other words, privatization has served to create a class of capitalists or 'oligarchs' who perform none of the 'tasks' associated with capitalist enterprises: they neither invested in training labour, invested capital in infrastructure, innovated nor located new markets. Privatization in the context of the ex-communist and nationalist countries most closely resembles *pillage* rather than *investment*. The process of privatization follows one of two paths: either direct buyouts by foreign capital or theft in public properties by former state managers and/or their oligarchic-gangsters, the emerging 'national bourgeoisie'. During a second phase many of the national oligarchs sell part or all their shares to foreign capitalists/MNCs. These political 'incentives' for foreign capital and oligarchic groups are justified by 'free-market' ideological dogma of the governing elite or by reference to the huge body of studies commissioned and prepared by international organizations such as the World Bank and the OECD (Nelson and Mahbodor, 2000).

The infamous author of Russia's disastrous privatization (Anatoli Chubais), which led to the massive disarticulation of the economy and the impoverishment of the Russian people, justified his 'shock' policy by citing the need to make capitalism irreversible – to undermine any effort to sustain a mixed social economy. In other words, the policy of privatization was a matter of ideology and, in fact, without any foundation in empirical fact. Corruption, vast concentrations of wealth, and a drastic fall in living standards, including an unprecedented decline in life expectancy, were the accepted costs to establishing capitalism at any price.

Denationalization of Natural Monopolies

One of the key justifications of foreign investment is that is encourages 'competition' with local monopolies, increases productivity, lowers costs and prices and increases employment (Odle, 1993; Heather, 1997; ECLAC, 2004; UNCTAD, 2004). Most available data, however, allows us to argue otherwise.

One of the favourite targets of foreign investors and one of the prime incentives offered by neoliberal regimes is the privatization of public utilities (electricity, power, energy, gas, highways and communications), which could be considered 'natural monopolies'. Classical examples of such privatizations, offered as an incentive to foreign investment, are the public offerings of Aguas Argentinas and Petrobas Telebras in Brazil as well as the privatization under Margaret Thatcher's government of the water and electrical utilities. Prior to that point privatization had been restricted to or prioritized those strategic industries that had been placed in the public sector via the nationalizations of the 1950s and 1960s. The aim and real effect of these privatizations is not to increase 'efficiency' but to transfer public monopolies to foreign-owned private monopolies, leading to an increase in charges for services, decline in services to less profitable regions or low income consumers, an end to subsidies to emerging industries and the impoverishment of the urban and rural poor. These effects have been well documented in recent years, leading to a growing resistance to the further privatization in the sector of public utilities and services.

One of the most powerful 'incentives' which foreign investors demand and pliable regimes offer is the privatization of energy sources. Once held up as strategic publicly-owned national assets, the most lucrative oil and gas fields and associated economic enterprises (an entire industry) in many countries have been effectively turned over to the private sector – and, in many cases, to foreign investors – by compliant rulers. Fortunately, in some countries such as Mexico constitutional provisions have sheltered public firms in strategic sectors or industries from privatization and thus denationalization – not without the strenuous efforts to advance the process of 'structural reforms' (privatization), as exemplified by Vicente Fox in Mexico (see Chapter 5).

The electricity industry has been another favourite target of the MNCs in their drive to accumulate lucrative already established and well-capitalized assets put on the auction bloc by Third world governments in their drive to attract foreign investment. In the 1990s some of the world's largest multinationals, ranked by foreign assets, took the opportunity to expand and invest in the newly privatized firms in the electricity sector of the energy industry. By 2002, nine of the world's 100 largest nonfinancial multinationals, ranked by foreign assets, were in the electricity industry (generation, transmission, distribution) – a remarkable ascendancy, considering that in 1990 there were hardly any multinationals in the industry.

The obvious result of such 'structural reform' (foreign investment in the form of privatization) has been a huge transfer of wealth from the national economy to the multinationals under the assumption that new investments and foreign 'know-how' will provide compensatory benefits. In Mexico, the state-owned and -controlled oil industry, and public utilities in the energy sector, such as the generation of electric power, are experiencing strong pressures from both the World Bank and the all-too-compliant regime established by Vicente Fox, who continues to strenuously represent the interests and the position of foreign investors in these matters, to turn over both oil production and electric power generation to 'the private sector' in the name of much-needed 'structural reform'. Fortunately for workers and the country, the Mexican constitution protects state ownership and public ownership of these industries. Not so, however, in the countries that make up the former USSR. The new post-communist leaders in these countries have proven themselves all too compliant to the demands of foreign investors for a piece of the action – an ownership share in the country's natural resources and the enterprises allowed to exploit them.

There a numerous problems associated with this policy of compliance. One of these problems, at least in the energy sector, is that the multinationals in this sector (and others, for that matter) are notorious in not fulfilling their investment obligations and charging local consumers international prices, pricing endogenous producers out of international markets and impoverishing low-income local energy users. But while the privatization of energy and utilities attracts foreign investors (indeed it is one of the most favored incentives for foreign investment), it has several strategic drawbacks: Higher charges make local competitive firms less competitive; it deprives the capital-starved state of a source of public revenues; and it heightens inequalities between the foreign rich and their local associates and the rest of the population.

In today's globalized economy the energy sector is by no means the only target for foreign investment and takeover. Other favourite targets include: telecommunications (especially cell phones), transportation systems, high-demand raw materials such as iron and cobalt, and agricultural products such as soya and forest products.

Telecommunications have been a particularly favoured target of foreign investors in the 1990s. Privatization, UNCTAD (2004, 117) notes, was the dominant form of investment in this sector, accounting for around two-thirds of the $274 billion invested in telecoms between 1987 and 2002. Rather than heightened competition telecom contracts with foreign investment have frequently led to the demise of local high-tech enterprises (admittedly often subsidized and betimes inefficient) and the emergence of virtual monopolies, leading eventually to monopoly profits. Foreign investors have also targeted the transport sectors: railroads, airlines, ports, and highways. Once again whenever these investors have been invited to the party, and to participate in the play for the country's strategic resources and economic enterprises, the inevitable end result is monopoly markets and increased costs to the consumer.

In the process leading up to the privatization of public assets, foreign investors generally demand that the state assume the costs of 'transition' – firing workers, paying pensions or severance pay – and provide diverse incentives including the abolition of regulatory controls over pricing, the assumption by the government of any liabilities accrued by the firm put up for public auction, a deferral of taxes, and a 'good deal' on royalty payments. To create the political climate for privatization the state usually disinvests in public enterprises, decapitalizing them, and runs deficits via high tax rate policies, thus worsening public services, in order to provoke popular discontent with the public sector. Given the government-induced debts and deficits, the public transport systems are sold at low prices to foreign investors, who are enticed by promises of rate increases, tax concessions, reduced staff and cuts in less profitable routes. Most important no independent regulatory system is put in place to check the inevitable abuses of the FI. The result is the disarticulation of the transport system, as only major routes to large metropolitan centres are kept operating while the outlying regions suffer severe reductions in transport, undermining local economies. Privatization and the denationalization of airlines have led to the stripping of assets, decline of services and ultimately the bankruptcy of the firm. Iberia's purchase of Argentine Airlines, stripping assets and running the airlines into bankruptcy, illustrates this pattern.[1]

Foreign investors have never shown any interest in maintaining and upgrading any railroad lines and port facilities that fail to generate the profit ratios, which their influential shareholders demand. Where regulators are in place they either lack authority to enforce contract obligations on foreign investors, are co-opted, or subject to political pressure to overlook the not infrequent failure of foreign investors to comply with investment agreements. When foreign investments in infrastructure – for example highway construction and toll roads in Mexico – fail to provide the necessary profits or high rates force users to secondary roads, investors frequently demand compensation or the re-purchase by the state at inflated prices.

The most highly publicized and disastrous privatization with foreign investment at issue was in water distribution in Bolivia (Cochabamba and El Alto) and in Peru, where mass popular uprisings protested the high rates and the failure to connect the majority of working poor with water lines (Galiani, Gertler and Schargrodsky, 2002; Grusky, 2003; Inter Press Service News Agency, 2003; Torero and Pascó-Font, 2000). For a number of reasons (including difficulties of balancing 'commercial requirements' against wider social needs) TNCs have been slow to invest in water services. Private investment – and with it FDI – in developing countries in water services (mostly in Latin America) seems to have peaked in 1997 (UNCTAD, 2004, 122) and then declined, probably because of the resistance from the local population (and the indigenous communities in the case of Bolivia, Peru and Ecuador). However, in both Argentina and Chile, 100 per cent of water and sewage services are under foreign ownership and control, with a rather significantly negative impact on the

1 On the policy dynamics of this and other cases of privatization in Latin America see, among many other studies, studies collected in Azpiazu (2002) and Petras and Veltmeyer (2004).

local population who have seen water rates rise as much as 88 per cent since 1993 (Enciso, 2005).

While foreign investors have been deeply involved in most of the disastrous privatization activities in the Third World, and the ex-Communist countries, many similar experiences have taken place in the imperialist countries themselves. The privatization of the electric power generation in California led to major blackouts and exorbitant price hikes due to corporate malfeasance. The privatization of the passenger rail services in the UK led to safety hazards, exorbitant rates and unprecedented delays due to ancient equipment. The privatization of water in England led to health problems forcing public investigations and a move to renationalize.

In summary, by offering choice profitable economic sectors as incentives to foreign investors, Third World regimes have fostered private monopolies, not competition, and a high-cost infrastructure, which fails to integrate regions because of narrow corporate calculations of cost-benefits. Incentives to MNCs have prejudiced long-term, large-scale industrial diversification by offering raw materials, energy and natural resources as incentives to attract foreign investment.

Using privatization as an incentive for attracting foreign investment has had an extremely harmful impact on the deep structures of the economy, polarizing society by privileging elite enclaves and local oligarchs and influential public figures.

Construction of a Foreign Investment Regime

The neoliberal program of structural reform, including the privatization of economic enterprise, market deregulation, financial and trade liberalization, decentralization and 'democratic' form of 'governance', is designed to establish an institutional framework for the free movement and operation of foreign investors and their capital. The conditions for this 'economic freedom' were created in the 1980s and 1990s in the context of several rounds of 'structural reform' under the 'Washington Consensus'. However, it turns out that for foreign investors it was not enough for developing country governments to open their economies to foreign investment and associated operations. Investors demanded greater legal security for their investments than that provided by the neoliberal reform process. To respond to this need and demand, the US and European state initiated a strategy of bilateral investment treaties (BITs) to provide foreign investors with the required degree of legal security.

BITs, the foundation of an emerging regional and hemispheric investment regime, are primarily about protecting the rights of investors – 'to secure additional and higher standards of legal protection and guarantees for the investments of its firms than those offered under national laws' (UNCTAD (2000b, 1). In effect, BITs are signed for their 'demonstration effect', signalling to potential investors that the developing country is willing and legally obliged to protect foreign investment. In addition, the US has used its BIT program to diffuse a particularly American conception of investment rights.

Despite these facts, and notwithstanding the reluctance of developing countries such as India, Brazil and India to sign off on the hemispheric and regional investment regulatory regimes promoted by the US and the EU, UNCTAD has reported on an astounding rise in the use of BITs during the 1990s, together with a heightened liberalization of domestic foreign investment regimes, marking thereby 'a global liberalization of the environment in which foreign capital operates'. By 2003, UNCTAD estimates, at least 2,265 BITs covering investment and other business services had been concluded between a total of 175 countries, reflecting both the increased interest of signing BITs between developing countries, and the rapid increase in BITs recorded in the latter part of the 1990s (UNCTAD, 2004, p. 221). In 1999, alone, 20 BITs were concluded in Latin America and the Caribbean (UNCTAD, 2000a, p. 8). Latin America arrived at the BIT trend relatively late, beginning in the late 1980s, but the total climbed to 300 by 1999, a total of 366 if the Caribbean countries are included.

BITs are not the only institutional mechanism involved in the construction of a foreign investment regime in developing countries. Other such mechanisms include a series of agreements in the form of TRIMs (Trade Related Investment.), TRIPs (Trade related Investment....) and GATT (General Agreements on Tariffs and Trade) as well as a state-investor dispute mechanism. Negotiations to establish the and other such institutions of a foreign investment regime have been advanced in diverse forums, including trade talks at the WTO and other such international organizations available to the imperial state. However, negotiations on these fronts in diverse forums have not been entirely successful or satisfactory, particularly as viewed from the perspective of the US Government, the dominant player in this global game.

A particularly thorny set of issues for the institution of a foreign investment regime came up at the WTO trade talks at Cancún in September 2003. These talks collapsed in face of the intransigence of a group of approximately 20 developing countries led by India and Brazil (later termed the G-20) over a series of trade issues and agriculture. A refused to negotiate investment rules demanded by the US, EU and Canada in the form of TRIPs, TRIMs and GATS. The G-20 naturally enough insisted on a level playing field in the arena of world trade in exchange for a guarantee of investor rights. In addition these countries have viewed thee proposed disciplines on investment contained in TRIMs and GATT as unnecessarily restrictive of their ability to enact development and industrial policies. And naturally enough the US and Canadian governments, as well as their counterparts in Europe, were unable or unwilling to accede to this demand for greater 'flexibility for development' and free trade – to open up the imperial economies to developing country exports. As a result, it would appear that both the EU and the US were prepared to abandon further negotiations rather than accede to the demands of the Group of 20, whose intransigence was blamed for the collapse of trade talks.

With the debacles in Cancún and Miami, and continuing opposition from the group of 20, serious negotiations to complete the FTAA as originally envisaged by 2005, and the setbacks in the Doha 'development' Round, various regional and multilateral attempts to establish a hemispheric regime to regulate foreign direct investment have been left in tatters. As for the US Government it has shifted towards a global strategy of 'competitive liberalization'. The idea is to increase the pressure on those countries resistant to signing up to the US approach on trade and investment by signing bilateral deals with neighbouring countries. This approach increases the risk to developing countries such as Brazil who refuse to negotiate with the US at the multilateral level, as they, but not their competitors, find themselves marginalized from US markets.

Since 'competitive liberalization' was adopted, the US, in the western hemisphere alone has concluded free trade agreements with state-of-the-art investment 'disciplines' with Chile, Costa Rica, the Dominican Republic, El Salvador, Honduras, Guatemala and Nicaragua, and has ongoing FTA negotiations with Bolivia Colombia, Ecuador, Panama and Peru, and a BIT negotiation with Uruguay. 'Taken together, the United States is on track to gain the benefits of free trade with more than two-thirds of the western hemisphere through sub-regional and bilateral FTAs' (USTR, 2004, p. 4; INVEST-SD 05/03/04). The idea is to increase the pressure on those countries resistant to signing up to the US approach and to bring them around.

Observing this panorama of bilateral negotiations, the International Institute for Sustainable Development (IISD) concludes that 'by pursuing negotiations with so many individual players in the hemisphere, the United States would appear to be in a strong position – should the FTAA fail – to achieve most of its objectives on investment through a multitude of sub-regional negotiations' (INVEST-SD, 14/11/030).

Subsidies, Tax Exemptions and Export Processing Zones

Many foreign investors demand and obtain, from pliable Third World regimes, direct and indirect subsidies in the form of lengthy tax exemptions or reduced tax rates for periods between 10 to 40 years on imports, exports, corporate earnings and foreign executives salaries. In addition, regimes seeking to attract FI frequently provide land for enterprise construction free of cost or at minimum price, and subsidize utility and energy prices, state-financed infrastructure, labour training and policing. The net result is that poor developing countries pay to be exploited. Frequently the only 'benefit' to the country is a minimum tax, and low wages to highly regimented workers confined to export processing zones. By not paying taxes, foreign investors deny Third World states revenue for public investment in education, health and skill upgrading. States that lack tax revenues frequently resort to borrowing, setting in motion new concessions to foreign investors as a condition for receiving loans from the IFIs.

UNCTAD, in its 2004 *World Investment Report*, which provides the most systematic report and data available on multinationals and FDI, outlines in considerable detail the range of 'incentives' provided by host governments to multinationals as a means of attracting FDI. These incentives include subsidies of all sorts (on this see the WTO, 2004), duty-free imports, income tax holidays or exemptions, direct grants, even 'equity injections', and other fiscal, financial and procedural incentives, not to mention incentives in the form of 'structural reforms' (privatizations, financial liberalization and deregulation of labour markets, etc.). In regard to such 'reforms' UNCTAD (2004, p. 8) reports that from 1991 to 2003 a minimum of 35 countries a year (82 in 2003) made a total of 3,385 regulatory changes in their investment regime, all but 114 more favourable to FDI, designed to attract it.

Export Processing Zones

Among the most striking developments in the Third World has been the massive growth of export processing zones (EPZs). By 2005 there were some 5,000 EPZs, employing 40 million workers under the most arduous repressive work conditions and the lowest pay in absolute terms (living standards) and relative terms (output / productivity to wages). The EPZs are not what they might appear to be: the first step toward higher skill, higher wage, technically advanced forms of industrialization that takes place outside of, or parallel to, the EPZ. EPZs are attractive to foreign investors because owners and managers have absolute control over labour and the environment and are able to operate freely – free of environmental, health and safety regulations that reduce profits. Many regimes which conceived of EPZ as the first stage of a process of 'deeper industrialization' have been disappointed: EPZs are simply 'pieces' in the MNC production strategies – a locus for cheap labour in the labour intensive 'assembly stage' of manufacturing. They are generally not well integrated into the national or local economy via backward or forward linkages. They are integrated instead into the circuits of global production in which employment and other possible local 'benefits' are greatly outweighed by the severe social and economic costs associated with them.

Tax Privileges

The tax incentives for the MNC means a higher tax burden on local workers, peasants, professionals, public employees, and small and medium sized business, if their children are to receive an adequate education and health care. The people pay to produce healthy, literate workers to be exploited at low wages by tax exempt multinationals who then transfer their untaxed profits to millionaire (billionaire) CEOs, stockholders and speculators. The list of tax 'incentives' or privileges is lengthy and extremely costly to the countries, and working population because what the MNC and foreign investors do not pay, is shouldered by the local taxpayers or else public services suffer dire consequences.

Tax revenues finance on-going basic social services and pay for the maintenance of the state and infrastructure as well as potential public investment for long-term growth. Tax privileges for foreign investors lower state revenues and hence expenditures on upgrading (or even maintaining) basic services as well as undercutting national investments to diversity the economy and move beyond a foreign investment 'enclave' economy.

The better known and most common tax privileges extended to foreign investors include exemptions on imports of parts and other inputs as well as exports, low or non-existent property taxes, minimal profit and revenue taxes, generous depreciation allowances, tax holidays of between five and 20 years. In addition, expatriate managers and CEOs receive their salaries, bonuses and stock options tax-free. If we add the cumulative sum of tax losses which the state does not receive to the vast expenditure of state resources invested in infrastructure, severance pay, and 'restructuring' costs to attract FI, it is clear that the total cost of attracting foreign investment far exceeds the benefits in employment and future taxes which might accrue over the foreseeable future.

If we add the loss of tax revenue from displaced local business-driven to bankruptcy – we face even fewer benefits resulting from foreign investment. Finally it is common practice of foreign investors to relocate their enterprises when their tax holidays expire, or when workers salaries begin to increase. The idea propounded by apologists of foreign investment that present sacrifices and for future gains is an illusion – an ideological ploy to secure current privileges.

Market Liberalization

Under conditions of total liberalization, the strategy advocated by the IFIs and followed by many Latin American and ex-communist rulers, all barriers to foreign investors entering the local economy have been lifted. Studies have demonstrated that where local establishments go head to head with large MNC, they almost always lose out, either going bankrupt, being bought out by the bigger firm or becoming a satellite supplier. Since most employment in the Third World takes place in small and medium size enterprises, the result of the entry of FI leads to an increase of unemployment as millions of firms providing jobs go bankrupt.

FI relies heavily on suppliers, experts and consultants from their home base to externalize costs (and maximize profits) and to maintain control, thus savaging existing local suppliers who were linked to local small and medium size producers. Only a small number of local firms survive the large-scale entry of foreign-owned MNCs. This is not surprising given the tax incentives, credit access, economies of scale and 'monopoly tactics' which they employ to capture markets (initially lower prices to drive out competition and then price increases once monopoly is established). The emergence of a minority of locally owned competitive firms is commonly publicized by neoliberal ideologues as part of their success story, excluding the much bigger story of failed enterprises and the foreign takeovers of majority shares of the local market.

The invasion by foreign investors of local economies seriously compromises efforts to construct 'regional integration'. This occurs because the principal beneficiaries of broader markets are precisely the large foreign-owned enterprises, not the national firms. This is particularly evident in MERCOSUR (the association of Brazil, Argentina, Uruguay and Paraguay). By locating in the country with the lowest labour and tax costs, the MNCs can dominate regional markets, undermine protected industries in neighboring countries and generate severe and destabilizing trade imbalances between different members of the regional integration pact.

Contrary to much 'progressive' opinion, regional integration, far from being a nationalist or regionalist alternative to imperial domination becomes an FI launching pad for entry into broader markets. What gives a particular reactionary cast to 'regional integration' proposals is that they skip over the more obvious problems of the lack of national integration within the participating countries: the decline of the domestic rural market because of inequalities of land tenure, the concentration of wealth in the urban central city and the vast impoverishment of sprawling suburban slums, the growth of dynamic enclaves in a sea of low paid, precarious, informal economic activities.

'Regional integration', anchored in big national or foreign-owned multinationals, essentially is a strategy to expand sales without changing the national class structure or the unequal distribution of land and income.

Opening the economy to FI is almost always accompanied by the 'deregulation' of the economy, or more accurately, a change in rules that facilitate the movements of capital in and out of the country. In particular the 'liberalization' of financial markets, meaning the decline of public oversight of financial transactions, allows FI to 'launder' unreported revenues and profits and transfer funds overseas.

The net effect of increasing market access for FI is to replace a market attuned to transaction between local producers, with a market that is constructed in the image of FI – with a heavy import content and deleterious nutritional effects (like soft drinks and fast foods) accompanied by colonial ideological-cultural propaganda.

Cheap Labor: Unskilled, Skilled and Professional

One of the most striking incentives to FI offered by Third World and ex-communist states is state-promoted cheap labor in manufacturing, services and the primary sector. In order to attract FI, states frequently following IFI directions have initiated a whole series of decrees and laws dramatically favoring capital over labour: wages and salaries have been reduced, frozen or kept below the rate of inflation; job protection legislation has been abolished or severely modified to allow investors to hire and fire without any restrictions or due process; severance pay has been eliminated or reduced; the work day and working conditions have been revised, extending and intensifying exploitation; pension and health benefits have been reduced, eliminated and privatized, trade unions have effectively lost the right to strike, have been repressed or incorporated in state-run, investor-dominated 'tri-partite' pacts.

By concentrating power in the hands of capital (euphemistically called 'labour flexibility') the neoliberal regimes compete with each other in bidding for FI. Favourable anti-labour legislation and draconian restrictions on trade unions have lowered labour costs and have favored foreign investors in labor-intensive manufacturing.

Since the 1990s, however, FI has increasingly looked toward 'outsourcing' skilled jobs to low-wage/salary regions (Agrawal and Farrell, 2003; Bardhan and Kroll, 2003; Dicken, 2003; Kobayashi-Hillary, 2004). This requires state promotion of an educated low-paid work force and financing of local business elites to act as recruiters and pointmen for the FI. Overseas relocation, the reality and the threat, is a common policy to lower wages, pensions, health benefits and job security in the imperial countries. Foreign investors benefit from both ends: exploiting skilled and unskilled labor in both assembly plants and high-tech (IT) industries in the Third World and ex-communist countries and reducing labor costs within the imperial countries, playing off one against the other and securing labor incentives from neo-liberal states in both. The net effect is to increase profitability by squeezing out greater productivity per worker at lower costs, expand market shares and create lucrative export platforms to sell back into the home market.

The same practice and logic which applied to the outsourcing of unskilled labor to low-wage areas has been extended to high end skilled labor in an array of activities from specialized software programming, accounting, engineering, research and development and design. The notion propagated by neoliberal apologists that the loss of manufacturing jobs would be 'compensated' by the growth of skilled service positions fails to recognize that corporations would follow the same logic with regard to skilled service jobs.

The net result of low-cost labor incentives to attract or retain FI has been to widen the economic gap between labor and capital, deepen the inequalities in political and social power, and dissociate growing productivity and profitability from wage returns. Wages and salaries increasingly lag behind capital gains in productivity, profits and export earnings largely as a result of the vast and profound labor incentives – privileges to FI. Under the rule of labour incentives to FI, growth of GNP has few spread effects to the rest of society, creating highly polarized growth.

One of the primary concerns of FI is securing ironclad legal guarantees against nationalization, expropriation or new regulations, no matter what the circumstances or non-compliance of MNCs. To attract FI, neoliberal regimes legislate or decree measures, which over-ride constitutional, health, environmental and other laws, in order to provide the absolute security which FI demand. The pursuit of 'low risk' status by many Third World and ex-communist countries in order to attract FI undermines the countries' sovereignty in several ways. In the first place, it opens the country to international judicial processes; embargoes and heavy fines if and when a future government decides that the non-nationalization and expropriation agreements violated the country's laws, were signed under duress, lacked transparency or simply gave undue privileges to FI. In other words, the pursuit of 'low-risk' status sacrifices future options and raises 'risks' for future governments intent on restructuring or transforming the country or merely altering the balance between public, private and foreign investment. 'Low-risk' agreements for investors may close the book or make it costly or 'high-risk' for future regimes designing new strategies, as the economy outgrows the FI-dependent stage.

In practice, there cannot be any durable investment 'guarantees' against expropriation, new regulatory or tax regimes or even confiscation because the conditions for FI vary with the fortunes of the class struggle, national liberation movements, global economic conditions and the changing priorities and internal dynamics of MNCs. The 'low-risk' agreements between an authoritarian regime and FI will last as long as the regime can silence or co-opt opposition.

Elected regimes that single-mindedly provide generous contracts and opportunities to FI while imposing prejudicial austerity programs on working majorities have caused the greatest damage among more highly developed economies, like Argentina and Russia, with a highly trained labour force, a developed home market, reasonably, sound infrastructure and an advanced social welfare system.

Large-scale privatization and denationalization promoted by regime ideologues, aided and abetted by US free market academics have provided innumerable incentives for FI buyouts, promoting in the process a fierce form of untrammeled free market capitalism in Russia, not to mention unprecedented levels of corruption. In both Argentina and the former USSR, privatization and financial deregulation did attract FI but with catastrophic results for the economy and the population. FI bought public enterprises at bargain prices, especially oil and gas fields, communications and other lucrative areas; financial deregulation led to massive bank frauds, and transfers of huge sums out of the country. The economies collapsed and foreign debt payments overwhelmed the countries' capacity to pay. Living standards plunged, with over one-third of the workforce unemployed: Over half fell below the poverty line. The ranks of the truly indigent climbed to over 15 per cent. Pension plans; advanced medical systems, educational and scientific facilities crumbled and skilled professionals fled the country in droves. Foreign investors initially prospered with their privileged access to the economy, but uncontrolled plunder led to a general crisis, which eventually engulfed the very speculators who brought it about.

Given the severe drawbacks in providing long-term, large-scale privileges to attract FI, what is the response of FI to a shift in policy, from providing corporate incentives to progressive social reforms, economic regulation, re-nationalizations, prosecution of tax evaders and money launderers and environment protection?

Strategies to Counter Social Reform and Popular Responses

For policymakers intent on constructing an alternative development model to the FI centred approach it is important to *anticipate* the strategies of opposition, which FI will adopt and be prepared to put in place timely counter-measures.

The most likely first move of FI, to counter policies designed to enhance the national economy and popular living standards, is to threaten or practice disinvestment in local facilities. This involves lowering production, closing facilities, reducing or withdrawing capital to destabilize the economy and force the government to withdraw, rescind or not implement legislation or executive rulings. Disinvestment can be accompanied by the threat of a 'strategy' – putting in jeopardy the employment of local workers, suppliers and other satellite enterprises.

Knowing this to be a real probability, the state can raise the stakes by insisting that disinvestment can lead to the cancellation or re-negotiation of the original investment agreement and/or state intervention into the enterprise, followed by outright state takeover in the public interest to safeguard employment, production, maintenance and shares of export markets. In other words, firm assertion of state purpose makes FI disinvestment a two-edged sword: either abide by the new legislation or lose access to the local market, exploitation of local resources and supply of strategic goods. The state can also affirm that there is 'no return' once an 'exit strategy' is adopted.

To back up the counter-strategy and make it more credible, the state should be ready to replace senior corporate personnel with local specialists from within the plant, or from other agencies or from the outside. Negotiations with suppliers and purchasers should be in place. Most of all the employees, workers and professionals in the affected economic sector should be mobilized, consulted, organized to respond favourably to the impending confrontation. They and the larger public – workers, peasants, lower middle class, professionals – should be informed and prepared for a period of transition to the new socio-economic model, in case there are sacrifices and temporary hardships.

A reduction or the elimination of privileged place of FI in the economy will likely lead to a run of liquid assets, which will certainly cause financial disruption. Here decisive and rapid action is essential – including the freezing of assets, generalized capital controls and other restrictive measures on the movement of capital, while maximizing the role of state-sponsored policies to maintain levels of credit and to maintain production even if it means a spike in inflation and monetary emissions, requiring price controls or subsidies on basic items of popular consumption.

Failing to intimidate the progressive regime through economic threats or actions, FI will turn to their imperial state to exert bilateral or multilateral pressures. These can range from threats to cut off loans from IFI, to restrictions on imports and exports, to destabilization efforts and/or threats of military intervention. Several contingencies may influence the effectiveness of these political pressures. In many cases, the key competing imperial countries may not be in agreement on these measures, especially if they affect mostly one or another imperial power. Secondly, the global economy is neither homogenous nor 'unipolar' in trading or military policy: losses by one imperial power can be gains for another. Thirdly threats to cut off financing by the IFI is a two-edged sword: ending of financing can lead to debt default, the refusal to pay past loans, setting a precedent for other debtor countries, and escalating the conflict to the global level. Once debt payments are suspended, the 'extra revenues' can be used to compensate enterprises prejudiced by IFI cut-offs. The larger the debt, the greater the destabilizing impact of a debt moratorium will have on international financial markets.

Clearly in anticipating this escalation of the conflict with FI, the state must view the problem through political lens in order to best prepare its counter-attack. Imperial threats usually radicalize and mobilize popular movements, isolate elite allies of the imperial power, and polarize the country in a way favorable to the regime, if the latter has clearly defined and demonstrated the socio-economic advantages of pursuing its new development model. If the imperial state pursues a military-political interventionist strategy, the regime in consultation with its mass constituency must rapidly pursue a multi-layered national defense strategy, which can range from anti-terrorist measures, to legislation outlawing imperial funding of political parties, NGOs and media outlets.

Clearly significant changes in one vital sector of the economy imply changes in the totality of the society and state. By regulating or redefining the state-FI relationship, new political actors are drawn in as the conflict spills over to other sectors of the economy and across frontiers, leading to the need for further changes in the economy and state security structure. Looking at the problem of FI conflict in narrow economic terms of a state-investment framework, can lead to unanticipated attacks and likely defeats and retreats.

FI can rely on their associates in the mass media to launch 'scare propaganda campaigns', which demonize progressive regimes: labeling them terrorists, rogue states and communists – part of the battle of ideas. The regime must be prepared to counter elite media warfare through its own mass media within the country and via progressive social movements and media throughout the world. Internet sites, community radios, videos and international solidarity organizations can be effectively mobilized to reach the active populations who would respond to the positive changes initiated by the progressive regime. What is essential is to move beyond criticizing the power of the adversarial corporate media toward the creation of multiple mass outlets and activities to gain political support.

It needs to be emphasized that 'changes' in relation to FI are interconnected with and activate other structures of the state and economy. The media, ideological and cultural wars are essential to sustaining or undermining efforts to limit or eliminate the dominant privileged role of FI.

A third strategy to undermine progressive legislation, which is almost always adopted by FI, is the corruption of government officials – especially regulators – trade union officials and the political elite. This involves cash payoffs in foreign accounts, job offers to relatives or promises of managerial positions after serving office, visiting professorships to prestigious universities with lucrative stipends, and a host of other remunerative rewards. Judges appointed by the pliable executives can be expected to rule against state measures to revise FI contracts or to rule in favor of extra-territorial judicial sites (lawsuits in imperial jurisdictions).

While 'international' and NGO investigatory agencies have established 'transparency' ratings for countries, few if any have examined or established corruption ratings for MNCs and FI, despite their widespread use of bribes and illicit activities and the devastating effects it has in undermining progressive changes. Corruption by FI can be limited by introducing a number of institutional changes: by creating workers, consumers and environmental oversight committees with open access to all accounts, transactions and especially government contracts. Secondly, corruption can be limited by publicizing all stages of negotiations between state and MNC and making it obligatory and subject to scrutiny by the classes and organizations most affected. Auditors and investigators who have no ties to FI interests can serve a technical advisory role in preparing evaluations of contracts and state-FI agreements. The reform of the public administrative structure must include deep ethical and political changes, inculcating members with a commitment to national and class values, from top to bottom. Ultimately technical and ethical/political commitments are the best safeguard for neutralizing the FI corruption designed to undermine the implementation of progressive legislation.

Finally FI may accept regulations and reforms, but resort to increasing prices, and lowering labor costs to maintain profits. State intervention fixing rates is an obvious counter-measure, along with threats to re-nationalize if FI decides to hold back on promised new investments. Enforcement of labour legislation and price constraints monitored by organized consumers can block corporate efforts to pass on the costs of state reform to the consumer.

Conclusion

FI incentives usually come at an unacceptable cost to workers, consumers, taxpayers, local producers and environmentalists – all have to pay for state subsidies which privilege FI in the way of higher taxes, lower social services, scarce and more expensive credit, and higher prices. Alternatives to incentives and privileges to FI are readily available, feasible and beneficial when a regime is prepared to withstand the inevitable threat, pressures and propaganda, which emanate from the imperial state linked to FI. A broad strategic approach prepares the state – allowing it to develop effective countermeasures to the reprisals taken by the FI or their colleagues in the IFI and the imperial state.

Chapter 7

Anti-Imperialism and Foreign Investment

Over the past 40 years, diverse socialist and nationalist regimes have attempted to combine public enterprise with private investment, including foreign capital. At first, decisions were made to limit the scope of foreign investment to particular sectors and in some cases to a defined time frame via 'fade-out formulas' (over time the foreign shares would be bought out by the public sector).

In the last decade of the regimes in 'socialist' USSR and East Europe the governing elites widened the scope of private and foreign capital and, in some cases, even signed agreements with the IMF accelerating the process. But with the collapse of these regimes and the ascendancy of pro-capitalist policies, the ruling elites and foreign capital proceeded to pillage the public sector of these countries to an unprecedented degree. Foreign capital and newly minted local oligarchs ran amok, grabbing and stripping public assets, public treasury, natural resources, public utilities, mass media and energy resources. This led to unprecedented and rapid impoverishment of the working population who were stripped of their social wages (ending the regime of free health, education and other social benefits) in the context of the growth of monstrous socioeconomic inequalities between a small stratum of multi-millionaires and the vast majority of the population, impoverished in the process, laid low by the 'forces of (economic and political) freedom.' The story of these developments has many facets to it and at least two sides. On the one side, incredible concentrations of wealth and prosperity for those individuals and groups, and some countries, integrated into the globalization process under relatively favourable conditions. On the other side, widespread poverty and the immiseration of the working class in its multitudinous forms, the newly dispossessed, excluded and oppressed. What this has meant is massive outmigration, corruption on an unprecedented scale, powerful murderous international gangs trading in hundreds of thousands of women and girls (sex slaves for international brothels), the proliferation of narcotics and illicit arms sales, ethnic and class conflicts, a so-called 'clash of civilisations' and imperialist wars waged against 'rogue regimes' and 'failed states' – those opposed to the forces of 'freedom, democracy and private enterprise' and the projection of imperial power to advance these forces.

Sell-offs of public assets in Latin America, Asia and to a lesser extent Africa were accompanied by large-scale corruption, and in many cases loss of control over the economy, economic stagnation and the growth of unprecedented social inequalities.

By the end of the 1990s, the disastrous political socioeconomic consequences of the rapid and massive conversion to capitalism and the unregulated invasion of foreign capital in the former 'socialist' bloc and strongly nationalist countries became evident to those regimes and individuals not prepared to take the leap into the abyss of 'free market' capitalism. Debates and discussions about the role of foreign capital in national development emerged, both among the political class and the wider public of intellectuals, workers, and political activists. A category of intellectuals and politicians identifying themselves as 'market socialists' argued for a greater or lesser role for foreign capital, while others, often referred to as 'orthodox Marxists' and citing the debacle in the former USSR, argued against large-scale, long-term openings towards foreign capital in any form.

The debate continues, the issues shifting with circumstance and context. The 'market socialists', however, now emphasize a new dimension of the issue – 'globalization' (integration into the global economy governed by principles of a 'new world economic order'). The dynamics of the globalization process they argue, are inescapable, requiring every society to adapt to it the best or any way they can, and striking the best deal possible with foreign capital. On the other hand, 'orthodox' Marxists continue to reject foreign investment in one form or the other (direct and portfolio) (FI), pointing out the links between FDI and 'militarist imperialism', here citing the US-EU's Balkans Wars, US-led invasions of Yugoslavia, Iraq, Afghanistan, and Haiti, the US sponsored coup in Venezuela and the overt military threats against Iran, Syria and Cuba. These orthodox Marxists argue for a rejection of, or fewer openings to, foreign capital for reasons of national security and opposition to the militarist machinations of the imperialist powers. However, 'market socialists' (the market itself has not been at issue, more a question of what institutions in which it should be embedded) have been unable to effectively counter the facts about imperialist aggression except to cite the possibility of 'separating' the role of foreign capital from the behaviour and interests of the bellicose imperialist state, an argument not without merit under certain circumstances. Nevertheless the *economic* arguments of market socialists still carry weight and have had considerable influence over state policies, leading to 'piecemeal' adoption of their ideas and policy prescriptions by orthodox Marxists.

In this chapter we review the various theoretical, policy and political debates that surround these issues. First, we identify the myths that continue to dominate the economic development discourse on FDI; we then review and critically discuss the arguments of the 'market socialist', neoliberals and other advocates of foreign capital. This is followed by a critique of these arguments from our unorthodox Marxist position and the presentation of alternatives to a reliance on foreign capital in a process of national development of the economy.

Myths of Foreign Investment

Myth #1 – FDI is an Important Engine of Economic Growth

It is widely assumed that foreign investment, or the private inflow of capital, is an absolutely critical factor in the development process, the only way for a developing country to overcome a shortage of capital. There is an as yet unsettled debate as to which form of capital inflow, or which type of capital – bank loans, portfolio investment or FDI – is superior (i.e. provides the greatest benefits at the lowest cost) but many economists share the view of the IMF that FDI is 'the backbone of development finance', a vital source of capital needed by developing countries to jump-start their economies. However, the evidence suggests otherwise – that MNCs with their investments seek out and enter, rather than create, economically dynamic industries and countries. In other words, economic growth leads to FDI rather than the other way around as suggested by so many neoliberals (Milberg, 1998).

In addition, there is considerable evidence that locational decisions of the MNCs as to their operation and FDI have less to with specific incentives and regulations governing FDI than the dynamism of existing production factors, the size of the domestic market, the presence of a sound infrastructure and a well-educated and disciplined labour force (World Bank, 1995; UNCTAD, 2001, 2004). Thus the bulk of FDI over the years and today is directed not towards the emerging markets in developing countries but to the developed countries themselves. In fact, an analysis of FDI flows over the years shows that FDI has generally pursued and followed rather than led economic growth. Recent patterns of change in FDI flows provide further evidence of this. For example, the success of China and Socialist Republic of Vietnam in attracting FDI does not in any way reflect a liberalized approach towards FDI. On the contrary. Both countries continue to aggressively regulate the operations of MNCs and foreign investment. Their success in attracting foreign investment has to do with their dynamics of economic growth and the enormous size of the potential market, providing profit 'opportunities' that the MNCs are anxious to exploit.

Myth #2 – FI creates new enterprises that are productive and competitive, transferring technology and in the process introducing superior managerial techniques and business practices, stimulating new research and the development of local technological 'know-how'

As a point of fact, FI has been generally directed toward purchasing the assets of privatized and often quite profitable existing public enterprises and private firms, taking over existing markets and selling – renting, more of the than not – technology developed at the 'home office'. In the 1990s over one-half of foreign investment in Latin America was used to purchase the assets of existing enterprises, usually well below market valuation. Instead of complementing local public or private capital, FI tends to 'crowd out' local capital and public initiative, undermining emerging technological research centres.

As for technological transfer, long a major presumed accompaniment and benefit of FDI, the evidence suggest that little technology is in fact actually transferred in the sense that local or national firms have access to it. A recent multi-regional, multi-volume study of the dynamics of technological transfer and transformation that this is a major difference in the economic development path traced out by a number of 'rapidly-growing countries' in Asia (the vaunted 'Asian Miracle') and countries in Latin America (and Africa). The difference in their development paths and their rates of economic growth can be traced back to the nature and economic role of the state – 'developmental' (also interventionist and protectionist) in the case of the former and 'neoliberal' (minimalist and oriented towards the free market and private sector). However, the most striking difference is in the degree of reliance on FDI and the rate of technology transfer: these two factors of economic growth appear to be almost inversely related – respectively low and high for the rapidly growing Asian countries, and high and low for the Latin American countries. The evidence is that Japan, Korea and Taiwan built their industrial foundations on the basis of a highly restrictive policies towards FDI.

More generally, the experience of most developing countries with FI and technological transfers by and large has been negative: over 80 per cent of R&D is normally carried out in the main office. Thus, the 'transfer of technology' means the rental or sale of techniques developed elsewhere rather than local design. Also, given that MNCs tend to charge their subsidiaries rather excessive royalty, service and management fees, to artificially or fraudulently lower profits and taxes payable to local governments. The costs of the little technology that is actually transferred are very high, well in excess of any received benefits.

As for market expansion, the record is mixed: in some sectors where public enterprises were starved for funds, like telecommunications, the new foreign owners may have expanded the number of users and enlarged the market. In other cases, like water, electricity and transportation, the new foreign owners have reduced the market, especially to low-income classes, by raising charges beyond the means of most consumers.

Myth # 3 – FDI is beneficial to developing countries because it provides important links with and access to foreign markets, increasing export competitiveness and stimulating the local economy via secondary and tertiary purchases and sales

In fact, FDI is often used to buy up lucrative natural resources and export them with little or no value added. Most of these resources, minerals, etc.and so on are converted into semi-finished or finished value added goods – processed, refined, manufactured – in home countries or elsewhere, creating jobs, diversified economies and skills in these countries. For example, the privatization of the lucrative giant iron mine Vale del Doce in Brazil in the 1990s has led to huge profits for the new owners and the sale of raw ore overseas, particularly to China in the twentieth century. As for China, it converts iron ore to steel for transport, machine industries and a host of job-generating metallurgical enterprises, with a major boost to export-led growth. In Bolivia, the privatization of the gas and petrol industry in the mid-1990s led to billions of dollars in repatriated profits and the loss of hundreds of thousands of jobs in processing and conversion of petroleum and gas into value added goods. In addition the MNCs export oil and gas, failing to supply local low-income consumers. The extraction of raw materials is capital-intensive, employing few workers relative to the many displaced in the process of foreign investment. One of the most noxious effects of foreign investment is reduced domestic production capacity and increased dependence on foreign imports. Mexico is a case in point. In 2005, the country has to import a third of its basic consumer goods (Balboa, 2005). The problem is particularly severe in the countryside, where in studies undertaken by associations of agricultural and peasant producers conditions are described as a 'true calamity', with producers and the rural population having to import 39 per cent of their basic consumer goods.

Myth # 4 – Foreign investors provide tax revenue to bolster the local treasury and hard currency earnings to finance imports

The reality is that FI entails massive tax frauds, swindles in purchasing public enterprises and large scale money laundering. For example, in May 2005, Venezuela announced a massive billion-dollar tax evasion and fraud committed by major overseas petroleum companies that signed on to service contracts since the 1990s. The entire Russian petroleum and gas sector was literally stolen by a new class of billionaire robber oligarchs associated with foreign investors, who subsequently evaded taxes. The trial and conviction of two oligarchs, Platon Lebedev and Mikhail Khodorkovsky for tax evasion to the tune of $29 billion facilitated by US and European banks is illustrative of this point.

The impact of MNCs on the balance of payments over the long run tends to be negative. For example, most assembly plants in export zones import all their inputs, machinery, design and know-how and export the semi-finished or finished product. The resulting trade balance depends on the cost of the inputs relative to the value of exports. In many cases, the imported components charged to the local economy are greater than the value added in the export zone. Also, most of the revenues from the export platform accrue to the capitalists since the key to success is low wages leading to the creation of personal empires.

Brazil's experience over the past decade and a half is illustrative of the negative external balances resulting from FI and external funded investment. In 2004, Brazil paid foreign bankers USD46bn in interest and principle while receiving only USD16bn in new loans, leading to a net outflow of 30 billion dollars (SOBEET, 2006). Between January and April 2005 Brazil was bled for USD4.6bn in interest payments, USD3.7bn in profit remittances by MNC, USD1.7bn for 'external services' and 7.3 billion in payments of principle in the debt. The total drain of USD17.3bn far exceeded the positive commercial trade balance of USD12.2bn (SOBEET, 2006) in other words, the FI-led export model led to new indebtedness to pay for the shortfall, the loss of employment by small and medium farmers at the mercy of the agro-business elites and the destruction of the environment.

Myth #5 – Maintaining debt payments is essential to securing financial good standing in international markets and maintaining the integrity of the financial system. Both are crucial to sound development.

The historical record reveals that incurring debt under dubious circumstances and paying back illegally contracted loans by non-representative governments jeopardized the long-term financial standing and integrity of the domestic financial system and led to a financial collapse. Argentina's experience from 1976 to 2001 is illustrative.

A substantial part of the public external and internal debt was illegally contracted and had little development utility. A lawsuit launched by an Argentine economist, Olmos, against payment of the Argentine foreign debt revealed that the foreign private debts of Citibank, First National Bank of Boston, Deutsch Bank, Chase Manhattan Bank and Bank of America were taken over by the Argentine Government. The same is true of debts of subsidiaries of overseas banks. The Olmos lawsuit also documented how the Argentine dictatorship and subsequent regimes borrowed to secure hard currency to facilitate capital flight in dollars. The foreign loans went directly to the Central Bank, which made the dollars available to the rich who recycled the dollars to their overseas accounts. Between 1978 and 1981 over USD38bn fled the country. Most of the foreign loans were used to finance the 'economic' openings, luxury imports and non-productive goods, especially military equipment. The Olmos case pointed to a perverse source of greater indebtedness: the Argentine regime borrowed at high interest rates and then deposited the funds with the same lender banks at lower interest rates leaving a net loss of several billion dollars, added to the foreign debt.

Myth # 6 – Most Third World countries depend on FI to provide needed capital for development since local sources are not available or inadequate

Contrary to the opinion of most neoliberal economists, most of what is called *foreign* investment is really *foreign borrowing of national savings* to buy local enterprises and finance investments. Foreign investors and MNCs secure overseas loans backed by local governments, or directly receive loans from local pension funds and banks – drawing on the local deposits and worker pension payments. Recent reports on pension fund financing of US multinationals in Mexico shows that Banamex secured a 28.9 billion peso (about USD2.6bn) loan, American Movil (Telcel) 13 billion pesos (USD1.2bn), Ford Motors (in long-term loans) (9.556 billion pesos) and one billion pesos (in short term loans), and General Motors (financial sector) received 6.555 billion pesos. This pattern of foreign borrowing to take over local markets and productive facilities is common practice, dispelling the notion that foreign investors bring 'fresh capital' into a country. Equally important it refutes the notion that Third World countries 'need' FI because of capital scarcity. Invitations to foreign investors divert local savings from local public and private investors, crowd out local borrowers and force them to seek 'informal' moneylenders charging exorbitant interest rates. Rather than complementing local investors FI competes for local savings from a privileged position in the credit market, bringing to bear their greater (overseas) assets and political influence in securing loans from local lending agencies.

Myth # 7 – The entry of FI serves as an anchor for attracting further investment and thus functioning as a 'pole of development'.

Nothing could be further from the truth. The experiences of foreign-owned assembly plants in the Caribbean, Central America and Mexico speak to the great instability and insecurity with the emergence of new sources of cheaper labour in Asia, especially China and Socialist Republic of Vietnam. Foreign investors are more likely than local manufacturers to relocate to new low-wage areas, creating a boom and bust economy. The practice of FI, in Mexico, the Caribbean and Central America, faced with competition from Asia is to relocate, not to upgrade technology and skills or to move up to quality products.

The connection between economic growth and FI upon closer analysis can be seen to result from a tendency for private capital flows to concentrate in those countries that have already inaugurated what economists regard as a 'virtuous cycle' of growth, investment and rising productivity. Contrary to the neoliberal claim, foreign private capital inflows follow from rather than create rapid growth. Thus, the developing countries (especially the poorest) might as well (or should) institute the interventionist policies that worked so well in Taiwan, Korea and China, initiating in these countries a sustainable growth path as a precondition for private capital inflows.

Arguments in Favor of Foreign Investment

The most common arguments in favour of foreign capital (Brittan, 1995) derive from the following propositions:

- Foreign capital is needed to compensate for a domestic shortage of capital, an absolutely critical factor of economic production and social development.
- Foreign capital provides a fundamental source of 'know how', as well as the superior managerial techniques and business practices needed – associated management and marketing skills needed to secure a comparative advantage in export markets. This proposition assumes that the world market, when freed from government interference and control, is a fundamental engine of economic growth.
- Foreign investment provides advanced technologies needed to modernize the economy, upgrade productivity, increase market competitiveness.
- Foreign capital increases the competitiveness of local production, driving out inefficient firms and forcing local firms to become more economically efficient. Foreign capital lowers prices to consumers, extending as well as improving services, providing thereby both effective competition and more rational production.
- Foreign capital promotes the integration into the global economy and will increase the propensity of a nation to export its social product and secure overseas markets.
- Foreign capital provides an additional source of employment and it remunerates labour better than local producers and business operators, paying higher wages and providing improved working conditions; in addition it pays more taxes than local producers and contributes to a healthy external balance.

Advocates of FDI argue that it is a 'win-win' proposition for developing countries and that it is superior to all other forms of intentional private capital flows. The stability of FDI, as well as its propensity towards 'productive' investment, renders it far preferable to foreign bank borrowing and PI. In this connection, what is good for the MNCs that make these investments is also good for the economies that host them. The restrictive policies towards MNCs that were popular in developing countries in the 1960s and 1970s [promoted by the UNCTC] were products of misguided ideologies. The problem, it has been argued, is that MNCs will not locate in countries that restrict their activities or that discriminate against FDI. The positive-sum effects on developing countries of FDI is partially explained in terms of the essentially state-less nature of today's corporations. In the new global economy MNCs have no reason to exploit their hosts because, it is argued, they have no national interest to advance.

Notwithstanding the virtual consensus on FDI's supposed benefits, there are differences among the diverse ideologues and advocates. In fact, there are two supportive but different schools of thought on multinationals and FDI. The one is predicated on the neoliberal model of a global free market capitalist economy. The other school supportive of FDI – (neo)structuralist rather than (neo)liberal – is exemplified by UNCTAD and ECLAC. The position of scholars associated with this school is that the multinationals (that is, FDI) can be converted into development agents provided that their activities are regulated and FDI is restricted. This was in fact the position of UNCTC, leading to the efforts (successful, as it turns out) of the Heritage Foundation to do away with it, viewing the UNCTC as a stalking horse for socialism.

Points of differences between the two groups of FDI supporters include questions as to:

1. Whether foreign capital should be allowed the same terms as local enterprises, or whether there should be differential tax rates, restrictions in areas of investments (some argue 'strategic areas' like energy should remain under state or national ownership). In the case of export processing zones, advocates of FDI encourage lower tax rates, rents and labour standards.
2. Whether foreign-owned enterprises should only produce for the export market or for the internal market (export trading zones) as well.
3. Whether foreign capital should be obligated to reinvest a percentage of its profits into the domestic economy or whether it can remit all its profits to the Home Office.
4. Whether foreign-owned firms should be obligated to invest substantial sums to upgrade firms and modernize production.
5. Whether foreign firms can own majority, minority or all shares in an enterprise. Similar differences exist on management rights between foreign and national owners.
6. What kinds of incentives to offer foreign firms, in terms of tax concessions, land grants, infrastructure investment by the state, job training by the local government, and so on.
7. The longevity of foreign ownership especially of mineral and subsoil rights; should it be on perpetuity, leases overextended or shorter time periods; renewal and options of existing contracts, sanctions for non-compliance, etc.
8. Management of FDI by host governments.

Structuralists argue that FDI *can* be beneficial to developing countries if properly managed by host governments within a country's national development strategy. But neoliberals view any management regime, even a national development strategy, as interference with the free market. A common form of host government management strategy in the 1960s and 1970s had to do with restrictions of FDI in certain strategic sectors that the government identified as strategic to the national interest. Japan, Korea and Taiwan, for example, like China today – or, for that matter, France (which defines huge sections of its corporate sector as strategic assets immune from foreign acquisitions) – built their industrial base on restrictive policies towards FDI. Like Cuba these countries permitted FDI only in certain sectors, and (except in special cases) prohibited more than majority foreign ownership in key sectors. Another form of management involved regulations that mandated 'local content' or employment requirements (that specified, for example, the proportion of local inputs in the production process) in subsidiaries of MNCs. See also # 1–5 above.

To sum up, among the advocates of foreign investment there is a range of positions on the scope and depth of concessions that accompany the promotion of foreign capital. In the 1970s and the 1980s the tendency was for governments to expand concessions to foreign investors within a framework of financial liberalization; as of the 1990s the dominant tendency has been to weaken the public regulations that govern the entry and operations of foreign capital, to deregulate both capital and labour markets.

As a result of the Washington Consensus on the need for globalization and a laissez-faire approach towards national development – a view that eschews the state-led approach that dominated the 1960s and 1970s – any debate on FDI over the past two decades has been conducted almost entirely *within* the paradigm of the 'new economic model' (neoliberalism). Voices on the left fringe of political economy, so loud in the 1960s and 1970s, were effectively silenced or totally sidelined. In this ideological and political context the debate on foreign investment has been generally limited to the questions of how many and what types of incentives to offer foreign capital, without evaluating whether foreign capital brings in its wake greater development problems than it is purported to solve. That is, in the mainstream of development economics (see, for example, Wolf, 2004) the emphasis has been on the positive contributions and benefits of globalization and FI, discounting if not totally ignoring the costs, both economic, social and political. We need hardly mention that the critics of FI, including ourselves, tend to focus on these costs, raising questions about weighing the overall balance of costs and benefits as well as their distribution – who receives the benefits and who bears the costs? These questions are central to the arguments that can be advanced against FI.

Arguments Against Foreign Investment: The Critics

The decision to open a country to foreign investment raises profound political, economic, social and cultural questions that go beyond short-term calculus of costs and benefits. In most cases the 'openings' leads to subsequent large-scale, long-term strategic consequences affecting a whole series of unanticipated but rather predictable outcomes.

1. First, foreign ownership of strategic industries and resources leads to a loss by the state of its decision-making capacity in regard to shaping investment

decisions, pricing, production, and future growth. Within a foreign investment regime these decisions are made by the foreign owners of capital. It is these owners who decide which enterprise in their empire will expand, stagnate or decline depending on their labour costs, taxes, transport and communication networks and other profit-making considerations. It is the new owners of erstwhile public but now privatized enterprises who will decide whether to conduct research within the enterprise or at the 'home office'. In this context, foreign investment, especially that involved in large-scale buyouts of strategic enterprises, severely compromises national sovereignty, converting political regimes into 'hostages' of the foreign capital. Multinationals in this context are able to exercise enormous monopoly power over political and economic conditions within host economies, a fact attested to by the widespread convergence in the 1980s and 1990s in the policy regimes established by countries across the world as well as the dominance of corporate capital. No doubt prior agreements between foreign investors and regimes establish rules that may be applied to each case, but these rules are subordinated to and conditioned by the willingness and ability to enforce them and the foreign investors' willingness to abide by them. But experience suggests that in most Third World states the initial agreements to privatize are rife with corruption, and the subsequent presence of large-scale foreign enterprise can easily and frequently lead to influencing administrators and regulators into lax enforcement of contracts.

2. Even where foreign investment induces an initial capital inflow it leads to long-term, large-scale outflows of profits to the Home Office, contributing to the decapitalization of the economy and, contrary to the neoliberal argument, a worsening of problems with the balance of payments. Turning over state enterprises to foreign investors (or local oligarchs) leads to a decline in state revenues, increased unemployment and plant closures in regions where the rates of return to the company are below expectations. Foreign ownership or takeover of a developing country's capitalist enterprises might well – and often does – lead to a process of 'rationalization' and 'restructuring' but the evidence suggests that this is likely to increase enterprise profits while activating a *negative multiplier effect* in the primary and tertiary sectors of the local and national economy. For example, a multinational firm may close down a rail-line and its attendant machine and maintenance shop because the rate of return is only two per cent in order to increase overall profit to 15 percent. However, the attendant closures may lead to a 25 per cent decline in commercial, industrial and agricultural production; a 20 per cent increase in bankruptcy and a 15 per cent increase in unemployment [source]. Thus, a net gain by the MNC means an absolute loss to the region and its labour force. [elaborate]. Increased (economic) 'efficiency' at the firm or micro-level means decreased (social) inefficiency at the macro-level.
3. Foreign investment leads to unbalanced and overly specialized production, principally the expansion of highly volatile commodities at the expense of a diversified economy with a broader production and trade base. Most foreign investment seeks to earn hard currency by investing in commodities with a high

export component, like oil, soya, iron, copper to complement their domestic requirements or those of industrializing economies. The result is a 'boom and bust' cycle in which high exports and revenues inflate regime revenues and imports prior to a harsh deflation and serious trade deficits, leading to sharp cuts in spending, rising unemployment and increase indebtedness.

4. Foreign enterprises frequently secure long-term tax concessions and large-scale public investments in infrastructure (transport and communications) as a condition for investment. Moreover, through transfer pricing and 'imaginative accounting' foreign capital more often than not is able to manage large-scale tax evasion. The net result is that foreign capital's tax payments are incommensurate with the payments required of the state to 'attract' and retain foreign investment and investors. [data. Elaborate]
5. Foreign capital in many cases neither creates new enterprises nor expands the market for the social product of developing countries in which it operates. More often than not they buy out local enterprises, in many cases profitable firms, at a high 'political cost' under conditions of widespread 'corruption' (stacked bidding contests, kickbacks and 'commissions'), which is then viewed as an attribute of a developing country with a weak state subject to rentierism, etc. In many cases, state telecommunications or oil monopolies are taken over and converted into private monopolies, thus imposing monopoly prices unhindered by the need for public accountability or responding to social needs. Moreover, as noted earlier, foreign investors frequently do not bring in 'new capital': rather, they borrow from local banks (the savings of local depositors), convert devalued debt paper to buy enterprises at nominal prices, and receive state-backed loans from international financial institutions. In effect, strategic and financial assets are privatized while liabilities and costs are socialized – and borne by the population or taxpayers at large.

   Even worse from the standpoint of national development is that when as in Mexico foreign investors take over the major domestic source of credit – the big banks – the end result is a significant loss of business and enterprise development credit, with a noticeably negative effect on the rate of economic growth. This point was made in a recent study by Steinfield (2004), commissioned by the Carnegie Endowment for Peace and Democracy. What he found was that with the foreign control over the entire banking system domestic credit to the private sector as a percentage of gross domestic product (GDP) fell in Mexico from 17.5 per cent in 1990 to 12.6 per cent in 2002. This is extremely low compared to the global average, which expanded from 97.5 per cent to 118.1 per cent from 1990 to 2002, and the developing-country average, which increased from 39.3 per cent in 1990 to 55.9 per cent in 2002. Furthermore, domestic credit provided by the banking sector as a percentage of GDP also fell from 46.5 per cent in 1994 to 26.6 in 2002.

   Is there a connection between the rise of FDI in the banking sector and the fall in domestic credit to the private sector as well as domestic credit provided by the banking sector? Undoubtedly. And whatever its cause, the credit crunch has a profound impact on the ability of small and medium enterprises (SMEs) to create jobs, innovate, and expand production. This is the main reason, according to the Mexican Banking Association in its 2004 convention, why Mexico's 'entrepreneurial spirit' has been sapped and why so many now claim that the banks have betrayed the public trust.

6. Foreign capital tends to create 'enterprise enclaves' that import technology (charging royalty fees) and are linked to outside production and distribution networks, thus having a minimal impact on the local economy. There are numerous examples of this: the better known are assembly plants in which the manufacturing and distribution is done elsewhere, by other subsidiaries of the MNCs, and the only contribution to the local economy is the payment of subsistence wages. Primary materials exporters, for example, extract iron and copper and soya and it is processed overseas where value added and jobs accrue to the recipient country. Raw material exporters employ few workers, the countries are converted into 'monocultures' and their economies are subject to volatile shifts in their revenue base. Dependence on income from a few exports or a single export (like oil) and overseas remittances does not constitute a sound political economy.
7. In a number of countries, especially in Latin America, foreign investors in a neoliberal policy environment have taken over the critically important banking sector, allowing them to shape state credit and interest policy and, more importantly, to decide what sectors and enterprise might be extended credit and at what interest rates. It is the insistence of Chinese authorities to restrict such 'opportunities' – regulating the financial sector and closing out foreign investors – that continues to provoke the ire of so many members of the US Congress, leading them to push for retaliatory measures.

   Among other things, foreign ownership of the banks and other financial institutions leads to privileging and lending to foreign-owned firms (the 'most credit-worthy'), that earn hard foreign currency, systematically excluding small businesses, farmers and peasants producing for the local market and employing the majority of the labor force. This leads the latter to turn towards usurious moneylenders that frequently extend credit at an interest rate up to 50 per cent or so a month or to divert capital from production to speculation.

   The broader and perhaps even more critical issue involved in the takeover of the banks is the capacity of the government to control and manage the economy as a whole. This issue can be exemplified in the difference between China and Mexico. In the interest of 'acquiring dynamic commercial enterprises' (via the injection of FI, viewed as a source of dynamic growth) while yet 'retaining ultimate control of the economy's commanding heights' China has recently listed its biggest banks internationally but the state assiduously maintains ownership of most of their equity (*Financial Times*, November 2 2005: 12). Foreign investment is limited to a 25 per cent share and therefore with limited say in management. This policy contrasts markedly with that of Mexico, where all but one big bank has fallen under ownership and control of foreign investors. Needless to say, the government is unable to exercise the influence, if not control, over foreign-owned enterprises and banks that it is able to do over banks under control of national capital. In regard to the so-called 'Asian model' of economic growth and development this influence and control is absolutely critical. Government control over the overall direction and dynamism of the national economy is also the reason why the Canadian Government restricts foreign ownership in the banking sector, keeping it as a strategic preserve of national capital. This difference in the degree of financial liberalization and foreign ownership in the banking sector of development finance, is the critical difference between the economic structure of the 'rapidly growing countries' of Asia and Latin America.

8. Given the apparent preference of foreign capital for extractive industries, their influence and power among local government elites and their backing by the IFIs, have placed many foreign investors at the forefront of environmental devastation in the Developing World. Timber barons and soya exporters are demolishing the Amazonian rain forest. Oil companies devastate the land and water in Nigeria and around the Caspian Sea. The increase in revenues to the federal state is rarely used to compensate for the destruction of the local agricultural and fishing economy. Instead state revenues are recycled to build roads and ports linking environmental predators to external markets.

Foreign Investment in the Third World and the Ex-communist Countries

Foreign investment plays a large role in the Third World and the ex-Communist countries in large part because of the liberalization policies imposed or promoted by the IFIs. As part of the liberalization process, restrictive tariffs and regulations are lifted regarding foreign ownership but also the massive entry of subsidized food and cheap industrial products. In this context, whatever dubious benefits foreign investors might provide is offset by the loss of local agriculture and manufacturing production and jobs due to the cheap imports. Moreover, foreign 'competition' between MNCs and local established and start-up companies is so lopsided that few survive. The net result is not to increase the competitiveness of local firms but to drive them out of business, or forcing them to sell out to the larger firms. Even when foreign owners relocate plants in the ex-communist countries and the Third World, the move is conditioned on maintaining labour and social benefits at low levels. With the growing demand of labour for wage increases and the end of tax holidays and other incentives, capital relocates. This has been a pronounced trend in the construction of a new international division of labour and the process of global transformation – a trend that has been documented and analyzed from diverse perspectives over the past three decades.

The political influence of foreign investors increases with their greater presence in the local market, their control of strategic sectors of the economy and the emergence of western-trained political leaders promoting 'free enterprise'. Equally important, foreign owned enterprises employ executives, managers, lawyers, publicists and economists, with linkages to the political elite, who frequently move into key political positions (presidents of the Central Banks, Ministers of Economy and Finance) and who implement macro-economic neo-liberal policies which maximize benefits to the foreign investors at the expense of the local labour force and treasury. In addition, foreign-owned enterprises play a lead role in banking, industrial and other business associations, leveraging them to secure policies favourable to their interests.

Finally foreign-owned firms gain management control over 'national' enterprises, either through purchases, 'management contracts' and subcontracting to satellite medium-size firms which become dependent on the 'core' foreign-owned forms, and frequently and forcible back their policies. Foreign, especially US-owned MNC frequently act as conduits for imperial state policies. They do so by *disinvesting* in countries that are on the US State Department blacklist and *relocating* productive facilities in Pro-US countries. American multinationals 'house' and provide a false cover to intelligence agents, pass on economic intelligence to the CIA, refuse to supply repair parts to countries in conflict with the US. US banks facilitate capital flight, tax evasion and laundering money for wealthy elites and, in the process, weaken US adversaries and competitors frequently reducing production, refining or services to countries in conflict with the imperial state. 'Marginal corporations', or even subsidiaries of major corporations, do not follow the line of the imperial state, either because the profits are too lucrative to overlook, competitive pressures from other MNC are intense, and/or because the long-term incentives offered by the targeted state offset the risks of antagonizing imperial policymakers.

Foreign-owned firms, at least initially, are usually run by expatriates who dominate the most senior positions. 'National' executives are usually hired to handle 1) links with the local regime, 2) labour relations, 3) tax evasion or to secure exonerations from payments and 4) public relations campaigns and political advice.

Contrary to the 'expectations' or the propaganda of neoliberal ideologues, foreign-owned firms do not usually transfer technological research and development (R&D) to Third World countries. Over 80 per cent of R&D is conducted in the Home Office in the imperial state. What are transferred are the results of R&D and at a stiff price in royalty payments over an extended period of time. In fact foreign investors frequently buy out local productive units, strip their assets, take over their customers, markets and distributive networks and then either close out the firm or merge it with the enlarged foreign-owned conglomerate, resulting in mass firings, reductions in services and higher costs to consumers.

To sum up, foreign investment has strategic disadvantages, endangering national independence, popular sovereignty, and severely compromising the capacity of the state to represent its citizens, especially the working class and the peasants. Equally important foreign investment has built-in mechanisms, which contribute to low re-investment rates, de-capitalization of the economy and balance of payments problems.

Foreign investment increases inequalities, and produces a polarized social structure, as a result of the low tax rates, the high rates of return and the pro-foreign investor outlook of the state. The 'residual benefits' to the 'receiving country' are usually appropriated by local 'political facilitators', top and middle management, and subcontractors and distributors. Large-scale, long-term foreign investment furthers the goals of the imperialist state; indeed it embodies imperialism, being one of its economic engines and driving forces.

Conclusion

Reliance on FI is a risky, costly and limiting development strategy. The benefits and costs are unevenly distributed between the subject and object of FI. In the larger historical picture it is not surprising that none of the early, or late developing countries put FI at the centre of their development scheme. Neither the US, Germany and Japan in the nineteenth and twentieth centuries; nor Russia, China, South Korea and Taiwan in the twentieth century depended on FI to advance their industrial and financial institutions. Given the disadvantages cited in the text, it is clear that the way ahead for developing countries is through minimizing FI and maximizing national ownership and investment of local financial resources, skills and enlarging and deepening local and overseas markets through a diversified economy.

Because the negative economic, social and political costs of FI are so evident to increasing numbers of people it is a major detonator of mass social movements, even revolutionary struggles, as in Bolivia during 2005. Since FI is a direct result of political decisions adopted at the highest level of government, mass social struggles are as much or even more so directed against the incumbent political regime responsible for promoting and mollycoddling FI. The increasing turn of social movements toward political struggles for state power is directly related to the increasing recognition that political power and FI are intimately connected. In the twentieth century, at least in Latin America, all of the electoral regimes, which have been overthrown by popular majorities, had deep structural links to FI: Gutierrez in Ecuador, Sanchez de Losada and Mesa in Bolivia and Fujimori in Peru.

The leader with the greatest sustained support in Latin America, President Chavez in Venezuela, is the only one who has increased regulations and taxes on FI and redistributed the increased revenues to the poor, working class and peasants. The question remains whether this new infusion of energy and class awareness can go beyond defeating pro-FI regimes to constructing a state based on a broad alliance of class forces that goes beyond 'nationalization' towards 'socialism'.

Chapter 8

Anti-Imperialist Regime Dynamics

Martin Wolf (2005) in a Financial Times column labelled 'Chirac, leader of a civilized nation (France)', as 'an enemy [of] those who recognize the case for sustaining a liberal world economy'. What provoked this tirade was Chirac's 'foolish, indeed depraved' remarks to the effect that 'liberalism...is as dangerous an ideology as communism'. Chirac's anti-liberalism, as Wolf sees it, is manifest not only in his government's programmed subsidies and corporate incentives but its protection of a huge section of the economy's corporate sector as 'strategic assets', immune from foreign acquisition. Of course, France is not the only industrially advanced and 'civilized' nation that continues to pursue an anti-liberal line in its macroeconomic policies. The US government is just as protectionist and antiliberal in its approach towards strategic areas of domestic production and trade. Liberalism, more often than not, is practiced only when and where the domestic economic sectors are competitive. Above all, liberalism is a policy reserved for countries that constitute an 'emerging market' and that the US is able to subordinate by shaping their national policies. This applies in particular to countries in Latin America and elsewhere where the US has found the means to impose its will – that they adjust their national policy to the requirements of trade and the free movement of investment capital.

Alternatives to Foreign Investment

In the face of overwhelming historical and empirical regarding evidence regarding the limitations and negative impacts of foreign investment, its advocates have resorted to Thatcher's celebrated assertion that 'there is no alternative' (TINA). In this ideological context it is argued that without foreign investment there can be no development, no markets, no technological advance and no progress.

We argue to the contrary that there are very solid empirical and historical grounds for the view that there are substantial financial and economic resources available to the nation state and popular regimes that are more efficient in producing positive growth and that have none or fewer of the negative social and political outcomes of foreign investment. This is not to say that in *limited* circumstance under *specified political* conditions and *particular* sets of regulations foreign investment cannot make a useful contribution. But in general terms, foreign investment is incompatible with any notion of anti-imperialist politics and, more importantly, *there are alternatives* to foreign investment, which include:

1. *Reinvestment of profits* from lucrative export industries and strategic domestic enterprises within the institutional framework of public ownership. Profits that

would be remitted abroad under a foreign investment regime are channeled inward into expanding local production, producing a 'multiplier' effect, increasing local consumption and demand in a virtuous circle as opposed to the vicious cycle of foreign investment's east entry and fast exit.

2. *Control of foreign trade, which* would allow for the retention of foreign exchange earnings, to avoid overseas seepage and allocate hard currency to the small and medium enterprises (SMEs) geared to local production and popular consumption.
3. *Investment of pension funds* in productive activities rather than holding them in private banks or trust funds. Pension funds in many countries constitute one of the largest pools of capital in the country, which under a mixed (government-worker) management regime could be converted into a major source of productive and social investments.
4. *The creation of development banks for overseas workers' remittances* to channel a part of worker earnings into productive, job-creating activities. In many countries overseas remittances are among the leading source of hard currency, usually for local household consumption and marginal economic activities. The neoliberal state more often than not also uses some of this hard currency to service the foreign debt.
5. A moratorium *on debt payments*, a policy predicated on an investigation as to whether the original debt was incurred legitimately, used to finance development or part of a pattern of corrupt practices and unproductive uses (military expenditures). Determination should be made whether the original principle has been paid and if loans were originally contracted by private firms, in which case debt payments should be cancelled or privatized – referred back to original borrowers. The state should not socialize the bad debts of mismanaged private firms or compensate poor judgment in investment decisions or the careless high-risk loan decisions of creditors. Past lenders and borrowers should assume the risks of profits and losses, rather than saddling the populace with payment for loans for which they were neither consulted nor benefited.
6. *Recovery of treasury funds stolen* and property illicitly privatized by previous regimes. Overseas accounts based on illicit transfers especially by business and political elites should be impounded as part of an anti-corruption commission headed by independent tax lawyers and representatives of the mass organizations. Enterprises privatized under dubious circumstances should be renationalized.
7. *Recovery of unpaid taxes*, especially through tax evasion by MNCs and international firms, which should be investigated and prosecuted, including stiff penalties. The state should demand full recovery of back taxes or undertake seizure of physical and liquid assets of the delinquent foreign firms. The state can demand that the accounting sheets of MNCs be open to public inspection, to foil the common practice of intra-firm 'transfer pricing' and thus artificially and illegally lowering profits and income to evade adequate tax payments.
8. *Graduated land taxes and expropriation of underutilized or speculative land* can provide land for agrarian reform, increase agricultural productivity

and food for local consumption as well as exports. Extensive estates and plantations illegally occupied should be expropriated without compensation. Compensation in long-term bonds should be based on past tax-declared value – or at market value, if the estate owners are willing to pay the difference between the declared and market value.

9. *Overseas holdings or investments by public firms* should be liquidated and the returns reinvested in upgrading national productive infrastructure and processing industries. Excessive foreign reserves should be downsized and put to work in diversifying the economy. Reserves should be held in diverse currencies and should not be deposited in overseas banks, where an imperial adversary could hold the funds hostage. Holding a 'devaluating' currency because of past 'reputation' or because of 'neo-colonial' linkages is both bad politics and bad economics.
10. *Maximizing employment under-employed labour* – running in some cases to 80 per cent of the labour force – in large-scale infrastructure projects can compensate for 'scarce capital' and become a source for initial capital accumulation. Likewise, underutilized educated, skilled workers and professionals can provide innovations and organizational breakthroughs, which can increase total output and increase productivity.

Any serious examination of the social economy of most countries would discover there are multiple *national* sources of capital without relying on foreign capital. These sources have all the advantages of high rates of capital investment with none of the political uncertainty, economic vulnerabilities and social inequalities associated with foreign capital.

Worst Case Scenario: Foreign Investment as a Last Resort

Let us assume that a developing country has scant overseas earnings, sparse or non-existing pension funds, an honest tax administration but few taxable sources, but is rich in natural or productive resources requiring high initial capital investments and new technology. In this case external financing or expertise is required. The question then becomes what are the optimal short-term and strategic contracts that will minimize the negative effects enumerated above.

The optimal approach here would be to dis-assemble the 'foreign investment package' – to minimize direct foreign ownership and long-term management control. To maximize strategic national ownership and control it is preferable to sign short-term management contracts that include the training of national replacements over a fixed period, preferably from countries with a less intrusive non-imperial state. Likewise where technical assistance is required, for lack of know-how regarding specific processes, it is preferable to contract technical advisers to work in tandem with local specialists, while local technical expertise is prepared for future takeover. If foreign multinationals are required to construct local productive facilities, 'turnkey contracts' should be signed in which the multinationals are guaranteed a certain rate of profit over a specified time frame and then handed over to national owners.

Specific contracts with time limits allow the nation to maximize the employment of national skilled professionals, managers and workers. The widening pool of available high-skill specialists in the global market provides choice and practically eliminates dependence on a single country (particular imperialist countries) and avoids dependence on foreign investment with the long-term loss of ownership, control and strategic investment planning.

To limit entanglement with foreign capital, it is essential for the country to invest in professional and technical training, research and development, all of which can be done through selective overseas studies or by importing specialists from abroad.

An Alternative Model: Worker-Engineer Public Control (WEPC)

Historical experiences provide us with several examples of successful worker-managed enterprises (WME). In Yugoslavia, WME functioned for over 30 years, reconstructing and subsequently rapidly expanding industry, increasing incomes, financing free public health, education and recreation programs. Despite the emergence of inter-regional and inter-plant wage differentials, and a centralist political structure, WME unified the diverse ethnic groups and substantially lowered unemployment and gender inequality. The subsequent introduction of IMF market reforms led directly to mass unemployment, which was exploited by rabid ethnic nationalists, and led to a series of bloody destructive wars, and the conversion of the new mini-states into economic subsidiaries of the Euro-American Empire.

In Chile during the Presidency of Salvador Allende over a hundred factories were expropriated and converted to WME. Scholarly studies (Zimbalist and Espinosa, 1976; Winn, 1989) provide empirical evidence demonstrating greater productivity, higher worker motivation and substantial improvements in social, health and working conditions. The US-backed military coup led by General Pinochet destroyed the WME system and imposed the free market system, resulting in a massive increase in unemployment, a sharp decline in living standards and working conditions, and the bankruptcy of many consumer goods manufacturers.

One of Argentina's most important ceramic factories, ZANON, was mismanaged into bankruptcy. Faced with massive unemployment, the workers took over and ran the enterprise, luring back the original workers and additional new hires. The factory was a model of efficiency as engineers and accountants teamed up with worker leaders, elected in general assemblies, to resist repression, produce and market their product.

Thorsten Veblen, one of the US most critical and brilliiant economists in the early part of the 20th Century wrote a devastating critique of the role of business in the organization and direction of industrial enterprise. In *Engineers and the Price System* (1921), he identified the conflict between the innovative and productive orientation of engineers and the business obsession for short-term profits, and the economic waste of marketing and advertising. While Veblen's critique of business was on the mark, he overlooked the creative and productive capacities of the working class; he failed to appreciate the potential in an engineer-worker alliance. Most important he understated the tendency for concentrated and unaccountable technocratic power to reach an accommodation with business and financial groups. Worker self-management, based on direct democracy factory assemblies and councils serves as a corrective to the tendencies toward oligarchic rule and the re-emergence of social inequalities.

The fact of the matter is that almost all enterprises operate without any important contribution from the CEO's: the engineers design, the skilled workers operationalize, the worker operate the machinery, the packers ship the merchandise, the accountants calculate the costs, benefits, etc. The capitalists are not involved in the social division of production and distribution. Their 'capital' (and wealth) is derived from the profits they extract from the labour of engineers and workers; it is far more rational and efficient for the producers to allocate the 'profit' toward greater production and social and recreational activities, because they can thus eliminate the exorbitant portion that passes into conspicuous consumption.

The historical and empirical evidence is that the political, economic and social drawbacks of foreign investment far exceed any short-term benefits perceived by its defenders. Research has demonstrated that most economies possess the financial and capital resources and underutilized human and productive capacity to undertake successful development without the high political costs that FI brings to bear. An alternative Worker-Engineer Public Control (WEPC) model provides numerous advantages over dependence on international finance and investor capital. While FI has a general negative role, the WEPC model does not totally exclude FI in specific sets of circumstances, limited in time and location to implement endogenous development. The strategy directed toward drawing on international assistance to complement growth emphasizes specific contracts with a variety of providers, particularly with those not linked to the imperial state.

While the WEPC model provides an alternative approach, which maximizes national and working-class interests, it has serious potential drawbacks or internal contradictions, which require constant reflection, deliberation, debate and reforms. Nonetheless, the model provides the surest and most direct road to development with democracy, social justice and national independence. The success and sustainability of the WEPC does not depend merely on its socioeconomic viability but on national security and cultural policies and institutions.

There are a number of significant advantages in relying on WEPC over foreign-owned MNC in pursuing a development strategy. They include:

- *Tax evasions and tax revenues* Multinational corporations are masters in the art of evading taxes and corrupting local regulators. WEPC, operating with 'open books' and independent auditors responsive to workers and consumers can minimize tax evasion, leading to increases in revenues, sound fiscal balances and limiting corruption.
- *Social Investment versus profit remittances and privileged salaries* Profits under the MNC-dependent strategy are largely invested overseas, in exorbitant salaries, bonuses and expenses for the CEOs and other management elites. Under WEPC model profits are reinvested in expanding local production, social development programs and improvements in working conditions.
- *Capital flight versus high reinvestment ratios* The MNC-FDI model is based

on volatile movements of capital, including capital flight, leading to greater investment instability and fluctuations in state revenues. The WEPC leads to higher and steadier re-investment ratios, greater stability in employment, investment and public revenues.

- *Speculative investment versus long-term Investment in R & D* One of the basic demands of the multinationals is the deregulation of financial markets, in order to move capital back and forth between fixed to 'liquid' (speculative) investments. This has led to the growth of speculative investment, which has provoked severe crises throughout the capitalist world. Under the WEPC model, highly regulated financial transactions could minimize the flow of capital into speculative activity and maximize financing of product innovations, research and development.
- *Capitalist versus social welfare* Under the MNC model, the state provides enormous subsidies to foreign investors, in the way of tax exonerations, rent-free land, state-funded infrastructure development, low interest loans, cheap credit and de-regulation of labour and environmental laws. Under the WEPC model, both costs and profits are socialized – providing free health, guaranteed employment, liveable and fixed pensions, child care, safe work conditions, adequate vacations and continuing education to upgrade skills and productivity to increase leisure and study.
- *Mobile capital/fixed labour versus fixed capital/mobile labour* Under the MNC model capital will 'relocate' in order to maximize profits, lower taxes, undermine working conditions, avoid health and pension obligations. Under the WEPC model 'capital' is fixed to specific location and labour is trained and mobile to move up in skill level employment, rotate in leadership roles and move in and out of work and job training. There is no 'contracting out' or 'outsourcing' of 'temporary work contracts'. This model takes advantage of a stable skill accumulating work force to apply its experience to improving production without the frequent disorganization caused by worker turnover.

Potential Problems in the WEPC

Notwithstanding the advantages of WEPC over FI there are several problems that can occur under the WEPC. These include:

- Greater consumption over investment
- Bureaucratization of organization
- Worker indiscipline, decline in production and innovation
- Loss of competitiveness
- Excess or insufficient taxes to the central government
- Inter-sectoral inequalities due to differential rates of productivity or prices
- Over-emphasis on social benefits as opposed to individual consumption
- Marginalizing issues of gender, race and ecology.

To be effective the WEPC model requires that its leaders and supporters have a long-term view of the development process, in order to balance the demands for immediate consumption with investment in production. Inevitably – especially in the initial phase of the model – there will be strong pressure to 'make a difference' with regard to past capitalist approaches which perennially postponed popular satisfaction in order to 'increase the pie'. The new regime will have to adjust to this political demand by initially providing significant social impact programs – like free medical care and higher education, rent reductions and debt forgiveness – in order to gain the confidence of the working classes and to demonstrate that the new regime represents a break with the past. The social impact programs will also secure the loyalty of the popular classes and give them a stake in defending the regime, an important issue given the likely hostility of the imperial powers and the local ruling class.

The new model needs to guard against inevitable tendencies toward bureaucratization based on 'representative bodies', differential expertise and the prestige of particular leaders. Formal mechanisms including popular workplace and neighbourhood assemblies, popular access to the mass media, referendum on strategic socioeconomic decisions and, above all else, a politically educated working class which is exposed to public debate is the best antidote to bureaucratism.

Worker indiscipline should not occur under WEPC but it might. Some workers will try to lessen their official work in order to carry on 'under the table' work; others will take advantage of a lax regime or the apparent absence of sanction for absenteeism or the possibility of faking illness; others may be perennially late or fail to adequately perform duties or be negligent. Social education on rights and responsibilities must be inculcated in all workers, backed by sanctions including loss of pay, benefits and time off for chronic offenders. A combination of reward and penalties must continue for an indefinite time/ Otherwise most workers will have to carry extra societal burdens because of a few slackers.

While a WEPC economy functions in a world capitalist marketplace, the enterprises must combine humane social relations of production with improving competitiveness. All WEPCs regardless of size, resource base, proximity to imperial centres, level and diversity of production, need to invest in research and development (R&D), to encourage innovations in pharmaceuticals, technologies, quality products and so on to be able to have marketable products at competitive prices. There should be specialized production in countries with favourable endowments in locations, resource bases or skills. Productivity gains should reduce working hours and years, extend rest, recreation activities and continuing education as well as quality time for personal, family and friendships. Without constant innovations and competitiveness, market losses will severely hinder the growth of social relations.

The socialization of production may not signify a shift in racial and gender inequalities among the working and agricultural classes. A concerted 'cultural revolution', based on legal, educational and government initiatives will be necessary to begin the process of reversing institutional and attitudinal racism and sexism in all spheres of production, consumption and cultural representations. Direct representatives of racial and women's class-based organizations must be present in key positions. Likewise socialization of production requires the direct presence of representatives of environmental mass organizations to minimize the exploitation of non-renewable resources, environmental pollution, chemical agriculture and so on.

Finally the WEPC faces the problem of inequalities generated by different levels of productivity, value production, and market demand leading to inequalities between factories, sectors and regimes. Decentralized control will accentuate the advantages of some to the disadvantage of others, leading to the reproduction of class and regional inequalities. A system of progressive tax and wage and social subsidies as well as increased investment in upgrading less developed industries and regions can lower the inequalities.

Policies to Sustain Anti-Imperialist Regimes

Not infrequently regimes which embrace alternatives to FI-based neoliberal strategies are overthrown because they fail to elaborate defence, security and cultural policies compatible with the new approach.

The centrepiece to sustaining a WEPC regime requires a consistent and coherent set of anti-imperialist institutions and policies. First and foremost is the issue of national security, closing the entry points for a military coup, intervention or destabilization campaign. In surveying the abundant literature on 'alternatives' to neoliberalism, 'sustainable development', 'popular power' there is no discussion of the construction of institutions, which can protect the alternatives from the predictable political-military intervention of US or European imperialism. At best, there is a critique of existing security linkages to the US international military-intelligence apparatus but few if any ideas on alternative proposals.

There are at least six major institutional arrangements which provide the US imperial state with direct entry into a targeted country: Military bases, military missions, overseas training programs, joint military manoeuvres, regional military conferences and 'informal personal relations' through any of the above. In all these contexts there is an asymmetrical flow of influence – from the US to Latin American military officials. The content is a mix of the technical and the ideological. The centrepiece of these programs is the recruitment of 'agents', ideological converts and political activists, who can pressure, threaten or intervene against anti-imperialist regimes or policies. They are conduits of US policy and sources of political intelligence. The 'ideological converts' are a key entry point for US destabilization efforts and important agents for establishing political parameters which restrict electoral politicians from pursuing anti-imperialist policies.

One of the 'signals' that activates US military intervention are policies designed to exclude or modify the entry of foreign investment. To sustain the alternative workers-engineer model requires a series of institutional and policy changes in security policy.

These include the termination of military base agreements, overseas training missions, military advisory missions and joint exercises. Procurement policies should be reoriented toward domestic suppliers and the development of a 'home-based' state military industry. Joint ventures with non-imperial countries and enterprises may be necessary. Equally important military instructors, curricula and strategic planning will have to be revised to serve national defence against imperialist aggression rather than popular repression. A balance will have to be struck between technically competent military staff and political militancy. The key point is to ensure that the military intelligence apparatus is compatible with the 'alternative' popular regime. To overlook this issue is to invite a dangerous threat to the new democratic regime.

International political and military alignments must be reformed to undercut pretexts for military intervention. Particularly dangerous are 'regional military pacts' which are led and directed by the imperial powers, since these can be utilized to invade and occupy an independent country and put in jeopardy the independent democratic politics of any 'alternative'. Instead bilateral agreements, regional linkages, excluding the empire, can serve to isolate the imperial power. Military purchases from imperial competitors or adversaries can provide ordinance to buttress national defense against threats from surrogate imperial clients.

In place of dependence on high tech weaponry linked to imperial advisory and training missions, the key to national security rests on borrowing and learning from non-adversaries, and the creation of highly trained mass citizens' army and civil defense linked to a highly trained professional army.

Given the high priority of imperial military threats, the key to national defense is the creation of an in-depth ground force, which will inflict politically unacceptable casualties if and when the imperial boots touch the ground. Depending singly on a professional or citizens army will not withstand an imperial invasion: professionals provide strategic, tactical and technical know-how in weaponry and military planning and a citizens army provides a vast network to sustain prolonged guerrilla resistance against the occupying force. It is clearly in the interests of the popular regime to train a massive military reserve, and to combine security functions with educational and cultural community assemblies, which discuss the evolving political conflict. The entire military training curriculum has to be shaped to focus on external threats emanating from an imperial power, its local proxies and neighbouring client regimes. Every effort should be made to form mutual defence alliances with regimes, which are likewise threatened by the imperial power, as well as diplomatic and political pacts with regional countries to neutralize imperial efforts to politically encircle or isolate the progressive government. Training missions, exchanges of intelligence, and joint military industries between friendly regimes can counterbalance the expulsion of imperial military missions.

The sourcing of military ordinance – should be diversified and from reliable supplier-countries. However for security reasons the development of independent local military industries with dual-purpose usages are essential: guaranteeing supply in any emergency and adapting weaponry to local terrain.

International solidarity built around mass movements, intellectual and social forums are an important element in developing a democratic foreign policy and strengthening national security. Knowledge that any imperial military aggression would detonate large-scale, massive protests, popular uprisings and retaliation against US business interests is an important deterrent. Coordination of a common agenda based on shared programmatic transformations and social values can facilitate rapid responses in time of imperial induced crises.

Mass media outlets, which can provide international reports to national and international audiences, are essential in the battle of ideas with imperial powers. Alternative news services, printed and electronic media linked to activist movements and mass audiences is essential to informing the public of the social advances, economic realities and the working class side in any disputes with the imperial power and their MNCs.

In the education field, basic texts in history and social studies, which propagandized the benign role of the imperial powers and local ruling classes, should be discarded and a 'new peoples' history and social analysis 'from below' should replace them. Emphasis should be placed on public service, cooperation and repudiation of all forms of exploitation and discrimination by imperial and national institutions.

National security is a comprehensive strategic approach that goes far beyond the professional services of the state, to encompass the social, cultural and political context of everyday work and life.

Sustaining Anti-Imperialist Regimes: Political, Social and Cultural Conditions

The private mass media (MM), particularly linked to FI-owned media, is a major transmission belt for propaganda promoting FI. Several mechanisms are obvious. Propaganda for 'products' from imperial countries and consumer habits favour imperial penetration. Pro-imperial propaganda is passed off as 'news reports'. Life styles that feature class and racial stereotypes, de-contextualized from class and ethnic relations, and mercantile values promote self-centred individual mobility against values of social solidarity and public service. Equally nefarious local MM reproduces pro-imperialist violent crime, spy and terrorist 'stories' which justify the crimes of imperialist interventions and degrades liberation movements.

Clearly all media productions and programs reflect the values and interests of the dominant groups in society. Where a workers government is in power, media programming should promote films, TV, radio and video programs which affirm resistance, solidarity and collective improvements, while encouraging critical confrontation with the contradictions and challenges facing society. Restrictions on violent crime stories and sexual exploitation should be promoted. The promotion of locally produced and written films and TV productions should be promoted by fixing quotas on foreign imports. Repeated foul language should be replaced by a richer vocabulary – the purpose being to raise literacy not to descend to 'lumpen' language.

The national language should be used in all advertisements, promotions, technical and political contexts. Multilingual classes should be promoted to deepen international solidarity, learning and communication. Everyone should attend public school from nursery school through university education, which should be free and accessible to all, and of equal quality, in order to mitigate class-based educational privileges and networks. Teacher training should include a critical history of imperialist power and anti-imperialist struggles. Promotion of mass participation in sports, arts, crafts and hobbies should be encouraged and facilities, teachers and trainers should be available. Cultural and sports events should be priced at affordable prices and tickets available on first-come, first-serve basis. Community and workplace based teams, performing arts, Internet facilities should be encouraged and linked with the national identity. Promotion of international people to people, sister city programs and cultural exchanges should be facilitated to encourage international understanding and undercut 'demonizing' campaigns by imperial leaders and media. International cultural exchanges should be based on equality, reciprocity and non-intervention. In summary – cosmopolitanism should be fused with popular culture and have strong national and class roots.

Science, Technology and National Liberation

The subjects chosen for scientific inquiry, beneficiaries, sponsors, uses and abuses are based on politics and economic structures. There is no such thing as apolitical science. While scientific methods are not political, their subjects, treatments and products are politically determined. The work of many scientists is dictated if not directly financed by the profit-maximizing behavior of the MNCs: pharmaceutical companies finance research to produce 'blockbuster' drugs, which would be made available to ameliorate diseases which affect the affluent in the imperial or wealthy countries while out of reach to the poor. Scientists work for military industries, private mineral and petrol corporations, which exploit non-renewable resources. Under a popular regime, scientist would work on disease prevention, public health, drugs and vaccines against diseases, which affect the poor (malaria, typhoid and yellow fever). Scientists would work to increase production of goods for popular consumption – nutritious food, household appliances and public transport. Scientific research priorities are dictated by national-class necessities. The science policy perspective of the government should be directed toward making social improvements in the living and working conditions of the popular classes. Ethics and public health take priority in applying scientific discoveries against corporate patents, which charge exorbitant prices to cure a few and sacrifice the many. Public policy must be oriented toward a national preventative medicine program covering everyone: education, treatment, nutrition and exercise should be promoted through voluntary membership in nationwide health groups organized according to the needs of specific groups of people.

The state, while promoting practical and preventive medicine, should also finance advanced experimental medicine toward finding new treatments for major diseases.

Science should also serve to develop new weaponry to deter imperial invaders – heat detecting missiles to knock out invading helicopters, missiles to defend against air assaults, tank piercing shells to disable tanks and armoured carriers. Scientific knowledge of strategic weaponry is essential in deterring imperial invasions and intervention: the higher the personnel costs of an imperial attack, the greater the domestic popular opposition in the imperialist country, the greater the discredit of the military and political elites and the more likely that an imperial attack will not be launched or prolonged.

Basic skills in informatics should be imparted along with languages, scientific method, history, ethics as well as training in specialized areas. *Independent* national research and development centres – divorced from 'prestigious' imperial centres – should carry on studies and elaborate policy proposals to popular assemblies and political leaders for debate discussion, approval and implementation. International cooperation, joint research and scholarly exchanges should take place with centres that share similar class interests or ethics.

Scientists, skilled workers, specialists and professionals throughout their education should study the ethical and political principles which sustain their society and learn of their civic obligations and social responsibility to all the workers, soldiers, farmers and professionals who collectively provide these skilled workers with the means for free education and self-realization. Only through a deep and abiding commitment to the social system that fosters individual success can the state resist the attempts by the imperial powers to induce the flight of skilled workers or their recruitment as paid 'dissidents'.

Conclusion

In the past many progressive, left and self-styled 'anti-imperialist' regimes have attempted to combine anti-imperialist foreign policy statements with invitations, partnerships and other forms of collaboration with foreign investors, including those from hostile imperialist states. The assumption of many of these regimes is that they can 'control' the FI or subordinate them to national goals and interests as if they are dealing with a 'fixed relation'. As we have demonstrated throughout this study, once a 'beachhead' is established for it, FI has a powerful tendency to expand into the wider economy, to corrupt local officials, to bribe regulators and to present a different 'role model' for state executives – one attuned to luxury living, big salaries, privileges and, above all, an ideology more attuned to liberalism than anti-imperialism. As we have shown FI is not merely economic agents, they are political actors who have the backing of their states, the international media and courts, as well as 'networks of local supporters' in and out of the state. FI generally moves from minority shares toward majority ownership, from advisers to executive positions, from particular economic sectors to the general economy. In the process, FI tips the balance, which the anti-imperialist regimes try to manage between FI and national private and public capital. Early on FI investors look for 'strategic partners' among the 'national bourgeois' offering lucrative buyouts, a down payment in building future monopolies.

What we are emphasizing is that anti-imperialist regimes, which claim to be 'pragmatic' in including FI in their strategic sectors, are in fact 'idealistic', un-historical and lack a realistic understanding of past and present strategies of FI.

FI may offer a shortcut to capital, legitimacy in capital markets, business knowhow and marketing networks, but the cost is the gradual subversion of the anti-imperialist policy, the corruption of state officials, and the reproduction of a new class society based on the power of FI over the national state.

A clear, coherent anti-imperialist regime cannot operate with double bookkeeping: sooner or later, foreign policy will be dictated by the domestic power of the emerging FI in alliance with the national bourgeoisie. While windfall profits or commodity booms can allow an anti-imperialist regime to sustain the contradictory discourse of an anti-imperialist foreign policy and large-scale entry of foreign investments, this is not sustainable over time. In the meantime, FI investments and its accompanying high profits and political connections corrode the social basis of the regime by highlighting the gap between anti-imperialist speeches and domestic policy collaboration.

We have demonstrated that the decay of anti-imperialist regimes is not inevitable, and that feasible alternatives are possible, only if anti-imperialist foreign policies are rooted in profound domestic social transformations, which puts the worker-engineer public sector-led model at the centre of development.

Bibliography

Aglietta, M. (1982), 'World Capitalism in the 1980s', *New Left Review*, 136 (November/December), 5–41.

Albritton, R., Itoh, M., Westra, R. and Zuege, A. (2001), *Phases of Capitalist Development: Booms, Crises and Globalizations* (New York: Palgrave), 2001.

Ames, B. et al. (2000), *Macroeconomic Issues: PRSP Sourcebook*, September.

Amin, S. (1976), *Unequal Development* (New York: Monthly Review Press).

Amin, S. (1997), *Capitalism in the Age of Globalization* (London: Zed Books).

Amsden, A.H. (1989), *Asia's Next Giant: South Korea and Late Industrialization* (New York: Oxford University Press).

Amsden, A.H. (1989), *Asia's Next Giant: South Korea and Late Industrialization* (New York: Oxford University Press).

Annan, K. (1998), 'The Quiet Revolution,' *Global Governance*, 4(2), 123–138.

Armijo, L.E., ed., *Financial Globalization and Democracy in Emerging* (Markets, NY: St. Martin's Press).

Asnand, S. and Kanbur, R. (1993), 'Inequality and Development: A Critique,' *Journal of Development Economics*, Vol. 41, June.

Azpiazu, D., ed. (2002), "Privatizaciones y poder económico. La consolidación de una sociedad excluyente," Buenos Aires: FLACSO / Universidad Nacional de Quilmes/IDEP.

Barro, R. (1996), *Determinants of Economic Growth* (Cambridge: The MIT Press).

Becht, M. (1997), *Corporate Ownership and Control: The European Experience* (Brussels: ECGN).

Bello, W.F., Cunningham, S. and Rau, B. (1994), *Dark Victory: United States, Structural Adjustment and Global Poverty*. Transnational Institute Series (London: Pluto).

Bhagwati, J. (2004), *In Defense of Globalization* (Oxford University Press).

Biel, R. (2000), *The New Imperialism: Crisis and Contradictions in North/South Relations* (London: Zed Books).

Bienefield, M. (1988), 'The Significance of the Newly Industrializing Countries for the Development Debate', *Studies in Political Economy*, 25(2), 7–39.

Birdsall, N. (1997), 'On Growth And Poverty Reduction: Distribution Matters', *Remarks at the Conference On Poverty Reduction, Harvard Institute For International Development, February 8.*

Birdsall, N., Ross, D. and Sabot, R. (1999), 'Inequality and Growth Reconsidered: Lessons from East Asia', *The World Bank Economic Observer*, 9(3).

Brenner, R. (1998), 'The Economics of Global Turbulence,' *New Left Review*, Vol. 229, May/June. [DOI: 10.1103/PhysRevLett.80.3668]

Brenner, R. (2000), *The Economics of Global Turbulence* (London: Verso).

Brightman, C. (2004), *Total Insecurity: The Myth of American Omnipotence* (London: Verso).

Bulmer-Thomas, V. (1996), *The New Economic Model in Latin America and its Impact on Income Distribution and Poverty* (London: Macmillan).

CEPAL (1998), Foreign Investment in Latin America and the Caribbean, (La inversión extranjera en America Latina y el Caribe (Santiago Chile).

CEPAL (2004), *La Inversion Extranjera En América Latina y el Caríbe* (Santiago, Chile: Naciones Unidos).

CEPAL Comisión Económica de América Latina y el Caríbe (2005). La panoramo social de américa Latina 2005. Santiago: naciones unidas.

Chalmers, J. (2000), *Blowback: The Costs and Consequences of American* (Empire, NY: Metropolitan Books).

Chan, Ha-Joon and Grabel, I. (2004), *Reclaiming Development: An Alternative Economic Policy Manual* (London and New York: Zed Books).

Chan, S. (1989), 'Income Inequality among LCDs: A Comparative Analysis of Alternative Perspectives,' *International Studies Quarterly*, 33(3), 45–65. [DOI: 10.2307/2600493]

Chang, Ha-Joon. (1998), 'Globalisation, Transnational Corporations and Economic Development,' in *Globalisation and Progressive Economic Policy*, Baker, D., Epstein, G. and Pollin, R. (eds.) (Cambridge: Cambridge University Press).

Chibber, V. (2002), 'Bureaucratic Rationality and the Developmental State,' *American Journal of Sociology*, 107(4), 951–989. [DOI: 10.1086/341010]

Chomsky, N. (2003), *Hegemony or Survival: America's Quest for Global Dominance.* (New York: Metropolitan/Owl Books).

Christiaensen, L.M., L., Demery and Paternostro, S. (2002), *Reforms, Economic Growth and Poverty Reduction in Africa* (Washington, DC: World Bank).

Chul-Lee, H.O. and McNulty, M.P. (2003), 'East Asia's Dynamic Development Model and the Republic of Korea's Experiences,' The World Bank Institute, Policy Research Working Paper 2987,1–64.

CNIE (1988), *Informe*, 1983–1987. México: CNIE.

Cooper, R. (2002), 'The New Liberal Imperialism,' *Observer* Worldview, The Guardian, April 7.

Cornia, A., Jolly, R. and Stewart, F. (1987), *Ajuste con Rostro Humano* (Madrid: UNICEF).

Cornia, G.A. (2003), 'Globalisation and the Distribution of Income Between and Within Countries,' in *Rethinking Development Economics*, Chang, H.J. (ed.) (London: Anthem Press).

Crouch, C. and Pizzorno, A. (1978), *Resurgence of Class Conflict in Western Europe Since 1968* (London: Holmes & Meier).

Davis, M. (1984), 'The Political Economy of Late-Imperial America,' *New Left Review*, Vol. 143, January/February.

DC-EU—Departamento de Comercio de Estados Unidos (1999). U.S. Direct Investment Abroad: Operations of U.S. Parent Companies and Their Foreign Affiliates. Washington D.C, Bureau of Economic Analysis. Agosto.

Delgado Wise, R. (2004), 'Critical Dimensions of México-US Migration Under the Aegis of Neoliberalism and NAFTA,' *Canadian Journal of Development Studies*, 25(4).

Delgado-Wise, R. and Cypher, J. (2005), *The Strategic Role of Labor in Mexico's Subordinate Integration, Presented to the NAFTA and Beyond Conference* (Princeton University), December 2-3. http://www.estudiosdeldesarrollo.net.

Dicken, P. and Global Shift, *Transforming the World Economy*, 3rd edn (New York: Guilford).

DOF (1996), 'Decreto por el que reforman, adicionan y derogan la Ley de Inversión Extranjera', *Mexico, Diario Oficial de La Federación, diciembre*, 24.

Dollar, D. and Kraay, A. (2002), "Growth is Good for the Poor," *Journal of Economic Growth*, 7. [DOI: 10.1023/A%3A1020139631000]

Dominguez, J. and Lowenthal, A., eds. (1996), *Constructing Democratic Governance* (Baltimore: Johns Hopkins University Press).

Doremus, P., Kelly, W., Pauly, L. and Reich, S. (1999), *The Myth of the Global Corporation* (Princeton, NJ: Princeton University Press).

Dos Santos (1970), 'Structure of Dependence,' *American Economic Review*, 60(2).

Drezner, D. (1993), *Multinational Enterprises and the Global Economy* (Harrow: Addison-Wesley).

Drezner, D. (2004), 'The Outsourcing Bogeyman', *Foreign Affairs*, 83(3) (May/June), 22–34.

Dunning, John H. (1989), *Transnational Corporations and the Growth of Services: Some Conceptual and Theoretical* Issues. New York: United Nations.

Eastwood, R. and Lipton, L.M. (2001), 'Pro-Poor Growth and Pro-Poor Poverty Reduction', *Asian Development Review*, 18(2), 1–37.

ECLAC—Economic Commission for Latin America and the Caribbean (2002). Statistical Yearbook. Santiago de Chile: ECLAC.

Eland, I. (2002), 'The Empire Strikes Out: The "New Imperialism" and its Fatal Flaws,' *Policy Analysis*, 459(v), 26. [Cato Institute].

Enciso, A. (2005), 'El agua, Botín Para Trasnacionales; La privatizan Con Alto Costo Social,' *La Jornada*, 19 de Junio.

Evans, P. (1995), *Embedded Autonomy: States and Industrial Transformation* (Princeton, NJ: Princeton University Press).

Fallows, J.M. (1994), *Looking at the Sun: The Rise of the New East Asian Economic and Political* System. New York: Pantheon Press (System, NY: Pantheon Press).

Finance and Development (2005), 42(2), June.

Financial Times (2004), *Special Report: Global*, 500(May), 27.

Forbes (2000), 'A Reassessment of the Relationship between Inequality and Growth,' *American Economic Review*, 90(4), 869–887.

Foreign Direct Investment Magazine (2004). Date accessed: 12 of September 2004. http:// www.fdimagazine.com/news/categoryfront.php/id/111/Mexico.html.

Foster, J.B. and McChesney, R.W., eds. (2004), *Pox Americana: Exposing the American Empire* (New York: Monthly Review Press).

Friedman, T., *The Lexus and the Olive Tree* (1999) (New York: Farrar, Straus, Giroux).

Fröbel, F., Heinrichs, J. and Kreye, O. (1980), *The New International Division of Labour. Structural Unemployment in Industrialised Countries and Industrialisation in Developing Countries* (Cambridge University Press, Cambridge).

Gabetta, C., Calcagno, A. and Calcagno, E. (2002), 'Dossier: Attac Sevilla Debate,' *Le Monde Diplomatique*, Info-Diplo, 9 March.

Gardner, L.C. and Marilyn, B., Young, eds. (2005), *The New American Empire: A 21st Century Teach-in on US Foreign Policy* (New York: New Press).

George, S. (1990), *A Fate Worse than Debt the World Financial Crisis and the Poor* (London: Pluto Press).

Gereffi, G. and Wyman, D., eds. (1990), *Manufacturing Miracles: Paths of Industrialization in Latin America and East Asia* (Princeton, NJ: Princeton University Press).

González Amador, R. (2003), 'Más de dos billones de dólares: La Sangría De América Latina en DOS Décadas,' *La Jornada - Argenpress.info*, 29 de Noviembre. [PubMed 12347932]

Gowan, P. (1999), *The Global Gamble: Washington's Faustian Bid for World Domination* (London: Verso).

Grabel, L. (2003), 'International Private Capital Flows and Developing Countries,' pp. 325–41 in H.-J. Chang, ed, *Rethinking Development Economics* (Anthem Press).

Guillen, R. Hector (1997), *La Contra-Revolución Neoliberal*. México D.F: Era.

Hardt, M. and Negri, A. (2002), *Empire* (Cambridge: Harvard University Press).

Harris, J. (2001) *Depoliticising Development. The World Bank and Social Capital* (New Delhi: Left Word Books).

Hayami, Y. (1998), *Toward the Rural-Based Development of Commerce and Industry Selected Experiences from East Asia* EDI Learning Resources Series 18348, 1-310 (World Bank Institute).

Hayter, T. (1971), *Aid as Imperialism* (Harmondsmouth: Penguin Books).

Helleiner, G. (1989), 'Transnational Corporations and Direct Foreign Investment', in *Handbook of Development Economics*, Chenery, H. and Srinivasen, T.N. (eds.), Vol. 2. Amsterdam: Elsevier.

Hulme, D. and Edwards, M. (1997), *NGOs, States and Donors: Too Close for Comfort?* (New York: St. Martin's Press).

Huntington, S. (1999), 'The Lonely Super-Power,' *Foreign Affairs*, 788(2), March/April.

IFAD—International Fund for Agricultural and Development (2001), *Strategy for Rural Poverty Reduction in Latin America and the Caribbean.* Soc.Capitl/IFAD. Strategy.for.20Rural.Poverty.Reduction.html.

Ikenberry, John, Lake, D.A. and Mastanduno, M., eds. (1988), *The State and American Foreign Economic Policy* (Ithaca: Cornell University Press).

International Monetary Fund—IMF (1981, 2004, 2005), *International Financial Statistics Yearbook* (IMF).

Jazairy, I., Alamgir, M. and Panuccio, T. (1992), *The State of World Rural Poverty* (London: Intermediate Technology Publications).

Johnson, C. (2004), *The Sorrows of Empire: Militarism, Secrecy, and the End of the Republic* (New York: Metropolitan Books) 2004.

Julius, D. (1994), 'International Direct Investment: Strengthening the Policy Regime,', in G. Kenen (ed.), *Managing the World Economy* (Washington, DC: Institute for International Economics).

Kagan, R. (2003), *Of Paradise and Power: America and Europe in the New World* (Order, NY: Alfred A. Knopf).

Kakwani, N. and Pernia, E.M. (2000), 'What is Pro-Poor Growth?', *Asian Development Review*, 18(1), 1–16.

Kapstein, E. (1996), 'Workers and the World Economy,' *Foreign Affairs*, 75(3).

Kauffman, S. and Rubio, L. (1998), *Mexico under Zedillo* (Boulder, Co.: Lynne Rienner).

Kay, C. (1989), *Latin American Theories of Development and Underdevelopment* (London: Routledge).

Kennan, G. (1948), U.S. State Department Policy Planning, Study #23, February 24. .

Klasen, S. (2005), 'Economic Growth and Poverty Reduction: Measurement and Policy Issues', Paper prepared for POVNET—Pro-Poor Growth Work Program. povnet@povnet.com.

Kohl, B. (2002), 'Stabilizing Neoliberalism in Bolivia: Popular Participation and Privatization,' *Political Geography*, 21, 449–472. [DOI: 10.1016/S0962-6298%2801%2900078-6]

Kuczynski, P.-P. and Williamson, J., eds. (2003), *After the Washington Consensus* (Washington, DC: Institute for International Economics).

Leftwich, A. (1995), 'Bringing Politics Back In: Towards a Model of the Developmental State,' *The Journal of Development Studies*, 31(3), 400–427.

Linsu, K. and Nugent, J. (1994), *The Republic of Koreas's Small and Medium-Size Enterprises and their Support Systems*, World Bank Institute. World Bank Policy Research Paper, (1404), 1–84.

Lipietz, A. (1987), *Mirages and Miracles: The Crisis in Global Fordism* (London: Verso).

Lozano, Claudio, Ana Rameri and Tomás RaffoLozano, C., Rameri, A. and Raffo, T. (2006), 'Ingresos, Salarios y Convenios Colectivos En Argentina 2006: La Deuda Interna Se Acentúa,' *Argenpress*, 17/04/2006.

Lustig, N. (1991), 'From Structuralism to Neostructuralism: The Search for a Heterodox Paradigm,' pp. 27-43 in Meller, Patricio (ed.). *The Latin American Development Debate: Neostructuralism, Neomonetarism and Adjustment Processes* (Boulder, Colorado: Westview Press).

Maddison, A. (2003), *The World Economy: Historical Statistics* (Paris: OECD).

Magdoff, H. (2003), *Imperialism without Colonies* (New York: Monthly Review Press).

Mahajan, R. (2003), *Full Spectrum Dominance: US Power in Iraq and Beyond* (New York: Seven Stories Press).

Mallaby, S. (2002), 'The Reluctant Imperialist: Terrorism, Failed States and the Case for American Empire,' *Foreign Affairs*, 81(2), March/April.

Mann, M. (2003), *Incoherent Empire* (London: Verso).

Marcos, S. (1994), 'A Tourist Guide to Chiapas,' *Monthly Review*, 46(May), 8–18.

Mokhiber, R. and Weissman, R. (2001), 'Corporate Globalization and the Poor,' August 6. corp-focus-admin@lists.essential.org.

Nayyar, D. (1978), 'Transnational Corporations and Manufactured Exports from Poor Countries,' *Economic Journal*, March. [DOI: 10.2307/2232014]

Norberg, J. (2003), *Defense of Global Capitalism* (Washington, DC: Cato Institute).

OECD (1997). Final Report of the DAC Ad Hoc Working Group on Participatory Development and Good Governance. Paris.

Oficial de la Federación, DD.-A. (1993) Ley para Promover la Inversión Mexicana y Regular la Inversión Extranjera, Mexico, Diario Oficial de la Federación, marzo 9.

Patillo, H.P. and Ricci, L. (2002), 'External Debt and Growth,' *Finance and Development*, 39(2), June.

Paugam, S., ed. (1996), *L' Exclusion. L'Etat des Savoirs* (Paris: Ed. La Découverte).

Petras, J. (2006), 'The Pro-Israel Lobby and US Middle East Policy', Rebelión, June 4.

Petras, J. and Veltmeyer, H. (2001), *Unmasking Globalization: The New Face of Imperialism* (London: Zed Books / Halifax: Fernwood Books).

Petras, J. and Veltmeyer, H. (2003a), *Cardoso's Brazil: A Land for Sale* (Boulder Co./Rowman & Littlefield).

Petras, J. and Veltmeyer, H. (2003b), *System in Crisis: Free Market Capitalism* (London: Zed Books / Halifax: Fernwood Books).

Petras, J. and Veltmeyer, H. (2005a), *Social Movements and the State: Argentina, Bolivia, Brazil, Ecuador* (London: Pluto Press).

Petras, J. and Veltmeyer, H. (2005b), *Empire with Imperialism* (Halifax: Fernwood Books / London: Zed books).

Petras, J. and Veltmeyer, H., eds. (2004), *Las privatizaciónes y la desnacionalización en América Latina* (Buenos Aires: Libros Prometeo).

Pochmann, M. et al. (2004), *Atlas da exclusâo no mundo, 5 vols* (Sao Paulo: Cortez Editora).

Pollin, R. (2003), *Contours of Descent: U.S. Economic Fractures and the Landscape of Global Austerity* (London: Verso).

Prebisch, R. (1949), 'The Economic Development of Latin America and its Principal Problems,' CEPAL Manifesto (Santiago: CEPAL).

Prestowitz, C.V. (1988), *Trading Places: How We Allowed Japan to Take the Lead* (New York: Basic Books).

Rapley, J. (1996), *Understanding Development: Theory and Practice in the Third World* (Boulder, CO: Lynne Rienner).

Rieff, D. (1999), 'A New Age of Liberal Imperialism?', *World Policy Journal*, 14(2), summer.

Romer, P. (1990), 'Endogenous Technological Change,' *Journal of Political Economy*, 98(5), 1971–2102. [DOI: 10.1086/261725]

Rowbotham, M. (2000), *Goodbye America: Globalization, Debt and the Dollar Empire* (Concord, MA: Paul and Co.).

Sachs, J. and Warner, P. (1995), 'Economic Reform and the Process of Global Integration,' *Brooking Papers on Economic Activity*, 1, 1–95. [DOI: 10.2307/2534573]

Salop, J. (1992), 'Reducing Poverty: Spreading the Word,' *Finance and Development*, 29(4), December.

Samuel, M.A. (2001), *The Income Distribution Problem in Latin America and the Caribbean. Economic Cooperation for Latin America and the Caribbean (ECLAC)* (Santiago: ECLAC).

Saxe-Fernández, John and Núñez, O. (2001), 'Globalización e Imperialismo: La Transferencia De Excedentes De América Latina' in Saxe-Fernández et al. *Globalización, Imperialismo y Clase Social*, Buenos Aires/México, Editorial Lúmen.

Schutz, E.A. (2001), *Markets and Power: The 21st Century Command Economy* Armonk, NY: M.E. Sharpe (Armonk, NY: M.E. Sharpe).

Sclar, E.D. (2000), *You Don't Always Get What You Pay For: The Economics of Privatization*, Ithaca NY: Cornell University Press (Ithaca NY: Cornell University Press).

SECOFI–Secretaría de Comercio y Fomento Industrial (1994), 'Structure and Policy of Foreign Direct Investment,' México DF: SECOFI, Febrero.

Semmens, BrendynSemmens, B. (2002), 'Re Post WWII Hegemony', Posted at ipe@csf.colorado.edu, 16 December [bsemmens@ozemail.com.au.

Senate, U.S. (1999), '106th Congress. Private Banking and Money Laundering: A Case Study of Opportunities and Vulnerabilities Hearings before the Permanent Sub-Committee on Investigations of the Committee on Governmental Affairs', Report November 9-10.

Senate, U.S., Permanent Subcommittee on Investigations (2001), 'Minority Staff', *A Gateway to Money Laundering Minority Staff Report on Correspondent Banking*, February.

Sheshinski, E. and López-Calva, L.F. (2003), 'Privatization and its Benefits: Theory, Evidence, and Challenges', in *Markets and Governments*, Basu, K., Ray, R. and Nayak, P. eds. (New Delhi: Oxford University Press).

SOBEET (1999), Carta de Sobeet, No. 11, Fevereiro [Sao Paulo].

SOBEET (2006), *O estoque de investimentos estrangeiros diretos no Brasil* (Año, VI: Carta de SOBEET), No. 34.

Solow, R. (2000), 'Notes on Social Capital and Economic Performance', in *Social Capital: A Multi-Faceted Perspective*, Dasgupta, P. and Serageldin, I. (eds.) (Washington, DC: World Bank).

Stiglitz, J. (2002), *Globalization and its Discontents* (New York: Norton Press).

Story, D. (1986), *The Mexican Ruling Party: Stability and Authority* (New York: Praeger).

Teichman, J. (1996), 'Neoliberalism and the Transformation of Mexican Authoritarianism', CERLAC Working Paper Series 6.

Todd, E. (2003), *After the Empire: The Breakdown of the American Order*, trans. Delogu, C.J. (New York: Columbia University Press).

UNCTAD (1989), *Services and Development: The Role of Foreign Direct Investment and Trade* (New York: United Nations).

UNCTAD (1998), *World Investment Report 1998: Trends and Determinants* (New York and Geneva: United Nations).

UNCTAD (1999), *World Investment Report 1999: Foreign Direct Investment and the Challenge for Development* (New York and Geneva: United Nations).

UNCTAD (2000), *World Investment Report 2000: Cross-Border Mergers and Acquisitions and Development* (New York and Geneva: United Nations).

UNCTAD (2001), *World Investment Report 2001: Promoting Linkages* (New York and Geneva: United Nations).

UNCTAD (2003), *World Investment Report 2003: FDI Policies for Development – National and International Perspectives* (New York and Geneva: United Nations).

UNCTAD (2004), *Global Investment Prospects Assessment Research Note 3: A Worldwide Survey of the World's Largest Transnational Corporations, Prospects for F.D.I. Flows, TNC Strategies and Policy Developments: 2004–2007* (New York and Geneva: United Nations) (http://www.unctad.org/ sections/dite_dir/ docs//survey3.

UNCTAD (various years), *World Investment Report* (New York: UNCTAD).

UNDP (1996), 'Good Governance and Sustainable Human Development', Governance Policy Paper. http://magnet.undp. org/policy.

UNDP (2004), 'Human Development Index', Date accessed: 14 February 2005. www.undp.org.

UNDP, United Nations Development Program (various years), Human Development Report.

United Nations (2005), *The Inequality Predicament: Report on the World Social Situation 2005* (New York: United Nations).

United Nations Conference on Trade and Development, (UNCTAD), *World Investment Report (1993): Transnational Corporations and Integrated International Production*. New York and Geneva: United Nations.

United States, Board of Governors of the Federal Reserve System (2004). "Flows of Funds Accounts of the United States: Flows and Outstandings, 4th Quarter 2003", March 4. Washington DC: Board of Governors of the Federal Reserve System.

US Census Bureau (2002). US Direct Investment Position Abroad on a Historical Cost Basis. Washington DC.

US Government, White House (2002), 'The National Security Strategy of the United States of America,' September.

Veltmeyer, H. and Petras, J. (1997), *Economic Liberalism and Class Conflict in Latin America* (London: Macmillan Publishing).

Veltmeyer, H. and Petras, J. (2000), *The Dynamics of Social Change in Latin America* (London: Macmillan Publishing).

Wade, R. (1990), *Governing the Market: Economic Theory and the Role of Government in East Asian Industrialization* (Princeton, NJ: Princeton University Press).

Wallerstein, I. (2003), *The Decline of American Power* (NY: The New Press).

Webb, S. (2001), 'Pemex Shake Up,' *Business Mexico*, 11 (April 14), pp. 26-32.

Wee, K., Hwee and Mirza, H. (2004), 'ASEAN Investment Cooperation: Retrospect, Developments and Prospects,' in *The Future of Foreign Investment in SouthEast Asia*, Freeman, N. and Bartels, F. eds. (London: Routledge).

Weisbrot, M., Baker, D., Kraev, E. and Chen, J. (2001), *The Scorecard on Globalization 1980-2000* (Center for Economic Policy Research), September, http://www.cepr.net/globalization/scorecard-on-globalization.htm.

Weiss, L. (1998), *The Myth of the Powerless State: Governing the Economy in a Global Era* (Cambridge: Polity Press).

Weller, C. and Hersh, A. (2002), *The Long and Short of it: Global Liberalization, Poverty and Inequality, Unpublished Paper* (Washington, DC: Economic Policy Institute).

Williamson, J. ed. (1990), *Latin American Adjustment. How Much Has Happened?* (Washington, DC: Institute for International Economics).

Woo, J.E. (1991), *Race to the Swift: State and Finance in Korean Industrialization* (New York: Columbia University Press).

World Bank (2000), *World Development Report 2000/2001: Attacking Poverty*, (NY: Oxford University Press).

World Bank (2002), *Recent Trends in International Resource Flows* (Washington, DC: World Bank).

World Bank (2004), *How Regions Finance Themselves Externally, World Development Finance* (Washington, DC: World Bank).

World Bank (2005), *World Development Report 2006: Equity and Development* (New York: Oxford University Press).

World Bank (various years), *Global Development Finance* (Washington, DC: World Bank).

Zayago Lau, E. (2005), 'State-led Investment in Mexico'. MA thesis, Halifax: Saint Mary's University.

Index